THE POLITICOS GUIDE TO
THE NEW HOUSE OF COMMONS
2015

THE
POLITICOS GUIDE
TO THE NEW
HOUSE OF COMMONS

2015

PROFILES OF THE NEW MPS
AND ANALYSIS OF THE 2015
GENERAL ELECTION RESULTS

EDITED BY

TIM CARR, IAIN DALE
& ROBERT WALLER

Biteback Publishing

First published in Great Britain in 2015 by
Biteback Publishing Ltd
Westminster Tower
3 Albert Embankment
London SE1 7SP
Copyright © Tim Carr, Iain Dale and Robert Waller 2015

Tim Carr, Iain Dale and Robert Waller have asserted their rights
under the Copyright, Designs and Patents Act 1988 to be identified as the
editors of this work.

ISBN 978-1-84954-923-3

A CIP catalogue record for this book is available from the British Library.

Set in Minion Pro

Contents

Introduction..VII

The 2015 general election results 1

What would have happened under proportional representation?........9

The 2015 election in figures..11

The 25 most memorable quotes of the general election campaign.......15

Scotland
David Torrance..19

Party like it's 1992: polling at the 2015 general election
Joe Twyman..31

The media
Theo Usherwood...39

Fixed-Term Parliaments Act
Peter Riddell 45

Survey of regional results
Robert Waller...51

2015 general election statistics
Compiled by Tim Carr and Robert Waller;
commentary by Robert Waller 77

The demographics of the new House of Commons
Compiled by Robert Waller..95

The new intake of 2015..117

Index of new MPs
    by surname..133
    by party..138
    by constituency..143
    by region..148

New women MPs by party..155

New BME MPs by party..159

Defeated MPs..161

Retired or de-selected MPs..165

The class of 2015..169

Introduction

The national shock felt at 10 p.m. on Thursday 7 May 2015 will live with us all for a long time. It was the moment when the veteran broadcaster David Dimbleby, anchoring the BBC's election special for the last time, tore open the envelope in his hand and read the results of the official exit poll.

Politicians, journalists and commentators alike will use it as a sobering cautionary tale – at least until, as in the aftermath of 1992, collective amnesia sets in and they become convinced that it could never happen again. The now legions of pollsters will simply shudder at the memory. Apart, that is, from Professor John Curtice and his exit-poll team of eight analysts from the universities of Oxford, Plymouth and Manchester and the London School of Economics, who undoubtedly rule supreme in the discipline.

We had been told for months by the polls that this was going to be the closest-run election since 1992, that there was not a chance of any one party managing to get a majority in Britain's now six- or seven-party system. We were set for protracted negotiations between the parties to determine who would form the next government. There were seemingly endless possible scenarios, gloriously set out in whizzy graphics in our newspapers, each scenario somehow assigned a percentage chance of happening. And the constitutional experts were waiting on hand to explain the pitfalls and uncertainties that undoubtedly exist in our imprecise, oh-so-very-British democratic system.

What followed, of course, was a night – and day – of unforgettable political and human drama.

Before anyone was able to get a good night's sleep, the Conservatives were returned with a twelve-seat majority, the SNP had turned Scotland into a virtual one-party state, a host of leading political figures had lost their seats, and the leaders of Labour, the Liberal Democrats and UKIP had all resigned, although Nigel Farage was later to reverse his decision. It was undoubtedly one of the most dramatic defenestrations of the political class in British political history. The ramifications of the result will continue to be felt for a long time to come and there are still potentially enormous political uncertainties in the future, particularly around the state of the Union and Europe.

This book is only an early start at explaining what happened on 7 May 2015. We recognise that the outcome of the election and the manner in which it was achieved will be scrutinised and analysed for years to come. Much of this book is devoted to the new parliament and the 182 new men and women (the latter present in record number) who have been elected to serve us for the next five years. But, importantly, we also look at some of the main features of the campaign and analyse the election results in some detail. We are extremely grateful to a range of commentators for providing their expert insights so quickly after the event.

Joe Twyman of YouGov considers the vexed issue of polling and what lessons can be learnt for future elections. Theo Usherwood looks at the role of the media during the election and how the SNP grew to become one of the major stories of the campaign. Election expert Robert Waller provides a detailed analysis of the voting patterns across the regions of the UK, explaining how the election was won and lost. David Torrance looks at how the SNP came to dominate in Scotland, shaking the political world in Westminster, and constitutional expert Peter Riddell looks at how the Fixed-Term Parliaments Act restricts the options available to David Cameron as he seeks to govern with only a small majority.

If you are reading this, then you are already fascinated by British politics. We hope that this book can feed that fascination further.

The 2015 general election results

United Kingdom (650 seats)

- The Conservatives win a 12-seat majority, the first Conservative majority since John Major's victory in 1992.

- Before the final result (St Ives) has been declared, 3 party leaders have publicly resigned: Labour's Ed Miliband, the Liberal Democrats' Nick Clegg and UKIP's Nigel Farage (although his resignation was later rejected by the party and subsequently withdrawn).

- With Harriet Harman, Baroness Sal Brinton and Suzanne Evans acting as caretaker leaders for Labour, the Liberal Democrats and UKIP, 6 of the UK's 7 main political parties are led by women on the day following the election.

- The SNP win 56 out of 59 seats in Scotland, smashing every record.

- Labour lose 39 MPs, the Liberal Democrats lose 38 and the Conservatives 9, and 6 others are defeated.

- Both Labour and the Liberal Democrats lose senior MPs – Labour lose shadow Chancellor Ed Balls, shadow Foreign Secretary Douglas Alexander and Scottish leader Jim Murphy. The Liberal Democrats lose former Chief Secretary to the Treasury Danny Alexander, Business Secretary Vince Cable, Energy Secretary Ed Davey and former party leader Charles Kennedy. Nigel Farage fails to get elected.

- The majority is achieved with only a 36.9% share of the vote, compared to 41.9% in 1992.

- The only time since 1945 that Labour's 30.4% share of the vote has been worse was its 29.0% performance in 2010. You have to go back to 1987 to find a lower number of Labour MPs (229 in 2015).

- Losing 49 of their 57 seats held in 2010, the Liberal Democrats have fallen back to the territory they occupied in 1970, when they had 6 MPs.

- UKIP secure third place in voting numbers with 3.9 million votes, but only win 1 seat.

- UKIP finish second in 120 constituencies and third in 364, suggesting that they may be better placed to win seats in 2020.

- There are 182 newly elected Members of the House of Commons, 28% of the Chamber. When combined with the 232 new MPs in 2010, it means that 414 MPs (63.5%) have been MPs for only 5 years or less.

- A record number of 191 women are elected, 44 more than in 2010 and 71 more than in 1997, raising the proportion to 29% of the House of Commons. 81 of the 182 new MPs are women. The Liberal Democrats now have no female MPs.

- A record number of 41 BME MPs are elected, up from 27 at the last election. 23 are Labour, 17 Conservative and 1 SNP. 16 are from the new intake.

- The number of declared LGBT MPs has also increased from 26 to 28 in the new Parliament (4%).

- The day after the election, the British Polling Council announce an independent investigation into why all of the 10 main polling companies had all consistently underestimated the Conservative lead over Labour.

- In the local elections in 279 councils on 7 May 2015, the Conservatives

win control of 30 councils and gain just under 500 new councillors.
Labour lose 179 councillors and the Lib Dems lose 365.

Turnout: 66.1%
Electorate: 46,425,386

	PPCS	SEATS	GAIN	LOSS	+/-	VOTES	VOTE SHARE	+/-%
Conservative	647	331	35	11	+24	11,334,920	36.9	+0.8
Labour	631	232	22	48	-26	9,347,326	30.4	+1.5
SNP	59	56	50	0	+50	1,454,436	4.7	+3.1
Lib Dems	631	8	0	49	-49	2,415,888	7.9	-15.2
DUP	16	8	1	1	0	184,260	0.6	0.0
Sinn Féin	18	4	0	1	-1	176,232	0.6	0.0
Plaid Cymru	40	3	0	0	0	181,694	0.6	0.0
SDLP	18	3	0	0	0	99,809	0.3	0.0
UUP	15	2	2	0	+2	114,935	0.4	0.0
UKIP	624	1	1	0	+1	3,881,129	12.6	+9.5
Green	573	1	0	0	0	1,157,613	3.8	+2.8
Alliance	18	0	0	1	-1	61,556	0.2	+0.1
Ind (NI)	1	1	0	0	0	17,689	0.1	0.0
Others	680	0	0	0	0	270,723	0.9	-2.6
	3,971	650				30,698,210	100	

All figures are in comparison to 2010 (Respect's George Galloway won his seat in a 2012 by-election)

Abbreviations:

PPCs: prospective parliamentary candidates

SNP: Scottish National Party

DUP: Democratic Unionist Party

SDLP: Social Democratic & Labour Party

UUP: Ulster Unionist Party

England (533 seats)

- The last time the Conservatives won 319 seats in England was in 1992, the last time it had an overall majority, although its share of the vote in 2015 was 4.5% lower than in 1992. It may be blindingly obvious, but it was certainly England that won the election for the Tories. And the right votes in the right seats.

- The UK picture may suggest a different story, but the end of two-party politics in England still seems a long way off. The Conservatives and Labour hold a higher proportion of English seats than in any election since 1979.

- The constituency of Havant elected the UK's first MP of Chinese background. Alan Mak MP was born and raised in York but his parents are from Guangdong in southern China.

Turnout: 65.9%
Electorate: 38,811,622

	SEATS	GAIN	LOSS	+/-	VOTES	VOTE SHARE	+/-%
Conservative	319	32	11	+21	10,483,555	41.0	+1.4
Labour	206	21	6	+15	8,087,706	31.6	+3.6
Lib Dems	6	0	37	-37	2,098,430	8.2	-16.0
UKIP	1	1	0	+1	3,611,367	14.1	+10.7
Green	1	0	0	0	1,073,242	4.2	+3.2
Others	0	0	0	0	216,909	0.9	-2.9
	533				25,571,209	100	

All figures are in comparison to 2010

Scotland (59 seats)

- The SNP result in Scotland was stunning: the largest number of MPs ever, the highest share of the vote and the near wipe-out of all other parties. The SNP's previous high was in October 1974, when it received over 30% of the vote in Scotland and won 11 seats.

- With 50 MPs, comparable to the Liberal Democrats in the last 4 parliaments, the SNP will be seeking a similar share of time, influence and resources. Should they expect priority questions at PMQs, a seat on every Select Committee and Bill Committee and chairmanship of the Scottish Affairs Committee and one other?

- The share of the vote of all the other 'major' parties fell, with only UKIP and the Greens increasing their share of the vote.

- Labour's performance in Scotland was easily its worst since 1918 in terms of both seats and share of the vote.

- The Conservatives may have fared better than they did in 1997, when they failed to gain a single seat, but their 14.9% share of the vote was the lowest on record.

Turnout: 71.1%
Electorate: 4,094,784

	SEATS	GAIN	LOSS	+/-	VOTES	VOTE SHARE	+/-%
SNP	56	50	0	+50	1,454,436	50.0	+30.0
Labour	1	0	40	-40	707,147	24.3	-17.7
Conservative	1	0	0	0	434,097	14.9	-1.8
Lib Dems	1	0	10	-10	219,675	7.5	-11.3
UKIP	0	0	0	0	47,078	1.6	+0.9
Green	0	0	0	0	39,205	1.3	+0.7
Others	0	0	0	0	8,827	0.4	-0.8
	59				2,910,465	100	

All figures are in comparison to 2010

Wales (40 seats)

- The big winners in Wales were the Conservatives, gaining 3 seats at the expense of the Liberal Democrats and Labour.

- Plaid Cymru's performance once again suggests that there is little appetite for independence, even under the leadership of the competent Leanne Wood, who performed well during the campaign.

- Plaid Cymru only managed a modest increase in its share of the vote and no new MPs. It won 4 MPs in 1992, 1997 and 2001. Its 12.1% share of the vote is some way behind its all-time high of 14.3% in 2001.

- For a party frequently associated with English nationalism, UKIP's share of the vote in Wales was higher than Plaid Cymru's.

Turnout: 65.7%
Electorate: 2,282,297

	SEATS	GAIN	LOSS	+/-	VOTES	VOTE SHARE	+/-%
Labour	25	1	2	-1	552,473	36.9	+0.6
Conservative	11	3	0	+3	408,213	27.2	+1.1
Plaid Cymru	3	0	0	0	181,694	12.1	+0.8
Lib Dems	1	0	2	-2	97,783	6.5	-13.6
UKIP	0	0	0	0	204,360	13.6	+11.2
Green	0	0	0	0	38,344	2.6	+2.1
Others	0	0	0	0	15,566	1.1	-2.2
	40				1,498,433	100	

All figures are in comparison to 2010

Northern Ireland (18 seats)

- The Ulster Unionist Party (UUP) were the surprise winners in Northern Ireland, gaining 2 seats, 2 more than they had in the last parliament. The UUP was the dominant Northern Ireland party in Westminster as recently as 1997, when it had 10 seats.

- Although it retained its 3 seats, the Social Democratic & Labour Party (SDLP) slipped to its lowest share of the vote in a Westminster election since it was founded in 1970.

- The Alliance Party of Northern Ireland lost its single MP and its only MP ever elected (Naomi Long).

- Lady Sylvia Hermon, the MP for North Down, is now the UK Parliament's only Independent MP.

Turnout: 58.1%
Electorate: 1,236,683

	SEATS	GAIN	LOSS	+/-	VOTES	VOTE SHARE	+/-%
DUP	8	1	1	0	184,260	25.7	+0.7
Sinn Féin	4	0	1	-1	176,232	24.5	-1.0
SDLP	3	0	0	0	99,809	13.9	-2.6
UUP	2	2	0	-2	114,935	16.0	+0.8
Alliance	0	0	1	-1	61,556	8.6	+2.2
UKIP	0	0	0	0	18,324	2.6	+2.6

Conservative	0	0	0	0	16,538	1.3	+1.3
Green	0	0	0	0	9,055	1.0	+0.4
Ind	1	0	0	0	17,689	2.4	-0.3
Others	0	0	0	0	29,421	4.0	-4.1
	650				727,819	100	

All figures are in comparison to 2010

What would have happened under proportional representation?

With the smaller parties amassing millions of votes (UKIP 3.9 million, the Liberal Democrats 2.4 million and the Green Party 1.2 million) but very few seats (10 seats for roughly 7.5 million votes), compared to the 50 Scottish National Party (SNP) seats for 1.5 million votes, the argument over whether or not the UK's First Past the Post (FPTP) system is broken has already begun.

So how different would the 2015 election result have been under a form of proportional representation?

The Alternative Vote method was resoundingly rejected by the public in the 2011 referendum by 67.9% to 32.1% and so is unlikely to be proposed again soon.

The d'Hondt method of proportional representation is used for the devolved assemblies in Scotland and Wales and a modified version of the system is also used in the London Assembly. Proportional representation systems aim to allocate seats to parties in proportion to the number of votes received.

So if the d'Hondt system was applied to the 632 seats in England, Scotland and Wales (Northern Ireland excluded), how would the new House of Commons have looked?

	ACTUAL SEATS	PR (D'HONDT) SEATS	+/-
Conservative	331	242	-89
Labour	232	199	-33
SNP	56	31	-25
Lib Dems	8	51	+43
Plaid Cymru	3	3	0
UKIP	1	82	+81
Green	1	24	+23
	632	632	

Source: http://icon.cat/util/elections

The 2015 election in figures

The UK electorate at the 2015 general election was almost 46.5 million, the largest ever. The registers contained 900,000 more than names than in 2010.

30.7 million valid votes were cast, making the overall turnout figure 66.1%. This makes it higher than 2010 (65.1%), 2005 (61.4%) and 2001 (59.4%), but a long way behind the 71.4% in 1997 and the post-war high of 83.9% in 1950.

Some 469,047 registered to vote online on the final day for registration (20 April 2015).

Scotland had the highest turnout at 71.1%, followed by England at 65.8%, Wales at 65.7% and Northern Ireland at 58.1%.

Turnout rose in every country of the United Kingdom but was most dramatic in Scotland (up from 63.8% in 2010 to 71.1%) and only marginal in England (65.1% in 2010 to 66.1%). Even Scotland failed to hit the 71.3% figure achieved in 1997.

The highest turnout was 81.9% in Dunbartonshire East and the lowest was in Stoke-on-Trent Central at 49.9% (surpassing Manchester Central, which had been expected to be the lowest). Scotland also saw the biggest swing – 39.3% from Labour to the SNP in Glasgow North East.

Paisley & South Renfrewshire elected the SNP's 20-year-old Mhairi

Black, who became the youngest MP since 1667. Christopher Monck, 2nd Duke of Albemarle, was 13 years old when he was appointed his seat in the Commons, and joined the Lords 3 years later. Black is the youngest elected MP since the 1832 Reform Act.

Meanwhile, Gerald Kaufman became the oldest MP in the new parliament. The Manchester Gorton Labour MP is 84. The next oldest is Dennis Skinner, who is 83.

Gerald Kaufman is also set to be the new Father of the House, the longest-serving member of the Commons. He was first elected in 1970 alongside Dennis Skinner, Michael Meacher and Ken Clarke, but was the first of the four to be sworn in.

The lowest winning share was Alasdair McDonnell of the SDLP in Belfast South, with only 24.5% of the vote. In England, Liberal Democrat John Pugh was able to retain his seat of Stockport with just 31% of the vote.

Anthony Wells, director of YouGov and editor of the UKPollingReport website, has estimated that the anticipated new parliamentary boundary review in the next session (reducing the number of MPs from 650 to 600) will result in the following: Conservatives 322 seats (-9), Labour 204 (-28), the SNP 50 (all seats in Scotland) and the Lib Dems just 4 (-4). This would give the Conservatives a majority of 44 in a Commons of 600 MPs.

If the number of votes cast for the smaller parties is compared with the number of MPs elected, 1 MP equals 3.9 million votes for UKIP, 1.2 million for the Greens and roughly 300,000 for the Liberal Democrats, but 40,000 for Labour, 34,000 for the Conservatives and just 29,000 for the SNP.

A deceased candidate succeeded in securing 113 votes in Hampstead & Kilburn. Ronnie Carroll, a former UK Eurovision contestant, died at the age of 80 just a week after the nomination deadline for candidates had closed. Under UK electoral law, candidates' names are not allowed to be withdrawn from the ballot paper once the deadline has passed.

The Green Party lost the most in forfeited deposits (£221,000), receiving less than 5% of the vote in a seat and losing the £500 fee to stand, followed by the Liberal Democrats (£170,500), UKIP (£39,500), Conservatives (£9,000), Plaid Cymru (£4,000) and Labour (£1,500). Unsurprisingly, the SNP did not lose a single deposit. For the Liberal Democrats, this means that they got less than 5% of the vote in 341 constituencies. UKIP's loss of £39,500 is substantially down on the whopping £229,500 it lost in 2010.

The British National Party (BNP) won 564,321 votes in 2010. This fell to just 1,667 votes in 2015.

The BBC's election night broadcast was led for the 9th and last time by David Dimbleby. His first election was in 1964.

The BBC's *World at One* has compiled some of the quirkier facts from the general election campaign (using information sourced from each party):

- Labour sold 13,281 tea towels

- Nigel Farage ate 25 curries

- Twitter users shared 20,386 selfies with Nicola Sturgeon

- David Cameron travelled nearly 13,000 miles

- Leanne Wood used 540 kirby grips for her trademark hairstyle

- Natalie Bennett consumed 680 Lockets

- One pigeon was hit by the Lib Dem bus

The 25 most memorable quotes of the general election campaign

'It's Ajockalypse Now. People are looking at Ed Miliband and they're getting bad visuals of him popping out of Alex Salmond's sporran like a baffled baby kangaroo.'
Boris Johnson's views on the prospect of an SNP-backed Labour government.

'Oh, it's crats? I thought it was Liberal Demo-cats.'
Reality TV star Joey Essex tells Nick Clegg of his confusion over the Lib Dem party name.

'Am I tough enough? Hell yes, I'm tough enough.'
Ed Miliband's 'fiery' response to Jeremy Paxman when asked whether he was 'tough enough' to be PM.

'One can have a mental brain fade on these things.'
Green Party leader Natalie Bennett on her botched LBC interview.

'We're a shining example of a country where multiple identities work … Where you can support Man Utd, the Windies and Team GB all at the same time. Of course, I'd rather you supported West Ham.'
David Cameron forgets what football team he 'supports', confusing his beloved Aston Villa with West Ham.

'I stopped this morning to get some newspapers in a petrol station in Catford … Everybody was black, getting petrol, buying newspapers. It's

unbelievable, they all wanted selfies and pictures.'
Nigel Farage responds to claims that UKIP is racist.

'This is a real career-defining … country-defining election.'
David Cameron makes his priorities clear on the campaign trail.

'I don't remember.'
Jim Murphy, on being asked whether he had ever sniffed glue. A spokesman for the Scottish Labour leader later clarified: 'Just to be clear, Mr Murphy has never taken drugs.'

'There is an element of *Forrest Gump* about voting Liberal Democrat. It's like the box of chocolates, you don't know what you're gonna get.'
David Cameron snubs his former coalition partners.

'People who do not have HIV, to be frank. That's a good start.'
Nigel Farage, outlining what sort of people would be allowed to migrate to Britain under a UKIP government.

'He's not a Tory.'
Nicola Sturgeon's response when asked by Ruth Davidson, Scottish Conservative leader, to name three things that made Ed Miliband the right man to lead the country.

'Terms are like Shredded Wheat. Two are wonderful, but three might just be too many.'
David Cameron sets out his timetable for standing down as Prime Minister.

'If either of them still think they're going to win a majority, they need to go lie down in that darkened room.'
Nick Clegg's response to David Cameron and Ed Miliband's unsavoury characterisation of coalition negotiations.

'I'd rather have Russell Hobbs than Russell Brand as economic adviser.'
Boris Johnson on the comedian's late-declared support for Labour.

'I was only trying to get a selfie with Nick Clegg.'
Student Will Carrie after accidentally dropping his trousers in front of the Lib Dem leader.

'Ed Miliband unveils his tombstone even before he's been buried.'
Political commentator Iain Macwhirter responds to the stone tablet engraved

with election pledges unveiled by the Labour leader to widespread derision.

'If this exit poll is right, Andrew, I will publicly eat my hat on your programme.'
Former Lib Dem leader Paddy Ashdown giving a verdict he later came to regret.

'There's going to be a lion roaring tonight, a Scottish lion, and it's going to roar with a voice that no government of whatever political complexion is going to be able to ignore.'
Alex Salmond on the predicted SNP landslide in Scotland.

'Thank you for the selfies, thank you for the support, and thank you for the most unlikely cult of the twenty-first century: Milifandom.'
Ed Miliband thanks his more unusual avenues of support in his resignation speech.

'It is now painfully clear that this has been a cruel and punishing night for the Liberal Democrats.'
Nick Clegg comments on the extensive losses suffered by his party.

'Well, well, mate, better luck in 2020.'
Comedian and candidate for South Thanet Al Murray consoles Nigel Farage on the loss of his seat.

'So there are now more pandas in Scotland than Labour MPs.'
Political correspondent Tim Reid on Labour losses in Scotland.

'Quit? I'll be gone within ten minutes.'
Nigel Farage, when asked if he planned on sticking with his decision to resign upon losing South Thanet. The party later rejected his resignation.

'Never ever thought I'd be pleased to see a Tory win a seat.'
Author Irvine Welsh on Conservative candidate Craig Mackinlay seeing off Nigel Farage in South Thanet.

'Compared to my plane crash, this feels pretty damn good.'
Nigel Farage, taking to the podium upon losing South Thanet.

Scotland

David Torrance

Since 2007, when the SNP formed a minority government in Edinburgh, Scotland has got used to thinking constitutionally. This geekiness, a fascination with process and the machinery of government (often at the expense of policy) reached its peak during the 2012–14 independence referendum campaign and, for a few months in the run-up to the general election on 7 May, it afflicted the rest of the United Kingdom too.

Rarely have the territorial aspects of the famously un-codified British constitution appeared so evident, and almost everything about the election served as a reminder that, in Scotland, politics is increasingly subject to a completely different dynamic. In England, for example, the Labour Party was perceived as *too* left-wing, while north of the border it wasn't left-wing enough; south of the border the Tories went into the election a credible party of government, while in Scotland they campaigned like a small fringe party (largely because they were).

2014's independence referendum cast a long shadow, having created a peculiar dynamic of its own. As the journalist Iain Macwhirter observed in his book *Disunited Kingdom*, 'The Unionists didn't quite win, and the Yes campaign didn't quite lose.' And although the Scottish First Minister Nicola Sturgeon maintained the election wasn't *about* independence ('Even if we won every seat in Scotland,' she said, 'that would not be a mandate for a referendum'), both the SNP (of which she'd assumed leadership in November 2014) and its *raison d'être* loomed large: would there be a Nationalist 'tsunami' in Scotland? Would that mean a second independence referendum?

And, more to the point, would the SNP do a deal with Labour in another 'hung' parliament? That question, more than any other, came to dominate the election debate not only in Scotland but across the UK. Indeed, the 2015 general election was about Scotland in the same way that electoral contests in the late nineteenth and early twentieth centuries had hinged on the question of Irish Home Rule. 'Not quite' losing the referendum had provided a paradoxical boost to the SNP, whose membership and poll ratings swelled following Alex Salmond's resignation on 19 September 2014.

'Not quite' winning, meanwhile, had left the three Unionist parties – Labour, Conservative and Liberal Democrats – trying to find a role. The Tories and Lib Dems, of course, fought the general election as incumbents, while Labour lost one leader (Johann Lamont) and gained another (Jim Murphy). But, as the former Labour strategist Paul Sinclair later put it, while the SNP 'had prepared for defeat' in September 2014, Scottish Labour 'didn't prepare for victory'. So even before the campaign officially began in late March, it was obvious Scotland was going to be a major headache for Ed Miliband.

Ironically, Nicola Sturgeon had warned towards the end of the referendum campaign that if Scotland voted 'No' then it would be 'put back in its box' and forgotten about by Westminster. Scotland's fifty-nine MPs, she had also said, rarely made any difference to the outcome of a UK election. The 2015 general election proved her wrong on every count; although it's unlikely she lost any sleep over it.

Scottish National Party

Most elections produce a 'change agent', someone who appears to promise an alternative agenda: in 2010 it was Nick Clegg, and in 2015 it proved to be Nicola Sturgeon. Paradoxically, she wasn't even contesting a Westminster constituency (although her predecessor, Alex Salmond, was), but won a UK audience largely as a result of two network-televised leaders' debates (the same medium that had given rise to 'Cleggmania' five years before).

In the first, on 2 April, the SNP leader stood out because to most viewers she was fresh and new; and if they'd been expecting a female version of Alex Salmond – aggressive and prone to dancing on the head of a pin – they instead witnessed an articulate (not to mention stylish) politician saying lots of things they couldn't really disagree with. Afterwards, even senior Tories like Michael Gove and George Osborne talked up Sturgeon's performance, for her and the SNP doing well dovetailed perfectly with broader Conservative strategy.

Since early March, billboards across England (not Scotland, for obvious reasons) had featured a benign-looking Alex Salmond peering down at Ed Miliband in his top pocket (later, Salmond would be replaced by Sturgeon). As David Cameron put it on Facebook, 'everyone' knew that Labour would end up in the former First Minister's 'pocket'. 'On every vote, every budget, every decision, the SNP would exact a high price for his support,' added the Prime Minister. 'Everyone in Britain will pay with higher taxes, more spending, more debt and weaker defences in dangerous times.'

This was the 'competence versus chaos' message (copyright Lynton Crosby) that dominated the 2015 election campaign. Contrived to win back UKIP defectees and wavering Liberal Democrats, in Scotland it would bolster the SNP's core message – that for the first time in decades its MPs could hold the balance of power at Westminster – and thus reduce the number of Labour MPs. And while the SNP attacked the Tory campaign as cynical and 'anti-Scottish', pointing out that it contradicted the love bombing during the referendum campaign, privately it realised the electoral benefits it could bring.

Following the debate in Manchester, Nicola Sturgeon returned to a hero(ine)'s welcome in Edinburgh, mobbed by hundreds of supporters as if she were a rock star rather than leader of a devolved government. Her popularity in Scotland was longstanding, but the response in the rest of the UK was striking. Some polls suggested she had 'won' the first televised joust, while others in England asked Google if they could vote SNP. Tweeters dubbed her the 'Sturgeonator', while the *Daily Mail* opted for 'the most dangerous woman in Britain'.

In the second (opposition) leaders' debate two weeks later, Sturgeon appeared even more dangerous. When she challenged Ed Miliband to help 'lock' David Cameron out of Downing Street, he declined ('It's a no, I'm afraid'). 'Don't turn your back on that,' the First Minister later told him. 'People will never forgive you.' Again, several polls showed how well Sturgeon had fared across the UK while, after the debate, one snapper caught a memorable image: the Greens' Natalie Bennett, Plaid Cymru's Leanne Wood and the SNP leader hugging each other while Miliband looked on from the sidelines, cut adrift from the 'progressive alliance' repeatedly talked up by the First Minister.

To an extent, however, it was easy for Nicola Sturgeon to shine in a UK context, where her record (and, to a degree, her arguments) was not going to be rigorously scrutinised. In several Scottish leaders' debates, the SNP leader got a much rougher ride from her three Unionist opponents, Scottish Labour leader Jim Murphy, the Scottish Conservatives' Ruth Davidson and Scottish Liberal Democrat leader Willie Rennie. Challenged on her government's record on health and education (not as good as the rhetoric implied), her plans for 'full fiscal autonomy' (devolution of everything except defence and foreign affairs, from which she subtly backtracked as the campaign wore on) and the possibility of another independence referendum (all talk of 'once in a generation' having been dropped), Sturgeon appeared much less sure-footed, not that it did her any harm. Nevertheless, having been heckled in one debate for appearing to prevaricate about another plebiscite, she wielded a 'triple lock': not only would another referendum have to feature in the SNP's manifesto for the 2016 Holyrood election, but there would need to be 'material change' in public opinion, and then another yes/no vote.

The SNP's strategy regarding its 'influence' in a hung parliament was also unconvincing. Having ruled out any 'deal' with the Conservatives, which necessarily limited rather than maximised its potential leeway, the discourse shifted from talk of coalition (there were jokes about Alex Salmond becoming Foreign Secretary or Deputy Prime Minister) to confidence and supply, in which the SNP would support Labour as the Liberals had supported James Callaghan's government in the late 1970s, and finally to a vote-by-vote arrangement in which the Nationalists would back a Labour Queen's Speech and then seek to exert 'influence' over its spending plans, the renewal of Trident and so on. Sturgeon said this meant the SNP could 'change the direction of a government without bringing a government down', something she claimed was made easier by the Fixed-Term Parliaments Act.

With this in mind, the SNP's manifesto, launched at a visually impressive climbing centre outside Edinburgh, ostentatiously echoed Labour's commitments to restore the 50p tax rate, abolish 'non-dom' status, introduce a 'mansion tax' and tax bankers' bonuses, on which Nationalists had hitherto not taken a firm stance. Cleverly, Nicola Sturgeon spoke to the whole of the UK rather than just Scotland (repeating a neat trick from the TV debates), offering to extend the 'hand of friendship' to Labour and other 'progressive' politicians. Referencing the 1983 Labour manifesto, Defence Secretary Michael Fallon called it 'the most expensive ransom note in history'.

Central to the SNP's 'progressive' agenda, meanwhile, was a pledge to 'end austerity' by increasing public spending by 0.5 per cent a year. But, as the Institute for Fiscal Studies (IFS) pointed out, the SNP's 'stated plans do not necessarily match their anti-austerity rhetoric', actually resulting in a longer period of austerity, given that Labour, the Liberal Democrats and the Conservatives all proposed to increase public spending by the end of the 2015–20 parliament. The IFS also monstered plans for 'fiscal autonomy', saying they'd punch a £9.7 billion hole in Scotland's finances in 2019/20. Even the businessman Jim McColl, one of Nicola Sturgeon's economic advisers, said the economy might get 'screwed up' if such a plan went ahead, but the previous First Minister Alex Salmond simply said the figures were wrong, while his successor dismissed them as 'not relevant'.

But the SNP had so firmly entrenched itself in the public eye as the 'anti-austerity' party (a *Financial Times* audit of eight years of SNP rule also found its record 'at odds with its left-wing pretensions') none of this made any difference, enabling it to campaign as a plucky outsider – despite having run Scotland since 2007. Campaigning in Gordon, meanwhile, Alex Salmond claimed credit for policies (free personal care for the elderly and free bus passes) that had been introduced by a Labour/ Lib Dem coalition, while in Edinburgh South, the SNP's candidate Neil Hay got into trouble for some offensive social media utterances, as did twenty-year-old politics student Mhairi Black in Paisley (she had called No voters 'gullible'), although she (unlike Hay) managed to charm and impress her way out of a potentially difficult spot.

Again, these incidents generated media coverage but little else. A TNS poll even put the SNP on 54 per cent of the vote, enough to give them nearly all Scotland's fifty-nine seats. But while UK voters liked the SNP leader, most pollsters found a majority didn't want her to influence the next UK government in the event of a hung parliament. The icing on the cake was an endorsement from the *Scottish Sun* (whose UK edition backed the Conservatives, partly to stop the SNP 'running the country'). North of the border, however, it splashed with 'STUR WARS: A NEW HOPE' (complete with Sturgeon as Princess Leia), claiming the Tories didn't 'understand' Scotland. Scottish politics moves in mysterious ways and so, it seemed, did Rupert Murdoch.

Scottish Labour Party

The Scottish Labour Party entered the general election campaign with a relatively new leader (Jim Murphy) and a new constitution (committing the party to work 'for the patriotic interest' of Scotland), but a nagging feeling that the outcome would be nothing like 2010, when it had returned forty-one MPs and even increased its share of the vote in Scotland by 3 per cent.

With poll after poll showing the SNP likely to win between forty and fifty MPs rather than just six (as in 2010), some outgoing Scottish Labour MPs found solace in gallows humour. 'I'm now set to DEFCON f****d,' said one. 'I'm expecting to leave and never come back. It doesn't matter how good you are or how weak your [SNP] opponent is; it's over.' Another said the mood in Scotland resembled 'the last days of Rome' but 'without sex, or wine. In fact, with none of the fun bits.' Others simply described the apparent surge as 'like a tsunami'.

At a UK level, Labour also found it impossible to escape the dominant narrative about a potential SNP–Labour deal, and, repeatedly pressed to say how he'd respond if Labour emerged as the largest party but couldn't govern on its own, Ed Miliband eventually ruled out what no one was proposing (a formal coalition), while sensibly (but at the same time awkwardly) keeping his options open beyond that. Unfortunately for him, there were mixed messages: while frontbenchers David Lammy and Angela Eagle suggested a deal with the SNP was possible, Alistair Darling said the idea of an alliance was 'for the birds'.

Gradually, as Labour realised the Tory strategy was harming them in England, the rhetoric hardened. Shadow Chancellor Ed Balls said he thought it would 'not happen' because the SNP existed to 'undermine' the UK and Westminster. Then, finally, Miliband did what some had been urging him to do all along: unequivocally rule out any kind of deal with Nicola Sturgeon's party. 'No coalition,' he told Andrew Marr, 'no tie-ins, I have said no deals.' Although this reflected growing confidence that a minority Labour government would be able to call the SNP's bluff, Sturgeon suggested Miliband had been 'bullied' by the Conservatives. 'I think what [Ed Miliband] says the morning after the election', she added, 'will probably be different to what he says now.'

But later, before a *Question Time* audience, Miliband even claimed he would turn down office rather than accept any post-election deal with the SNP. 'If it meant we were not going to be in government by not doing a deal', he said, 'then so be it.' All this put Labour's Scottish leader Jim Murphy, busy defending his East Renfrewshire constituency, in a difficult position. Not only did he appear peripheral to events, but, having launched his manifesto, after which he claimed there would be no need for any spending cuts in Scotland beyond 2015–16, the UK Labour Party launched its manifesto with a commitment to do precisely the opposite. To make matters worse, when asked about the apparent discrepancy, Chuka Umunna said the leader of the Scottish Labour Party would 'not be in charge of the UK budget'. Murphy, taunted the SNP, had been 'hung out to dry'.

In late 2014, Murphy had maintained it was still possible to hold on to all of Labour's forty-one Scottish seats, but he became markedly less confident as the campaign wore on. Focus groups gave rise to a 'merchant of doom' image, with voters expressing concerns about Murphy's negativity. Indeed, at times it looked as if he were re-running what critics had called 'Project Fear', i.e. referendum-era scaremongering. That was but one of Murphy's electoral strategies, and none of them appeared to be working.

Meanwhile, Ed Miliband tried to lure back independence-supporting Labour voters by making the case for a 'radical Labour government' at the STUC conference in Ayr, and Gordon Brown was once again called upon to try to salvage an obviously bad situation. In a speech, the former Prime Minister said the time had come for 'new radical measures' to tackle food poverty, while later he accused David Cameron of 'whipping up English nationalism' by scaremongering about potential SNP influence on a Labour government. Miliband echoed this, saying the Prime Minister was trying to 'set one part of the United Kingdom against another'.

Events in Scotland appeared to baffle Labour grandees back in London. 'It's as though a great part of the Scottish nation', mused David Blunkett, 'have switched off, and that is so dangerous for the Union and for the future of Britain.' Some of what Labour had to endure during the election campaign was out of the ordinary by any measurement. Several candidates were followed, filmed and arguably intimidated by Nationalists, while a campaigning visit from the comedian Eddie Izzard was disrupted by several protestors, including two SNP members (later suspended), prompting Labour to brand it 'the ugly face of nationalism'.

Some of the same protestors gathered outside the Tollcross leisure centre in Glasgow prior to a final Labour rally. Under considerable pressure, Jim Murphy gave the speech of his life, a passionate defence of his party's history and record, combined with a penetrating critique of the SNP. Ed Miliband reiterated his vow not to co-operate with Nationalist MPs, urging Scotland not to 'gamble with the SNP when you can guarantee change with Labour'. That message went down well with the faithful, but they were far from representative of the Scottish electorate as a whole.

On 7 April 2015, the Prime Minister and his wife Samantha visited every constituent part of the United Kingdom in a single day, starting in Edinburgh before flying to Belfast and on to Cardiff before finishing up in north Cornwall. In retrospect, it was the most Unionist thing he did during the entire election campaign, for he spent most of it warning that the SNP influencing a Labour government was 'a frightening prospect' and a potential 'coalition of chaos'. He was back in Scotland just over a week later to help launch the Scottish Conservative manifesto, which included a promise to reintroduce the Right to Buy. The Tories, he said, were 'the real party of devolution'.

By general consensus, Ruth Davidson, the Scottish Tory leader, had a good campaign, performing well in the Scottish TV debates, visiting almost every constituency and taking part in a series of rather colourful photo-calls, including a Thatcher-like moment in a tank. To an extent, she echoed Cameron's warnings about a Labour–SNP deal, but one blogger (a former Scottish Tory press officer) said there was 'mouth-foaming anger' among some senior figures over aspects of the UK Conservative strategy. 'If the SNP could create the Tory campaign,' wrote Andy McIvor, 'they would have created the one we have seen for the last week. It has legitimised the left-wing paranoia which is feeding the army of monkeys required by the SNP's organ grinders.'

He was referring to the Prime Minister's 'Carlisle Principle', under which Cameron promised an annual review to investigate what impact decisions from the Scottish Parliament were having on the rest of the UK. Cameron also talked up plans for an England-only income tax and 'English Votes for English Laws', and launched the party's first 'English' manifesto, while on St George's Day, the Chancellor made like Nigel Farage by raising a pint and wielding a large England flag alongside a pub landlord. Scottish Labour leader Jim Murphy accused the Conservatives of a 'crude, nasty bid' to boost Scottish nationalism.

Hyperbole was ever present. A Labour government reliant on SNP votes would, according to Home Secretary Theresa May, amount to the 'biggest constitutional crisis since the abdication' of King Edward VIII in 1936 ('completely and utterly stupid' said Nicola Sturgeon), while Boris Johnson claimed the SNP would end up 'crouching' on Ed Miliband's back 'like a monkey'. The former Prime Minister Sir John Major also warned of Labour being subjected to a 'daily dose of political blackmail' from the SNP (which Sturgeon called 'silly and undemocratic').

Sir John's former colleague Lord (Michael) Forsyth, meanwhile, gave *The Guardian* a splash with his warning that his party was playing a 'short-term and dangerous' game in talking up the SNP, which reflected unease (and not just in Scotland) that Cameron et al. were playing fast and loose with the Union, no matter what the immediate logic of its campaign. Sir Malcolm Rifkind, the former Foreign Secretary, and Lord Tebbit, a former Conservative Party chairman, both urged Conservative voters in Scotland to consider voting Labour in order to keep out the SNP (although Ruth Davidson argued against tactical voting).

The Guardian also quoted one Tory activist saying that Lynton Crosby loved 'his shoals of Salmonds and Sturgeons', otherwise known as CCHQ teams attending Labour events while wearing masks of the former and current First Ministers. Voters were led to believe that the Prime Minister was taking a close personal interest in the minutiae of Nationalist campaigning. He even tweeted a fuzzy video clip of Alex Salmond (clearly) making a joke about writing Labour's Budget and, when a television presenter introduced his next guest as 'a man who can pinch your wallet, your watch and even your tie without you ever noticing', Cameron, also a guest, could be heard saying: 'Who's that, Alex Salmond?' Indeed, another Conservative campaign poster depicted the former SNP leader as a black-clad pickpocket. 'The Tories', retorted Salmond, 'have been picking Scotland's pocket for years.'

For weeks the warnings never stopped coming. Boris Johnson spoke of a 'constitutional crisis' or, more colourfully, 'Ajockalypse Now'. A week and a half out from polling day, the Prime Minister said he had 'ten days to save the United Kingdom', and that his 'duty' was to win an outright majority in order to avoid 'uncertainty, instability and resentment'. Then, on a final pre-election tour of the UK, Cameron said there was no need to 'imagine the chaos there would be if Ed Miliband became Prime Minister'. 'Just watch the news,' he added. 'Nicola Sturgeon is on the television all day every day, telling us she plans to put Ed Miliband into No. 10 – so that she could hold him to ransom every time there's a vote in the Commons.'

Scottish Liberal Democrats and other parties

When Nick Clegg refused to rule out the possibility of backing a Labour government, the Prime Minister widened his attack on Miliband and Sturgeon to include the Liberal Democrats, but in a Scottish context he needn't have bothered: for although the junior coalition party went into the election with eleven MPs and modest hopes of holding on to at least half that number, it found itself almost irrelevant amid the Tory/Labour and Labour/SNP dynamic. As with Labour, polling suggested the party could lose the vast majority of its Scottish seats, with even former Lib Dem leader Charles Kennedy at risk in the Ross, Skye & Lochaber constituency he'd held for more than thirty years.

Only early in the campaign did the Liberal Democrats impinge upon the Scottish campaign, and then not in a good way. Just after Nicola Sturgeon's triumph in the first leaders' debate, a Lib Dem Spad at the Scotland Office leaked a memo based on a conversation with the French consul general in Edinburgh, who had apparently passed on details of a meeting between the First Minister and France's ambassador to the UK, during which Sturgeon had indicated that her preferred election outcome was another Conservative government. #Nikileaks, as it was dubbed on Twitter, proved a storm in a teacup, swiftly closed down by the SNP leader, who denied saying any such thing, but it reflected badly on a party that had once dominated Scottish politics. (Shortly after the election, Alistair Carmichael, who, as Scottish Secretary, had denied being the source of the leak, apologised to the First Minister when a Cabinet Office inquiry concluded he had authorised it.)

The Scottish Liberal Democrat manifesto was launched in a café in South Queensferry, which said a lot about the party's reduced status north of the border. Leader Willie Rennie proposed reforms to health and education (both devolved areas) but no one was really listening. He also warned of another independence referendum by 2020 and urged Scots to 'vote intelligently' to keep out the SNP, a plea for tactical voting echoed by Nick Clegg on a campaign visit to Scotland.

Clegg also 'totally' ruled out any arrangement with the SNP, saying his party could never 'help establish a government which is basically on a life-support system, where Alex Salmond could pull the plug any time he wants'. Meanwhile, Charles Kennedy attacked the SNP for 'reopening' the referendum debate, breaking their 'once in a lifetime' promise, and the Conservatives for exploiting English nationalism. Danny Alexander agreed, saying the Prime Minister was 'playing with fire' by stirring up ill feeling between Scotland and England. As for Alexander's Highland seat, he joked it would be saved by the 'ginger lobby', while the actor Hugh Grant even tweeted his support. 'Dear People of Inverness (incl my friends and relations),' he wrote, 'I know Danny Alexander and think you're very lucky to have him.'

As for the other parties, a few left-wing groupings contested the odd seat in Scotland but received little or no media coverage, while the Scottish Green Party (constitutionally distinct from that in England and Wales) had to acknowledge that all the action was taking place south of the border. UKIP did have high hopes of making some inroads in Scotland (building on its success in electing an MEP the previous year), but its campaign was amateurish and its Scottish manifesto launch a car crash. David Coburn (the MEP in question) contested Falkirk, but his vow to abolish the Barnett formula, not to mention Nigel Farage's charge that the SNP was fuelling anti-English 'racism', wasn't exactly a vote-winner.

The implications for the Union

Given that so much speculation during the campaign had focused on the SNP and its potential influence in a hung parliament, the election outcome was both a triumph and a disaster for the SNP. A triumph because the SNP took fifty-six of Scotland's fifty-nine seats (not fifty-eight as predicted on the night), but a disaster because accompanying it was not only another Conservative government but one with a majority in the House of Commons.

Thus, Nicola Sturgeon's planned 'anti-Tory majority' crumbled with the broadcasters' exit poll at 10 p.m.; 'locking' David Cameron out of Downing Street was no longer an option and, as the Conservatives headed towards an overall majority, it became mathematically impossible. As she watched Labour lose seat after seat in Glasgow, the First Minister cautioned against triumphalism, although up in Gordon, where, as expected, Alex Salmond won, her predecessor declared that the 'Scottish lion' had 'roared'.

Indeed, the Scottish lion had devoured Douglas Alexander, Labour's campaign chief, pensions spokesman Gregg McClymont and Scottish party leader Jim Murphy. Even Kirkcaldy, where Gordon Brown had stood down after more than thirty years in Parliament, fell to the SNP on a massive swing. The Liberal Democrats, meanwhile, lost Danny Alexander, a key figure in the Conservative–Liberal Democrat coalition, and former leader Charles Kennedy. By the end of the night there were just three non-Nationalist MPs still standing: Scotland Office minister (and future Scottish Secretary) David Mundell (Conservative) in Dumfriesshire, Clydesdale & Tweeddale; former Scottish Secretary Alistair Carmichael (Liberal Democrat) in Orkney & Shetland; and Ian Murray (Labour) in Edinburgh South.

The turnout in Scotland was higher than in the rest of the UK, another legacy from the referendum, but, while the SNP had secured an overwhelming mandate (it got nearly 50 per cent of the Scottish vote), when 'the fifty-six', as they became known, made their way to Westminster – a journey recorded in a blizzard of selfies – it became clear their 'influence' would be more theoretical than real. On votes concerning more austerity, Trident renewal and an in/out EU referendum they would be noisy but powerless.

Speaking after the result, David Cameron sought to reclaim the mantle of 'One Nation' and promised to 'bring our country together', an ironic statement given his campaign strategy over the previous two months. The Prime Minister also pledged to bring forward a promised Scotland Bill 'as fast' as possible, and indeed yet 'more powers' for the Scottish Parliament was the focus of a conversation between Cameron and Nicola Sturgeon a few hours later. At the VE Day commemorations in London, photographers caught the First Minister apparently glaring at her UK counterpart, but in reality their dealings were courteous and businesslike, for both were courteous and businesslike politicians.

Even so, for the next five years the presence of fifty-six SNP MPs will serve as a constant reminder that the old British party political system is virtually dead. And while another independence referendum is unlikely any time soon – not least because Sturgeon keeps saying as much – there looms the prospect of a decade or more of Nationalist hegemony in Scotland, with support for independence rising amid further austerity, a possible 'Brexit' and general Tory unpopularity. As the journalist Peter Geoghegan put it, this risks turning the UK into a 'zombie union', 'not yet dead but listless, inert and lacking the vital human spark that nations, like people, need to prosper'.

David Torrance is a political writer and the author of The Battle for Britain.

Party like it's 1992: polling at the 2015 general election

Joe Twyman

From the beginning of the general election campaign, Conservative and Labour were neck and neck in the opinion polls. Commentators and pollsters alike predicted a hung parliament. The only question that remained was whether Labour or the Conservatives would win the most seats. In the end, and contrary to the polling, the Conservatives achieved not just the most seats, but an overall majority.

This was the story of the polls for the 2015 general election and there is, sadly, no getting away from it. Perhaps even more frustrating is that this was also the story of the polls for the 1992 general election – the *annus horribilis* of the political polling industry.

In both cases, all the pollsters got the story wrong. In 1992, however, even the exit poll for the broadcasters was incorrect. By 2015, the exit poll was substantially closer to the actual outcome, even though it too under-estimated the degree of success for the Conservatives.

So what had happened?

By lunchtime on Friday 8 May it was clear that the political landscape had changed significantly. In Scotland, the SNP had almost totally domi-nated the seats north of the border, winning fifty-six of the fifty-nine seats available. Meanwhile, UKIP support surged to win 3.9 million votes, more than double the number voting for the SNP, but the party still won only one seat. The Liberal Democrats, on the other hand, lost forty-eight of their seats, leaving them with just eight remaining, although their leader Nick Clegg did hang on to his seat in Sheffield Hallam.

While the pollsters largely predicted these headlines, where they were not as accurate was on the crucial matter of Labour versus Conservative – the battle that would decide who formed the next government. No poll predicted the Conservatives winning a majority, but in the end they won 37 per cent of the vote and 331 seats, compared to Labour's 30 per cent and 232 seats.

All this was in spite of the fact that the 2010–15 parliament was, by any measure, the most polled in the history of British politics. Throughout recent decades, newspapers and broadcasters have always commissioned polls, but the frequency of polling between 2010 and 2015 had never been seen before. Unlike in 1992, when the polls were broadly conducted in the same way, pollsters now use a variety of methods to carry out their work and a range of analytical techniques to maximise their accuracy: online, telephone, face-to-face, reallocation of 'Don't knows', allowance for differential turnout, simulated replication of ballot papers etc. etc.

In addition to national-level polls looking at the whole of the British electorate, Lord Ashcroft also privately funded a large number of polls in 167 specific key marginal constituencies during the twelve months from May 2014. This provided a new, additional dimension and granularity to the polling landscape as election day approached.

This new and heightened frequency of polling allowed for analysis not just of short-term fluctuations, as the ebb and flow of the news cycle exerted its influence on public opinion, but also the underlying long-term trends. By the start of the formal campaign for the election, a number of trends had become clear.

Most pronounced was the decline of the Liberal Democrats. They had won 24 per cent of the British vote at the 2010 election, but after joining the coalition their support plummeted. By the start of 2011 they were averaging around 9 per cent of the electorate selecting them in voting intention questions, a figure that occasionally dipped further down, but remained largely unchanged for the next four years.

While the Lib Dems suffered, UKIP surged. In 2010 they had won 3 per cent of the British vote, but as 2012 began they were still struggling to move beyond 5 per cent. Twelve months later they were up to 9 per cent – despite failing to correctly put down their party name on the nomination papers for the London mayoral elections – and 12 per cent by the end of 2013. Significant gains in successive local elections were followed by winning the most votes of any party at the European Parliament elections of 2014, and by the end of that year they had enjoyed highs of 19 per cent in the wake of achieving their first MP, albeit a former Conservative incumbent who had won a by-election.

However, at the start of the 2015, and as the election approached, UKIP's national vote share began to wane slightly. An average of 15 per cent in January became 14 per cent and then 12 per cent by the start of the formal campaign. Down on the highs of October 2014, but still an enormous step up from the 3 per cent of 2010.

In contrast to UKIP's decline, the performance of the Scottish National Party north of the border improved swiftly and then held. In the aftermath of the Scottish independence referendum result, some had expected support for both nationalist issues and nationalist parties to decline substantially. History had shown that to be the case in Scotland in the 1970s and Quebec in the 1990s.

Precisely the opposite happened in 2014. Back in June of that year, the SNP were getting 31 per cent for Westminster voting intention, but after the referendum that figure soared, reaching 47 per cent before the year was finished. As the election approached, the support was sustained, even rising slightly to just below 50 per cent.

In many ways, both the SNP and UKIP (and even the Greens to a lesser extent) were increasingly effective throughout the parliament at mopping up anti-establishment votes. They successfully courted support from voters who were dissatisfied, disapproving and distrusting of Westminster political institutions, political parties and politicians themselves. And though the socio-demographic profile of support varied from party to party, their followers often shared the feeling that they had been 'left behind' by recent changes to modern Britain, and not just in a belief that pork did not always have to be pulled and caramel salted.

For the Conservatives, the story of the voting intention data was, in a sense, far less exciting, as it had remained rather static for some time. The proportion of the electorate saying they would vote Conservative had fluctuated largely between 31 per cent and 33 per cent all the way back to the 'Omnishambles' Budget of March 2012.

Labour, on the other hand, had peaked as high as 45 per cent at various points during the parliament, but they had never been able to sustain it. From early in 2013, their support showed a gradual but steady decline, falling below 40 per cent in 2013 and then below 35 per cent in 2014.

At the start of the official campaign for the 2015 general election, the voting intention figures for the two main parties were generally where they had been at the start of that year: there was little to separate Labour and the Conservatives and neither had anything like the kind of vote share that would be required to get close to the all-important 326 seats in the House of Commons. Beyond the two leading parties, UKIP were still holding on to a strong third place in terms of share of the British vote, with the SNP continuing to dominate Scotland and the Lib Dems failing to show any signs of recovery.

Looking beyond voting intention data, however, the situation was more complicated than the sclerotic trends for that particular measure suggested.

Historical precedent showed it was extremely unusual for a party to come from behind in the polls on leadership ratings to win an election. Equally unusual was that a party could come from behind on economic management to win an election. Furthermore, it had never been the case that a party trailing on both of these metrics had won an election. But as 2015 progressed, the voting intention data suggested just such a situation was a possibility.

At the start of the year, 37 per cent of the British electorate thought David Cameron would make the best Prime Minister, compared to 19 per cent who chose Ed Miliband and 5 per cent who selected Nick Clegg. Meanwhile, 40 per cent thought Cameron was doing well as leader of his party, some way ahead of Miliband on just 18 per cent.

Though it was the Labour leader who improved his personal ratings most during the election campaign, he never caught up with Cameron. By the eve of the election, 44 per cent thought the Conservative leader would make the best Prime Minister and 47 per cent thought he was doing well – still some way ahead of his opponent: 29 per cent of Britain thought Miliband would make the best Prime Minister and 35 per cent thought he was doing well.

Even more positive for the Conservatives were their ratings on the issue of the economy, chosen by survey respondents as both the most important issue facing the country and the most important issue facing them and their families.

The Conservatives had held a lead over Labour since March 2013, when people were asked which party was best able to deal with the issue of the economy in general. At the start of 2014, that lead was 9 per cent. By the start of 2015, the lead had grown to 15 per cent, and by the eve of election day it had reached 19 per cent.

Another related trend moving in the right direction for the Conservatives was respondents' expectations of their own household's financial situation over the next twelve months – the all-important 'feel-good factor'. From a net low of -48 per cent in December 2011, this had steadily risen ever since, albeit with a number of fluctuations along the way, moving up to -7 per cent by the end of the campaign. Still in negative territory, but a great improvement.

Historically, incumbent governments usually get a boost in their vote share as election day approaches, and while it is true that the Conservatives had an Achilles heel on the economy in the form of their ratings on fairness, and Labour held a significant lead on the issue of the NHS, their ratings on the economy coupled with Cameron's scores on leadership were good news going into both 2015 and the official campaign. Many commentators expected them to achieve 'crossover' in the voting intention data at some point and then to pull ahead from their opponents.

But it didn't happen.

The polls didn't really move. On election day, the voting intention data for both Labour and the Conservatives was largely where it had been at the start of the official campaign, which was largely where it had been at the start of the year. Inevitably there were fluctuations along the way, with one party ahead on a given day, only to be caught or overtaken the next. However, in spite of the debates, the pseudo-debates, the leader interviews, the battle buses, the high-vis jackets, the hard hats and the small matter of the manifesto launches, none of that movement was significant and nothing really 'moved the dial'.

All published polls pointed to a statistical dead heat between the top two parties and a hung parliament. The reality turned out to be different. Historical precedent had held. It was still the economy, stupid – and leadership was important too. Why had this not shown in the polls?

Unfortunately, the simple answer to why the polls got it wrong is that there is no simple answer. All the companies who conduct political polls in Britain are in the process of a detailed analysis of exactly what happened, but so soon after the events it is not possible to say with any certainty what caused such a visible disconnect between the data and reality. Various possible explanations are being tested and their impact analysed. However, all that can really be said at this stage is that the final explanation is very unlikely to be a single issue and will instead almost certainly be a combination of a number of smaller issues, all having an impact.

One possible explanation that emerged very quickly and attracted some attention was the issue of 'late swing'. It was suggested that a proportion of the electorate had been won over and switched allegiances from Labour to Conservative at the very last minute, and that this proportion had been large enough to explain the difference between the polls and the result.

Support for this explanation was provided by one polling organisation who claimed, after the election result was known, to have conducted a survey at the last minute that showed the correct final result. Rather inconveniently for them, and for the rest of the industry, they had apparently chosen not to publicly publish the results of this survey, or even mention the fact they were conducting it, anywhere in advance.

Such behaviour is highly unusual for the political polling industry as a whole and judged as being akin to claiming that you bought a winning lottery ticket only after the draw has been made. After all, even if a given company really did conduct an unpublished survey of this type, they could just produce a series of unpublished polls, sampled and weighted to produce every conceivable result, and then subsequently only release the one that aligned with reality.

Instead, respected established pollsters are committed to transparency and publish all their polls of this type in advance, even if they are out of line with others. For example, publicly published polls predicting victories in contests as varied as the 2008 London mayoral elections and the first series of *Pop Idol* were out of line with others, but subsequently proved to be correct.

Casting further doubt on the 'late swing' explanation is that closer inspection of the data revealed that most of the supposed 'swing' could actually be explained by a more Conservative-leaning sample profile in later polls, rather than actual attitudinal change. Tracking respondents at an individual level showed very little significant change, and certainly nothing like the kind needed to bring about such a sudden transformation of the result.

Another explanation saw an old enemy of British political polling re-emerge: 'Shy Tories'. This phenomenon was thought to be (at least partly) to blame for the mistakes in 1992. The idea is that a certain proportion of respondents are unwilling, for a variety of both conscious and latent reasons, to say that they are intending to vote Conservative and instead tell pollsters something different. Poll results then underestimate the true percentage of Conservative voters.

With far more data being collected now than ever before, particularly at an individual level, it should be possible to investigate this explanation in some detail, but by definition the 'shy' nature of the data means it is a complex task.

A more straightforward explanation to test covers the issue of turnout. Specifically, are certain groups of voters more likely or less likely to say they intend to vote compared to actually doing so? Has a 'Lazy Labour' phenomenon emerged whereby Labour supporters say they will vote, but then do not actually get round to it? This can be tested by seeing how local authority voting records align with voting data for individuals, but the process is largely a manual one and so extremely time-consuming.

Of course, the political polling industry must also look at the issue of response rates. For example, anyone taking part in a survey via the internet must first register on a panel and then agree to take part in a subsequent survey. Even an internet pollster that spends many hundreds of thousands of pounds a year recruiting respondents to their panel will still only have around 500,000 people to choose from. Similarly (and depending on who you talk to), only between one in five and one in twenty people called for telephone interviews agrees to take part and even the absolute best face-to-face projects face refusal from half of the people they speak to.

Are these people who take part the same as those who do not? Or are there fundamental attitudinal differences? And if there are, how can results be analysed to mitigate for that difference? All these are important questions the polling industry will seek to answer, but none of those answers is arrived at easily.

Away from published polls, the week after the election result also saw the internal pollsters for the two main parties emerge into the limelight, both of whom claimed to have been more accurate in their own work than the public, published pollsters.

The Conservative's internal pollsters said that they always thought their party was performing better than the public polls and seat forecasts suggested, and that they might even be on for a small majority. This was due, in part at least, to more nuanced questions and analysis being used to determine 'true' voting intention. This prediction largely chimes with what Conservative insiders report being told in advance of polling day, even though many of them apparently seemed to have been sceptical.

Similarly, Labour's internal pollsters also subsequently claimed to know the result in advance, thanks this time to the positioning of the voting intention question after a number of introductory questions about the election campaign and the issues involved. After the election, they said that through this method they had identified the 'crossover' point when Labour had been overtaken by Conservatives, and it had been back in October 2014.

However, during the campaign, some months after 'crossover' is supposed to have been found, Labour Party insiders report being told either nothing of these findings or the opposite story: that Labour were on course for the most seats in a hung parliament.

Despite the differing opinions from insiders within the parties, both explanations for the increased accuracy of internal pollsters are interesting and also testable in the short to medium term.

Further explanations may emerge in due course and, in addition to the extensive internal work carried out by the polling companies, the British Polling Council has agreed to conduct an inquiry headed up by Professor Pat Sturgis, an independent academic from the University of Southampton.

Whatever the explanations, pollsters were affected whether they were small or large; whether they conducted their work via telephone or via the internet; and whether this was their first general election or their umpteenth. The whole political polling industry made a mistake.

Following on from similar mistakes in 1970 and 1992, the industry as a whole demonstrated once again that it certainly does not always get things right. However, its continued success in a wide variety of elections since 1997 – all the way up to getting the European Parliament elections in 2014 almost spot-on – shows clearly that it certainly does often get things right.

As in previous years, I fully expect the industry to adapt, rebuild and improve.

Joe Twyman is head of political and social research at YouGov.

The media

Theo Usherwood

In August 2014, Iain Dale asked me to write a chapter for his book, *The Politicos Guide to the 2015 General Election*. My brief was simple: to predict how newspapers and broadcasters would cover what promised to be the most exciting and unpredictable election in a generation. I titled my chapter 'When Three Becomes Four', and I anticipated that unlike in every other election for a generation we, the media, would spend the next nine months dividing our attention between four parties – the Tories, Labour, the Lib Dems … and then UKIP as well. By mid-October 2014, Nigel Farage's party was not only taking his fair share of media attention, he was dominating the agenda. Douglas Carswell had defected from the Tories to UKIP. He stood down as MP for Clacton, fought the seat in a by-election and won. Mark Reckless – the Conservative MP for Rochester & Strood – was on the verge of repeating the same trick. We were still waiting for David Cameron's speech on his terms for any renegotiations with the European Union and UKIP was riding high in the polls at 25 per cent. Then, on the evening of Thursday 30 October, a poll from Ipsos MORI dropped. It was to turn the narrative of this election on its head. The SNP, it found, were twenty-nine points ahead of Labour in Scotland. Ed Miliband's party would, the poll predicted, lose thirty-seven of its forty-one MPs to the SNP in the fall-out from the referendum on Scottish independence. The story led the bulletins that night. It featured heavily in the newspapers the next morning. There was still a fourth party on the scene; it just wasn't UKIP any longer.

For those journalists fortunate enough to cover the election, this campaign was to become about much more than the rise of the SNP and the obliteration of Labour in Scotland. It became a human story about the power of Nicola Sturgeon to dictate her terms to the established parties in Westminster, and in particular to Labour. Within three weeks of that devastating poll, she was sworn in as Scotland's new First Minister – taking over from Alex Salmond in the wake of the referendum defeat two months earlier. Journalists in Westminster knew Alex Salmond all too well from September's independence vote. But even as late as last November, Ms Sturgeon was still an unknown quantity. Nobody in London paid a huge amount of attention as she addressed the Scottish Parliament on 19 November. And nobody predicted that within three months every utterance the new Scottish leader made in public would be subject to the closest scrutiny.

If there is one speech that can be credited with announcing the arrival of Nicola Sturgeon as a force in this election, it was her address to University College London on 10 February. In it, she set out her price for supporting Labour: Ed Miliband must commit to ending austerity. To do that, she insisted any Labour–SNP government would borrow £180 billion – this proclamation coming at a time when Mr Miliband's team was trying to convince voters the party could be trusted to run the economy. Many Labour MPs on the left of the party were wondering why their leader wouldn't make the same spending commitments. Len McCluskey, the general secretary of the union Unite, would later speak of his admiration for the SNP. But what made this intervention from Ms Sturgeon so threatening to the English media – and in particular the right-wing press – was the idea that you could have a left-wing anti-austerity party, along the same lines as Syriza in Greece, dictating the terms of business to a weak, fledgling Miliband government. Added to that, voters were presented with a party that only six months earlier had come within a whisker of bringing about the break-up of the country. And yet in February, Ed Miliband would still not rule out a deal that could see Alex Salmond – the man at the helm on the independence campaign – being driven down Whitehall in a ministerial Jaguar. For Labour, the narrative had become toxic.

Following that Sturgeon speech, the pressure on Ed Miliband to rule out a coalition with the SNP was ramped up on a daily basis across the media. Fearing he would block his own path to Downing Street, the Labour leader resolutely refused to engage with the question about a possible coalition with the SNP. But on 16 March, in another speech in the capital, this time to the London School of Economics, Ms Sturgeon forced the issue with an offer to Mr Miliband to 'lock the Tories' out of power with a Labour–SNP deal. The Labour hierarchy had to act. Within hours, Mr Miliband had done the inevitable. There would be no formal coalition with the SNP. But there was still the hanging question – would he resort to a more informal pact with Nicola Sturgeon and, if he did, what would be the SNP's price for propping up a Labour minority government? On 4 April, the *Daily Mail* ran the front-page headline 'Most Dangerous Woman in Britain' above a picture of the SNP leader. Again, Ed Miliband and his team refused to rule out a pact with the Scottish Nats, even if it were on a vote-by-vote basis. It was only on 26 April, speaking to the BBC's Andrew Marr, that Mr Miliband retreated from the ground he hoped he would never have to surrender. There would be no deal of any kind. He would instead rely on the SNP voting with Labour on the basis that to vote against his party would leave Alex Salmond and his fellow MPs open to the accusation that they had let the Tories back into power. In truth, however, the damage had been done. The country was only eleven days from the election. The vision of the Labour leader hamstrung by the demands of the SNP had been firmly rooted in the mind of every English voter. And the image of a strong Nicola Sturgeon standing up for voters north of the border had been planted in the mindset of Scotland's electorate.

There's been a huge amount of debate as to the impetus behind the Scotland story. The truth is that it worked for every political party apart from Labour. For the SNP, it fed into the idea that both Sturgeon and Salmond were a coming force, ready to take on the Westminster power base of the established parties. It may seem irrelevant now, but Nick Clegg even tweaked the Liberal Democrat message: his party would be the stable force in government our country needed, unlike the SNP. And for the Tories, the idea of a Labour–SNP deal dovetailed with their core message that a Miliband government would bring chaos, while a Cameron-led administration meant security. In short, Nicola Sturgeon's pledge to end austerity with more borrowing if the SNP found itself in government with Labour slotted neatly in to that narrative. There was a choice, the Conservative spinners claimed, between the chaos of increased borrowing, more debt, higher interest rates and new taxes on the one hand, and then the stability of a David Cameron government on the other. With the SNP looming over its campaign all the while, Ed Miliband tried desperately to claim Labour was the party of fiscal prudence. His team even wrote a new section of the party's manifesto the weekend before its launch on 20 April, pledging the leadership would only make promises that were fully funded. However, with the threat of the Scottish Nationalists, there was a question mark about how much autonomy Mr Miliband would have when it came to managing the economy if he needed the support of the SNP. This was exploited ruthlessly by Tory campaign boss Lynton Crosby, who used the threat of the SNP as an axis on which to set his agenda.

On Wednesday 8 April, Ed Miliband announced that Labour would ban non-doms. The story was briefed to the newspapers and led the radio and television bulletins throughout the day. Tactically, it was a strong announcement. The arcane tax status, Mr Miliband said, had allowed the super-rich to avoid paying their dues to the Exchequer for too long. The proposal went down well with voters and it created a conundrum for the Tories, as it was difficult to defend a tax status they had allowed to exist for five years without appearing to be on the side of the ultra-wealthy. Coincidentally, I had been invited to do a short interview with the Chancellor George Osborne for LBC at a bicycle shop in south London. I wanted to tempt him in to the trap of defending non-doms as job creators. He wasn't having it and simply stuck to the party line that the coalition had clamped down on tax evasion over the previous five years. However, back at CCHQ, the Tories were devising a plan to prevent this story from surviving another day. They needed a distraction to stop voters talking about non-doms.

'Ed Miliband stabbed his own brother in the back to become Labour leader. Now he is willing to stab the United Kingdom in the back to become Prime Minister,' wrote the Defence Secretary Michael Fallon in *The Times* on Thursday 9 April. It was a claim he was to repeat on Radio 4's *Today* programme that morning. Mr Fallon posed a transparent front for the attack, announcing what everyone knew already: the Tories would renew the country's nuclear deterrent, Trident. Ed Miliband had also said he would spend £100 billion to secure its future. But the real purpose of Mr Fallon's intervention was to create a row by accusing the Labour leader of stabbing his brother David in the back to win the leadership of his party, and then claiming he would show the same level of treachery when it came to national security. By midday, Mr Miliband had gone for the bait, giving a clip to the broadcasters accusing the Cabinet minister of demeaning his office. The media had their row. For the spinners at CCHQ, it did not matter whether Mr Fallon won or lost. It didn't matter if he came across as a man lacking integrity. It didn't even matter if some voters thought Ed Miliband was still a decent man. What mattered, what really, really mattered, was that the broadcasters, the scribblers, the editors and producers across every major outlet, were no longer talking about the non-dom story. Instead, they were arguing about nuclear weapons and whether Ed Miliband would find himself held to ransom. And again, Nicola Sturgeon and the SNP provided the hook.

As I have mentioned before, Nicola Sturgeon was a relative unknown in England prior to this election. I'm not entirely sure many political journalists who gathered in the spin room in Westminster for the challengers' debate on 16 April knew about the SNP leader, let alone many of the nine million viewers who tuned in at home. But within the last three minutes of the debate, Ms Sturgeon cemented her position as the face of the 2015 general election. We were left with that killer quote – to be played over and over again – in response to Mr Miliband's decision to rule out a deal with the SNP. 'Don't turn your back on it. People will never forgive you.' That was widely regarded as a defining moment of the campaign, when the apparent threat of the SNP cut through to millions of voters usually unconcerned with politics. For the Tories, a chunk of those voters had been toying with voting UKIP. Now there was a reason to return to the Conservatives.

The irony of this election is that the media spent so much time talking about a hypothetical scenario that never transpired. The press office at Conservative Campaign Headquarters will of course claim the credit for a job well done. It is worth remembering, however, that the polls gave credence to the story. We were told every day the country was heading for another hung parliament. The Lib Dems were facing extinction. Nicola Sturgeon had ruled out any deal with the Tories. Had the pollsters been proved correct and a hung parliament emerged, the arithmetic suggested the most likely outcome was a Labour–SNP deal. It is also worth remembering that the campaigns themselves had been dragging on since the previous year's party conferences. They were narrow and they were boring. Neither Labour nor the Tories – both committed to cutting public spending – had a huge pot of money to pay for expensive new policies or giveaways. That created a vacuum that allowed the SNP story to gain legs. However, while we have been deprived of coalition wrangling potentially lasting weeks, the profiles of Nicola Sturgeon and Alex Salmond remain on an upward trajectory. At the time of writing this chapter, Labour is in the early stages of picking a new leader. That process will be complete by September and it will be up to Ed Miliband's successor to decide whether to join the SNP in trying to thwart Conservative plans or vote with the government. If the new Labour leader decides to work with the SNP in Parliament, especially on thorny issues like welfare reform, there is a good chance there will be some embarrassing defeats for Mr Cameron, who enjoys only a slim majority. There will be many on the Labour back benches who would support such a strategy. But working with the SNP carries the inherent risk that Labour will open itself up to accusations that it has still learnt nothing from past mistakes on public spending and it could potentially make it much more difficult to win over Tory voters. In short, this story may not have transpired in the way we were expecting. But it is not over yet.

Theo Usherwood is Political Editor at LBC.

Fixed-Term Parliaments Act

Peter Riddell

David Cameron has more limited options than his predecessors. Past prime ministers with a small Commons majority have always looked for the opportunity to improve their party's position at a general election well before the five-year limit. That option has now been restricted by the Fixed-Term Parliaments Act of 2011 (FTPA).

Anthony Eden went to the country in May 1955, barely three and a half years after his party had returned to office with a majority of seventeen, roughly the same as Mr Cameron after the 7 May general election. In March 1966, Harold Wilson sought to improve on the majority of four he had won eighteen months before, and in October 1974, Wilson sought to turn the minority position of minus thirty-three of the February election into a majority. In each case, these early elections were successful and resulted in an improvement in the incumbent's position, though with only a tiny overall majority in October 1974.

It is not hard to envisage circumstances in which Mr Cameron might seek a similar election before 2020 to improve the Conservatives' position – say, after the promised referendum on European Union membership if this result is seen as a victory for him; or at another opportunity when the Conservatives' political standing, and electoral prospects, are favourable compared with Labour's.

But this option no longer exists for him. The FTPA sets the date of the general election as the first Thursday in May in the fifth calendar year after the previous election. Under Section Two of the Act, early general elections can only occur if either of two conditions is met. First, if a motion for an early general election is agreed either by at least two-thirds of the whole Commons (including vacant seats) or without a division. Second, if a motion of no confidence is passed and no alternative government is confirmed by the Commons within fourteen days by means of a confidence motion. The precise wording of both motions is laid down in the Act.

The effect of the Act has been to end the prerogative power of the monarch to dissolve Parliament, always, in modern times, on the recommendation of the Prime Minister. Both the passage of the Act and its implications have proved to be controversial. There was criticism during debates on the Bill that it was being hurried and should have been subject to pre-legislative scrutiny. The relevant committees of both the Commons and the Lords were critical of the speed at which it was pushed through. The Constitution Committee of the Lords argued in a report in December 2010 that the origins and content of the measure 'owe more to short-term considerations than to a mature assessment of enduring constitutional principles or sustained public demand'. Various provisions, notably on the threshold required under Section Two to permit early general elections, were altered from the original announcement of the Bill to its publication and enactment.

In particular, there was much discussion about whether the length of term should be four years, rather than five. The Parliament Act of 1911 set the maximum term at five years, though the life of the parliament was extended in both the world wars. In practice, prime ministers whose parties have been ahead in the polls have usually sought re-election after four years – as Margaret Thatcher did in both 1983 and 1987, and Tony Blair did in 2001 and 2005 – while those with parties behind in the polls, or who have had a change of leaders, have often gone nearly to the full five years, as Sir John Major did from 1992 to 1997, and as Gordon Brown did from 2005 until 2010.

Complaints about the Act increased during the course of the 2010–15 parliament. They largely came from critics of the Liberal Democrats arguing that the five-year fixed term had become primarily a means of keeping the coalition together. Proposals to repeal the Act were brought forward by backbenchers in both Houses, primarily Conservative MPs in the Commons and Labour's Lord Grocott in the Lords. It is hard to determine whether the Act did prevent the coalition splitting apart at times of strain, though it probably helped. Another objection is that the FTPA permits a change of government, probably of coalition partners, within a single parliament without seeking the approval of voters in a fresh election. This is not unusual in some other European countries but would be novel in the modern, democratic era in the UK.

However, even without the Act, it is likely that the 2010–15 parliament would have gone nearly its full distance simply because it was not in the interests of either party to have an earlier election. Not only were the Liberal Democrats running at a third or less of their 2010 standing in the polls, but the Conservatives were running behind in the published polls, at least in early 2015 (flawed though those polls may have been).

The FTPA also came to prominence during the election campaign, when there was speculation about what would happen in a hung parliament, especially if the outcome was not clear and two rival parties both claimed the right to govern. There was a lengthy debate about whether the Act had replaced the normal conventions affecting when a Prime Minister has to resign when he or she has lost the confidence of the Commons on, for example, a vote on an amendment to the Queen's Speech. In the past, notably in January 1924, when Stanley Baldwin lost on a vote on the King's Speech, he resigned and was replaced by Ramsay MacDonald, the Leader of the Opposition.

One suggestion, however, was that the existence of the Act altered the convention, since a Prime Minister who had lost a vote on the Queen's Speech could in future remain in office seeking to form an arrangement with other parties, arguing that only a defeat on a specifically defined motion under the FTPA counted. In these circumstances, no doubt the Leader of the Opposition would table a motion of no confidence expressed in the language of the FTPA. This would trigger the fourteen-day period during which an alternative government would have to win a confidence vote. But the wording of the FTPA is unclear on who governs during the fourteen-day period. Does a Prime Minister who has lost the first vote have to resign immediately? It might not be clear that the Leader of the Opposition could successfully form a government and win the confidence of the Commons. Part of the problem was that the FTPA had never really been intended to cover the formation of government, as opposed to providing a means of ending a parliament after, say, two or three years if either of the two conditions were fulfilled.

After this discussion, a widespread – and, in the event, untested – view was that the fate of any minority government would be determined in traditional means by votes on the Queen's Speech rather than FTPA motions. But there is still the concern that the Act might permit later changes of government without a further general election. That might happen if a government lost a series of by-elections, or suffered a split and defections of its MPs, and sought to shore up its position by securing the formal support of another party.

At the end of the election campaign, there were renewed demands for repeal of the Act from Lord Lisvane, better known as the former Clerk of the Commons Sir Robert Rogers, and from Lord Pannick, the barrister and respected crossbench peer. Lord Lisvane argued in a letter to *The Times* that the Act made no 'provision for a government losing on a matter which previously would have been regarded as one of confidence: the Finance Bill, for example, or even the Queen's Speech; and having to limp on without the authority to govern'.

Simply repealing the Act could be complicated, since the 2011 Act replaced a prerogative power by a statutory mechanism. Constitutional authorities disagree about whether a prerogative power could be restored after being abolished, or whether the prerogative power was merely placed in abeyance and could be exercised again. The Treasury Solicitor's Department told the Public Administration Select Committee in an earlier inquiry, before the FTPA was conceived, that 'it is not altogether clear what happens where a prerogative power has been superseded by statute and the statutory provision is later repealed but it is likely to be the case that the prerogative will not revive unless the repealing enactment makes specific provision to that effect'.

A simple solution might simply be to replace Section Two of the Act with a requirement that Parliament can be dissolved by the vote of a simple majority of those MPs voting, not a higher proportion of all MPs. So the decision would still lie with the House of Commons but an earlier dissolution would be available to a government which could command a majority.

The discussions about a hung parliament also underlined the potential – though, in the end, not realised – problem of a long period of uncertainty before a government, incumbent or its replacement, could establish whether it had the confidence of the Commons. Under the 2015 timetable, the key votes on the Queen's Speech would have been in early June, nearly four weeks after polling day. An alternative approach, aired before the election but rejected by the government, would be to have a nomination or investiture vote soon after Parliament meets (the first business after the election of the Speaker and the swearing in of MPs). This is like the procedure adopted in the Scottish Parliament and the Welsh National Assembly and would clear up any uncertainty before the Queen's Speech. There is a strong case for reconsidering this idea as part of the post-election review of constitutional arrangements around the election.

In any event, Section Seven of the FTPA requires the prime ministers to make arrangements between June and November 2020 for a committee to carry out a review of the operation of the Act – and, if appropriate, to make recommendations for the repeal or amendment of the Act. A majority of members of the committee are to be MPs and its report and recommendations will be published. That does not, however, rule out amendment or repeal before then.

Peter Riddell has written extensively on constitutional matters and is director of the Institute for Government.

Survey of regional results

Robert Waller

Scotland

I make no apologies for starting with Scotland, rather than leaving it to the nether end of regional surveys, as it often is. Not only did Scotland make such a significant contribution towards the dashing of Labour's hopes of a majority government of the United Kingdom by removing all but one of its forty-one seats north of the border, but the apparent threat of Scottish National Party influence on such an administration was a major factor in Labour's surprisingly poor performance in England and Wales too.

The sheer scale of the SNP landslide deserves repeating: fifty-six out of fifty-nine seats, leaving Labour, the Liberal Democrats and Conservatives with only one seat each required unprecedented swings. The biggest of these was the 39.28 per cent in Glasgow NE, hitherto Labour's safest seat in Scotland, which was, as Alex Salmond delighted in pointing out, the largest shift anywhere in Britain's history since electoral records began in 1835. In Scotland as a whole, the SNP's share rose from 19.9 per cent in 2010 to almost exactly half – an *average* swing of 30 per cent. Fifty seats changing hands and fifty new MPs out of fifty-nine is also the largest turnover ever in personnel in any region. These include twenty-year-old Mhairi

Black, who had still to take her finals in Politics at Glasgow University – who became the youngest recorded MP since the seventeenth century. What is even more remarkable is that she defeated the Labour shadow Foreign Secretary and national campaign organiser Douglas Alexander.

As may be expected in the circumstances, he was not the only 'name' to be expunged. Those ousted included Tom Clarke (Coatbridge, Chryston & Bellshill), the longest-serving MP to be defeated anywhere, after thirty-three years as Member in seven parliaments, and, at the other end of the seniority scale, his neighbour Pamela Nash, the youngest Member of the 2010 intake. The Scottish Labour leader Jim Murphy, charged with saving his party from impending doom just five months before the general election, signally failed to do so, or to save himself in East Renfrewshire. The Liberal Democrats were the other major losers in Scotland, being stripped of ten seats, including that of a member of the senior governing 'Quad' in the last parliament, Danny Alexander of Inverness, Nairn, Badenoch & Strathspey, along with former party leader Charles Kennedy (Ross, Skye & Lochaber), who had entered Parliament as a 23-year-old in 1983.

However, there is no further point in reciting the litany of the defeated. As Edwina Currie said after the 1997 election, with rather less justification, 'We all lost.' One might rather ask, how did anyone else survive the SNP onslaught? The outgoing Scottish Secretary, Alistair Carmichael, held on (just) for the Liberal Democrats in Orkney & Shetland, their longest-standing seat in Britain (since gained by Jo Grimond in 1950) – but it has been argued that these most northerly of isles feel little kinship with Scotland, having been part of Norway till 1471. At the other end of the country, the lone Conservative elected in 2010, David Mundell, also managed a majority of under 1,000 in Dumfriesshire, Clydesdale & Tweeddale, which is very much on the border with England. It might be pointed out, though, that the Tories did maintain their share of the vote across Scotland relatively much better than the other two 'English-led' parties. Finally, the sole Labour hold was by Ian Murray in Edinburgh South (ironically where they recorded their smallest majority in 2010). He was keen to point to his hard work as a constituency MP over the previous five years, but it might also be remembered that the seat has an exceptionally high proportion of English-born voters and had a very low SNP share in 2010, and that he probably benefited from tactical voting in previously unfavourable parts of the seat like Morningside. The Labour majority in Edinburgh South was the highest of the survivors, but at 2,637 is paltry compared with almost all the SNP margins of victory. No one else really came close to holding on, although worthy of credit was Jo Swinson's effort in only losing 2 per cent of the LD share in losing by just over 2,000 in East Dunbartonshire, and the Conservative effort in Berwickshire, Roxburgh & Selkirk, just 328 behind the SNP.

Why all the above happened cannot be explained in a brief regional survey. Clearly, Scottish nationalism was immensely energised by the narrow failure of the campaign for full independence less than eight months earlier, reflected by the turnout of 70 per cent – 7 per cent higher than in 2010, and around 5 per cent higher than the UK-wide average in 2015. Yet the SNP share exceeded the 'Yes' vote. It might also be argued that many former Labour voters were attracted by the thought that they could gain a greater voice for Scotland while still getting a Labour-led government in the hung parliament predicted by all the polls during the pre-election period. This did not come to pass, and the upshot is that the Labour Party now looks further away from office than for a very long time, having being so aided for five decades by the hitherto reliable support of Britain's northern nation.

South West England

If Scotland was the nemesis for Labour in the 2015 general election, the South West of England was the region that most epitomised the disaster that befell the Liberal Democrats. Before the election, this was their strongest area in the whole of Britain, as they held fifteen seats across the counties of Cornwall, Devon, Somerset, Dorset, Gloucestershire and Wiltshire (compared with eleven in Scotland, their next strongest). They lost all fifteen – leaving the remaining rump of eight Lib Dem MPs spread across six regions. In terms of change in share of vote, the South West recorded the best Conservative performance (up 3.8 per cent since 2010) and the Liberal Democrats' worst (a staggering minus 19.6 per cent).

In other circumstances, in four constituencies defeat could have been accounted for merely by the retirement of popular incumbent MPs: Annette Brooke in the highly marginal Mid Dorset & North Poole, the former GP David Heath in Somerton & Frome, Jeremy Browne in Taunton Deane, and even in Bath, where the majority was much larger but had been built up over five general elections by Don Foster, who had originally defeated the Conservative chairman Chris Patten in the 'John

Major' election of 1992. The scale of the Conservative victories in some of these seats does confirm the size of the challenge facing replacement candidates – 15,000 in Taunton, 20,000 in Somerton & Frome. Yet the eleven established Liberal Democrat MPs were also all removed, suggesting the true depth of the rejection of the party in its traditional West Country heartland.

Cornwall, where the Lib Dems held every seat as recently as 2005, is now all Tory. The last result to declare in 2015, as in 2010, was St Ives, the westernmost of all, including as it does the Scilly Isles. It provided a fitting end to the declarations that so broke LD hearts, as Andrew George, a Cornishman to his bones, fell by 2,469 votes to the Conservative Derek Thomas. This was almost the closest his party came to victory in the region, except for the Pensions Minister Steve Webb, who held the Tory majority in Thornbury & Yate to just under 1,500. Elsewhere it was not even close. Perhaps the most signal defeat came in Yeovil, where David Laws, a chief architect of the coalition agreement five years before, reaped the bitter fruits of the fate that has befallen so many junior partners, in the seat that kick-started a Liberal revival which lasted over thirty years when Paddy Ashdown gained it back in 1979. Sir Nick Harvey also lost, like Laws, by over 5,000 votes, and this in a seat with an even longer tradition of Liberalism – Jeremy Thorpe's North Devon. Nor did the first-term incumbency effect work for the Liberal Democrats, as their youngest MP, Dan Rogerson, found after five years of hard work in North Cornwall; as too did Duncan Hames, thrashed in Chippenham and having to join his wife Jo Swinson in seeking new employment.

The Conservatives gained fourteen of the fifteen Liberal Democrat seats. The other one was Bristol West, where Stephen Williams suffered the indignity of dropping to third place behind the Greens (their second-best performance, 27 per cent, after Caroline Lucas) and the Labour victor. However, the South West did not provide any net advance for the Labour Party as a whole. This was because not only did they fail to gain one of their main targets in the region, the marginal Conservative seat of Plymouth Sutton & Devonport, but they actually lost the other Plymouth seat (Moor View) to the Tories. This was probably due to the much higher than average UKIP share and swing in this working-class, northern part of the city. Labour also went sharply backwards in all their other targets, Stroud, Gloucester, Kingswood and South Swindon – all comfortably held by first-term Tory MPs. This was partly due to the 'sophomore effect', whereby five years of representation generates most of the benefit a personal vote brings, but the Tory surge was much stronger than can be so explained.

The outcome of all the above is that the South West now looks almost like the South East on an electoral map: a sea of blue. Labour are now confined to four dots, the urban seats of Exeter and three in Bristol. Liberalism has been wiped out. This presents a very different picture from that we have become accustomed to. Ever since the nineteenth century, the further away from the South East of England one went, the less Conservative the electoral geography: Scotland, Wales and the far West have never been almost totally dominated by the Tories – due to political and social cleavages stretching back to the heyday of Nonconformity, for example. One wonders if, ironically, one major cause of this transformation was the threat posed so far away at the other end of Britain, that the Scottish Nationalists would have much power in a hung parliament. The South West decided, for whatever reason, that it wanted a clear overall majority, and by providing fifteen gains for the Conservatives (more than in any other region) it did more than its fair share of making sure that David Cameron got one.

South East England

Common wisdom has it that the South East of England has always been the solid, true-blue Conservative heartland. So, no change there then.

But in fact there *was* change in 2015. Not all of the region was Tory in 2010. The Liberal Democrats, for example, were defending four seats, one of which looked impregnable. It was no surprise that they lost Portsmouth South to the Conservative Flick Drummond. Their MP there since 1984, Mike Hancock, had been embroiled in controversy for some years and had resigned from the party in 2014. He did stand for re-election as a 'No Description' candidate, but scarcely split the vote by polling only 716 votes, the poorest performance of any sitting Member. But damage must have been done to the Liberal Democrat brand, and their new candidate Gerald Vernon-Jackson actually did quite well to finish in second place, though the share was more than halved.

Less widely predicted losses came in Eastleigh in Hampshire, where Mike Thornton had managed to stave off strong Conservative and UKIP challenges in a 2013 by-election occasioned by the unfavourable circumstances caused by the conviction and jailing of Chris Huhne for trying to pass points for a speeding offence to his now-estranged wife. However, in 2015, when a national government was being chosen, Thornton lost to the Tories by over 9,000. In Eastbourne, Sussex, constituency opinion polls before the campaign gave first-term incumbent Stephen Lloyd a huge lead; but he too was beaten, though by the smallest margin of any unsuccessful LD defence, 733 votes. The biggest shock, though, was the defeat of Norman Baker, the hyperactive constituency MP for Lewes since 1997 and Home Office Minister 2013–14. He lost over 16 per cent of his share in what was regarded as the safest LD seat in the region.

Not only did all the Liberal Democrats lose to Conservatives, but so did one of the four Labour seats. In Southampton Itchen, the eastern side of the city and traditionally its more left-inclined half, the very popular John Denham retired, and although he was replaced by a very attractive candidate in Rowenna Davis, this probably made the difference for Royston Smith, who had also been the Conservative candidate five years earlier without success. In the western Southampton division, Test, the sitting MP Alan Whitehead was returned with a positive swing. This would have left Labour with only Slough and Oxford East (where Andrew Smith massively increased his majority to over 15,000 due to the collapse of the Liberal Democrats) – except that they did also regain one seat, Hove, lost in 2010.

This was scarcely consolation, though, for Labour failed in all their other targets in a region in which they at least have to make some impact to challenge for government. Brighton Kemptown Labour needed a 2 per cent swing and achieved less than 1 per cent. In all their other hopes they suffered negative swings – that is, the Tories strengthened their position. Typical was the 'odd couple' seat Hastings & Rye, where Amber Rudd increased her majority from 1,993 to 4,796 to secure a more comfortable second term. It will be harder for Labour to advance in the South East next time, even discounting the effect of likely boundary changes, especially as they fell back from second to third place in some seats they had won in the Blair years, such as Sittingbourne & Sheppey in Kent.

The runner-up position there was taken by UKIP, as it was in the much higher-profile constituency of South Thanet – possibly the most media-covered contest in the whole country, because of the candidature of Nigel Farage – who through either confidence or bravado declared he would resign as party leader if he didn't win it. He lost by over 2,800. In fact, though, the South East did not turn out to be UKIP's best region – or even one of its best. Their share here was 14.7 per cent, less than in five other regions (top of the list was the North East of England). The South East is a relatively highly educated part of Britain; UKIP did best in seats with few university graduates. Their disappointments included the loss of Rochester & Strood (also in Kent – literally that most south-eastern of all counties), held by their second defector Mark Reckless in a by-election in their high-watermark year of 2014. Reckless lost by over 7,000. Finally, UKIP had to suspend and disown one candidate who allegedly threatened to shoot his British Asian Conservative opponent, in North East Hampshire. The outcome? Ranil Jayawardena was elected with the largest Tory majority anywhere, a margin of 29,918 votes. The next highest in the list were also to be found in this region, led by Theresa May in Maidenhead (29,059) and Dominic Raab in Esher & Walton (28,616). It is the Conservative Party, not UKIP, that can point to the South East as their strongest region of all, obtaining 50.8 per cent of the vote – an absolute majority, which they did not quite manage in 2010 (49.9 per cent). This was even despite the rise of UKIP and the Greens (who again won their only seat as Caroline Lucas greatly strengthened her position in Brighton Pavilion), which made 2015 much more of a multi-party contest. This is the measure of the Conservative dominance, which now looks still more unassailable.

London

London was Labour's great hope in 2015. Strong performances in the 2014 London borough elections, demographic change as the capital has become ever more cosmopolitan, and a vaunted 'ground operation' all contributed to a strong expectation that Labour would sweep many Conservative MPs out of the Commons, and thus lay the foundations for at least becoming the largest party – even if an overall majority was out of reach because of developments far from the metropolitan hub in Scotland. Such optimism was largely unjustified.

Yes, Greater London did turn out to be Labour's best region in 2015, even if this was only relative to the disappointments and disaster elsewhere. Four of their ten gains from the Conservatives were in the capital. These included the two that needed the largest swings. In Ilford North, where the British Asian population has grown rapidly since 2010, the new MP Wes Streeting, a former President of the National Union of Students, needed a 6 per cent swing to oust the Jewish Conservative Lee Scott; he achieved 6.3 per cent. This seat was No. 71 on the Labour versus Tory target list. Rupa Huq gained Ealing Central & Acton (No. 47) from Angie Bray by 274 votes, with a swing of over 4 per cent. The gains were spread around the sub-regions of London. To the west, Brentford & Isleworth fell, and in north London Joan Ryan regained the Enfield North constituency she lost five years before. Labour also took three from the Liberal Democrats. Overall, the Labour share rose by 7.1 per cent, more than in any region. However, much of the advance was where it didn't count most, and their showing in the crucial marginals was patchy.

For example, Labour did not succeed in gaining their top target in London, the super-marginal Hendon, where, in a re-run of 2010, Matthew Offord increased his majority over its previous MP Andrew Dismore from just 106 to 3,724. On paper, Hendon had been Labour's third most likely gain anywhere in Britain. Other seats Labour needed to win to form a government also eluded them: Croydon Central, Harrow East (where Bob Blackman remains the Tory with the lowest proportion of white constituents anywhere), Battersea; indeed, in the latter two there was actually a pro-Conservative swing. Across London as a whole, the Tories increased their share.

This was partly because of their surprising gains from the Liberal Democrats, who had done better in local elections in 2014 in Sutton than in 2010 – but still lost Sutton & Cheam. Also in outer south-west London, Kingston & Surbiton fell to the Conservatives, and the coalition Cabinet minister Ed Davey was out. This was not entirely unexpected, as Kingston Council had been gained by the Tories in 2014, but a real surprise was the disappearance of an even more prominent Liberal Democrat, Vince Cable. His majority of over 12,000 proved no defence against the Conservative flood; or rather, the Lib Dem collapse. Just as much a shock was the loss of Simon Hughes to Labour after thirty-two years as MP for the Bermondsey area; and Lynne Featherstone was beaten by over 10,000 in Hornsey & Wood Green. The worst performance in any 2010 Lib Dem seat was not entirely unexpected: following the retirement of a disillusioned Sarah Teather, the party's share in Brent Central fell from 44 per cent to 8 per cent (in third place) and Dawn Butler won for Labour by nearly 20,000. Only Tom Brake (Carshalton & Wallington) could parlay the LD dominance of Sutton Council into retention at parliamentary level.

There were some notable personal triumphs. In Richmond Park, Zac Goldsmith, an independently minded Conservative, played on his local role in increasing his majority to over 23,000 in a part of London historically known since the 1970s for very close contests with the Liberals in their various guises. The largest vote anywhere in Britain was for Labour's Stephen Timms in East Ham, the only one which exceeded 40,000. London was UKIP's worst region by far in England, as they polled only an 8.1 per cent share overall. They did finish a strong second with nearly 30 per cent in Dagenham & Rainham, though many would consider that effectively still part of their strongest county, Essex. Nor did the Greens challenge for victory anywhere, though their best performances were at Hackney North (14.6 per cent) and Holborn & St Pancras, where party leader Natalie Bennett got over 7,000 votes, though Sir Keir Starmer easily won the seat, formerly held by Frank Dobson, for Labour. There was no appearance for either George Galloway's Respect Party or Lutfur Rahman's Tower Hamlets First in the heart of the East End, which may have saved this neighbourhood from further controversy – for the time being at least.

With the virtual disappearance of the Liberal Democrats as a competitive force in Greater London, its divisions are now revealed more clearly. Labour majorities mushroomed in ethnically mixed areas such as in the boroughs of Redbridge and Waltham Forest, while the Conservatives strengthened their grip in leafy outer suburbs and wealthier zones nearer the centre. The capital does display stark contrasts between affluence and multiple deprivation, but having rapidly grown in electorate (over 90,000 were on the roll in West Ham, for example), it will not lose many of its seventy-three seats in the expected reduction of MPs from 650 to 600 for the 2020 election. London may offer too much internal variety and too many unique features to be regarded strictly as a microcosm of England as a whole, but there will still be plenty of key marginals to provide exciting contests next time.

East of England

The Conservatives won fifty-two of the fifty-eight seats in the East of England in 2010 – and fifty-two again in 2015. A flat result in this flattest of regions, then? Not quite, because this is where we must give pride of place to what is undeniably a dynamic new force in British politics – the United Kingdom Independence Party.

Some thought that UKIP's true heartland would be the county of Kent in the South East region, and that is where their leader Nigel Farage sought entry into Parliament in South Thanet. Yet it turned out that their two best performances – and solitary triumph – came in the East, in Essex ('land of the East Saxons'), and they challenged elsewhere in this region too, taking many second-place positions.

UKIP's one MP, as the smart observers predicted, is Douglas Carswell of Clacton. He had by far the best chance of actually winning as he had cemented his personal strength by contesting a very high-profile by-election in October 2014 after announcing his defection from the Conservatives on 28 August. There is something of a tradition of defectors winning one general election (Dick Taverne, Lincoln, in February 1974 after retaining his own seat in a 1973 by-election, and Eddie Milne in Blyth at that same general election), though as UKIP's own Mark Reckless found this time, it is not guaranteed. Carswell is much liked and respected, though, and he duly won Clacton again in 2015 with a majority of over 3,400. Whether he can hold on again may be moot – Taverne and Milne lost in their second post-defection general elections – but he should have a better chance than they did, as rather than being a lone operative he is a member of a party that has a serious chance of continuing to play a significant role in British politics. UKIP finished first in the 2014 European elections, and did of course finish this general election with 3,881,000 votes (12.6 per cent), even though with only this one seat. Europe (and indeed immigration, their other main issue) is still likely to be prominent in the 2020 general election, unless perhaps there is a 'Yes' vote in the putative 2017 referendum (in which the main party leaderships are likely to campaign for the UK to stay in the EU). If Britain chooses to stay in, UKIP may be energised thereafter, as the SNP were after *their* referendum.

This also means that UKIP's near-misses in 2015 should be considered closely. In Thurrock, also in Essex of course, they finished third but were still less than 1,000 votes and 2 per cent behind the Conservative winner, Jackie Doyle-Price. Thurrock was undoubtedly the best example of a three-way marginal anywhere in Britain this time. In Castle Point, UKIP finished a very clear second with over 14,000 votes. Across the region they averaged 16.2 per cent. If the Tories should prove unpopular in government, UKIP are now placed as the strongest challengers in a raft of constituencies.

Labour failed to gain any of their target seats from the Conservatives. They did have chances. In Waveney in Suffolk, based on Lowestoft, the easternmost seat of all, they only lost by 769 in 2010 but went backwards despite again fielding their former MP Bob Blizzard. They also suffered negative swings in Ipswich and Norwich North, just as the two football teams representing those communities vied to reach the Championship play-off final. They could only close the gap slightly in Bedford, another seat where the bookmakers' odds suggested Labour were strong favourites. Constituencies like Stevenage, Harlow, South Basildon & East Thurrock and Great Yarmouth now seem well beyond their ken, though they need to win them to have an overall majority again, as they did from 1997 to 2005. In Braintree, gained by Labour in the Blair landslide, the Tory majority is now over 17,000 – and UKIP are in second place.

The grim news for Labour was only slightly counteracted by two gains from the Liberal Democrats, in Cambridge, where the popular scientist Julian Huppert nearly hung on, and in Norwich South. In the latter, where the influence of the University of East Anglia is strong, Simon Wright had been expected to lose, but Labour had to contend with one of the two strongest Green challenges for a gain in the country (the other was in Bristol West); in the end, the Greens fell disappointingly short, in third place behind the Conservative and actually losing share of the vote. Wright fell more disastrously short, dropping from first to fourth – the only place where this happened to the Liberal Democrats.

The Lib Dems also lost Colchester, which the veteran Sir Bob Russell had held safely since 1997, to the Tories. Their single success in the region was that of Norman Lamb (North Norfolk), who was promptly installed as one of the favourites to be the leader of the much shrunken party. A final bitter pill for them to swallow on a night entirely lacking in positive news came in Watford. A three-way marginal in 2010, the Lib Dems had believed that this was their best chance of a gain in any region. This was because their candidate was Dorothy Thornhill, elected four times as Mayor of Watford from 2002 up to and including 2014. The result summed up the Eastern region and the general election as a whole. The Conservative Richard Harrington won, increasing his majority over Labour to a convincing 9,794 – and Dorothy Thornhill finished an even more distant third, the Liberal Democrat share dropping by 14 per cent. Even one of the most electorally successful local politicians of the recent era had been decisively rejected, showing how toxic the Liberal Democrat label was in 2015. In the East of England region, UKIP polled almost exactly double the vote total of the Liberal Democrats, confirming their position as the new third force in English politics.

East Midlands

If any region epitomised the Conservative victory over Labour in the 2015 general election it was the East Midlands. The Liberal Democrats did not really figure significantly here before the election, never mind after it. This was a 'major party' battleground, featuring eight very important key targets for Labour, who were trying to reverse as many of their losses in 2010 as possible. They regained precisely none of them. Even worse for Ed Miliband's party, they also lost the by-election gain in November 2012 of Corby in Northamptonshire that had given them so much optimism that they might return to government, as well as losing Derby North on a fresh swing to the Tories. The East Midlands was the only region in England that swung overall directly from Labour to Conservative in terms of both vote share and seats.

Derby North was the most obvious blow, as the former city council leader Chris Williamson was edged out by Amanda Solloway by forty-one votes. But the pattern of negative swing was also found in all the marginals Labour had hoped to gain. For example, in their No. 5 target in the whole country, Sherwood in Nottinghamshire, the Conservative MP elected in 2010, Mark Spencer, increased his apparently fragile lead of 214 to a healthy 4,647. Sherwood, though named after the forest, had once been an area dominated by the mining of the Dukeries coalfield, but that era has finally come to an end with the announcement in 2014 of the closure of the last pit, Thoresby Colliery near Edwinstowe. In Broxtowe, just west of Nottingham, a re-run of the 2010 contest saw a decisive victory, also by over 4,000, by Anna Soubry over the popular former MP Nick Palmer. The largest town in that constituency, Beeston, was named in 2015 as statistically 'boasting' the highest proportion of adultery in England and it too has not remained faithful to Labour. The divorce between Labour and its former East Midlands seats was not confined to Nottinghamshire. In Derbyshire, they needed a swing of well under 1 per cent to retake Amber Valley; there was a 4 per cent swing to the Tories and UKIP increased their share by 14 per cent. On the same day as the general election, the Conservatives took Amber Valley Council away from Labour's control. Nor was former local authority success a harbinger of Labour victory in Lincoln; and in Northampton North there was yet another swing to the Conservatives.

The last-named seat also witnessed one unique pattern of candidature, with no fewer than three former MPs all in the contest: in addition to

Sally Keeble trying to regain it from Michael Ellis, the ex-Northampton South Member Tony Clarke entered the lists as a Green in the North division. He finished fourth and lost his deposit. To return to the sorry saga of swings against Labour in key marginals, the sitting Tory MPs in Erewash (Derbyshire), the Education Secretary Nicky Morgan's Loughborough (Leicestershire); and High Peak all increased their majorities. In none of these seats could intervention by the declining Liberal Democrats or the rising Greens and UKIP account for the changes. There was a straight switch of preference between Labour and Conservative.

UKIP did harbour hopes elsewhere in the East Midlands region. In particular, academics as well as anecdotes had identified Boston & Skegness on the Lincolnshire coast as one of their strongest seats demographically, with its large numbers of Eastern European workers in the agricultural processing economic sector and its huge UKIP share in the 2014 European elections. However, they too could not cope with the Conservative surge, polling over a third of the vote but losing by 4,336. Perhaps the fact that their candidate, Robin Hunter-Clarke, was just twenty-two years old (having first been elected as a councillor in Skegness as a teenager) did not help in a party whose voting profile increases with age; in any case, his hopes of being the 'baby of the House' would have been dashed by the SNP's twenty-year-old Mhairi Black. UKIP did finish second in all the other rural Lincolnshire constituencies as well, doing best on the coast. Generally speaking, the nearer an English seat was physically to the continent of Europe, the higher the expressed desire by the voters to leave the EU.

The Liberal Democrats, never strong in the East Midlands, collapsed almost everywhere, most spectacularly in Chesterfield, where they held the seat until 2010 and finished fourth this time. They were runners-up only in Bosworth, site of a famous battle in ancient times. In political terms, they have joined Richard III as a discarded corpse buried in a car park. The Conservatives have emerged from the fray this year in the role of the Tudors, grasping power in their own hands and, maybe, commencing a long spell of dynastic rule over England.

West Midlands

A crude view of the political geography of Britain has suggested that Labour have traditionally held the north, the Conservatives the south, and that the Midlands has been the area where the overall victors are decided. There has been an element of truth in that, maybe enough to be applied to the 2015 contest: Labour were hammered in the far north, Scotland (by what the trending TV drama *Game of Thrones* might characterise as the wildlings beyond the Wall), and also lost decisively in central England. In the East Midlands, the Conservative share was 43.5 per cent compared with Labour's 31.6, and in the West Midlands they also triumphed, by 41.8 per cent to 32.9 per cent. In both regions Labour needed to be ahead to win the general election as a whole.

As in the East Midlands, Labour did not make net gains from their main rivals. They did at least pick up one seat, Wolverhampton South West, which has changed considerably since Enoch Powell was its MP. The sitting Conservative was Paul Uppal, of Asian descent, and it was regained by Labour's Rob Marris – who had himself beaten Powell's successor, Nicholas Budgen, back in 1997. However, Labour also lost one seat in the West Midlands, as in the East. This was far more unexpected; as in the general election as a whole, they were looking to advance significantly from five years before, when Gordon Brown had been struggling so much after thirteen years of Labour government and a mighty financial crash. That loss was in Telford in Shropshire, which had previously withstood the fate of new towns in the south, such as Crawley, Basildon and Stevenage – but Dave Wright was beaten by an adverse swing of 2 per cent to the Conservative Lucy Allan, who became yet another new Tory female MP. Also, as in the East Midlands, Labour made no progress at all in their key targets.

These included the most vulnerable Conservative seat anywhere in the United Kingdom, North Warwickshire, where the Tories did not even have the benefit of an incumbent. Dan Byles had announced his retirement after just one term. In July 2014 this former mountaineer, sailor, ocean rower and polar adventurer announced that he was seeking new challenges, and almost no one gave the new Tory candidate Craig Tracey a chance, defending as he was a majority of just fifty-four votes; but he won by nearly 3,000, and this on a swing of over 3 per cent against the former Labour MP for the constituency, Mike O'Brien, who would surely have had the benefit of more name recognition. This was an extraordinary result. In Labour's next target, the more urban Halesowen & Rowley Regis, there was almost no movement between the main parties. Nuneaton was the first genuine marginal in the country to declare on the night of 7/8 May. Perhaps the increase in the Conservative majority there might have suggested to more of the television pundits than it did that an overall majority for David Cameron was on the cards, if they had not already been reeling from the exit poll predictions. After that the next on the list in the West Midlands produced another astonishing outcome. Cannock Chase also had no incumbent, but Aidan Burley's departure had been under less admirable circumstances than that of Dan Byles. Burley had lost his job as a PPS in December 2011 after a stag party in France had involved the wearing of Nazi uniforms, and an internal party inquiry had found that he had 'caused deep offence'. Yet in 2015 the Conservative Amanda Milling held Cannock Chase by nearly 5,000.

With a region-wide picture like this, there was no chance for Labour to take more distant prospects such as Warwick & Leamington or Dudley South. They did, however, gain one on the national swing from the Liberal Democrats. John Hemming of Birmingham Yardley will now have to pursue his campaign to reform the family courts outside Parliament. The Lib Dems lost their only other seat in the region to the Conservatives, as, after two previous victories in ultra-middle-class Solihull that had astonished most observers, Lorely Burt was beaten by over 12,000 votes. UKIP also came nowhere near achieving any representation. In Dudley North, for example, where one of Lord Ashcroft's polls had suggested they would be competitive, they finished in third place. The Green Party's share across the region was lower than their national average. Finally, despite the betting odds, it looks like the end of the line for Dr Richard Taylor and the Independent Community and Health Concern cause in Wyre Forest in Worcestershire. After first gaining the seat in an attempt to restore the A&E department of Kidderminster Hospital in 2001, and finishing a close second in 2010, this time, at the age of eighty, he fell to third place, and did not even maintain his usual strongest performance of any 'Independent' in English constituencies – his share was surpassed by Claire Wright in East Devon, who managed a very creditable 13,000 votes (24 per cent).

Unless the boundary changes very much alter the pattern in the West Midlands, the increase in the Conservative leads in the marginals in 2015 means that it will look much harder for Labour to make gains next time. To make another awful allusion to *Game of Thrones*, having been expelled from the North, they also face a stark future in this critical region.

North West England

Labour's highest increase in share of the vote in any region apart from London came in the populous North West, which, with seventy-six seats in all and over twenty vital marginals, is always a key battleground. Yet even here they cannot be satisfied with their performance. A mere three gains from the Tories and two from the Liberal Democrats would have been nowhere near enough to elevate Labour even to the level of largest party, even if replicated elsewhere and even if the Scottish earthquake had not consumed them. What is more, they managed to lose a seat to the Conservatives as well, as Julie Hilling was ousted in Bolton West.

If Labour had managed to increase their share uniformly across the region by the average 5.1 per cent, that would have translated into a large enough swing (3 per cent) to gain Morecambe & Lunesdale, Carlisle, Weaver Vale, Warrington South, Bury North and Blackpool North & Cleveleys. They actually won none of these crucial targets. There are two main reasons for this failure. One is familiar in all regions – the ability of Conservative MPs who had served one term to generate a personal vote based on incumbency. The other explanation is unique to the North West. This huge European Parliament region is in fact composed of several sub-regions, which behave quite differently. In particular, we must consider the 'Merseyside effect'.

Liverpool and its environs have been trending towards Labour, compared with the rest of England, for over fifty years. Before the 1964 election, seats such as Liverpool Walton and West Derby were actually held by the Conservatives. Wallasey on the Wirral survived in the hands of Lynda Chalker till 1992. In the 2015 election, the safest Labour seat and highest share of the vote anywhere in Britain was recorded in Liverpool Walton, where Steve Rotheram took 81.3 per cent and won by 27,777 votes. The Conservative candidate lost his deposit, failing even to reach the 5 per cent threshold, at a time of national triumph for his party. Four of their five largest shares anywhere were in Merseyside, and in Wallasey a swing from the Tories of 8.64 per cent nearly doubled Angela Eagle's lead to over 16,000. The biggest majority recorded anywhere was George Howarth's 34,655 in Knowsley. It was in the Merseyside sub-region that two of Labour's 2015 gains occurred – Wirral West, where Esther McVey was probably the highest-profile Conservative loser on a swing of nearly 4 per cent, and the City of Chester (just within the orbit of Liverpool), where Labour's Chris Matheson squeaked home by ninety-three votes. Only two more difficult challenges were successful for Labour (both in London), and the Tories held 80 per cent of their seats that had narrower margins than these two. This local effect trumps even strong demographic indicators such as housing tenure: in Sefton Central, the seat with the highest proportion of owner-occupiers anywhere (87.2 per cent), the swing to Labour was over 8 per cent and they won by nearly 12,000. Merseyside just doesn't much like Conservatives.

Elsewhere in the North West, Labour only took Lancaster & Fleetwood, and two seats from the Liberal Democrats: Burnley, and the university-influenced Manchester Withington. The cull of the Liberal Democrat MPs also helped the Conservatives, as their two suburban seats in the borough of Stockport fell easily – Cheadle and Hazel Grove, which had had a majority of over 6,000. Despite this, the Lib Dems can take (scant) consolation from holding onto two constituencies in this region, jointly their best with Yorkshire and Humberside. Southport is in, yes, the former Merseyside metropolitan county. The other, though, stands out as quite clearly the party's best performance anywhere. The largest LD share, and largest numerical majority, now belong by some distance to Tim Farron in Westmorland & Lonsdale. He actually managed to get more than half of all the votes cast in the constituency. This achievement is based on two factors. One is the personal appeal of a man who, though not without enemies in his own party, was immediately established as the bookmakers' favourite to lead the Liberal Democrats out of the wilderness. The other is the party's very strong grip on local council elections within this Lake District seat. Even on the same day as the national catastrophe, they easily retained their overall majority on South Lakeland Council.

Whoever is leader of the Liberal Democrats, they will have a steep task in 2020. So will Labour: there is at least anecdotal evidence that they suffered in seats near the border, like Carlisle, from an almost ancestral fear of the Scots – in this case of their invasion of Westminster and any disproportionate influence over Labour. Labour went backwards elsewhere in Cumbria, not far from losing in Barrow & Furness, for example – a far cry from the Merseyside sub-region. The SNP strength does not look like it will dissipate any time soon, and so the issue of the reaction to a possible SNP–Labour informal bloc may yet arise again.

North East England

The North East is the smallest of our British regions (which are based on the European Parliament constituencies), with only twenty-nine seats. At first sight, relatively little changed here since 2010. There were no changes of hand between Conservative and Labour, and each of these parties picked up one from the Liberal Democrats, reducing the latter to zero. However, sometimes dogs that don't bark can tell a story, and there are some interesting features to analyse beneath the headline results.

This is where Labour performed relatively best in the United Kingdom, but only in terms of overall share – which went up by 3.3 per cent to 46.9 per cent. This was still enough for them to win twenty-six out of twenty-nine constituencies – that is, 89.7 per cent of them – as a clear effect of the first-past-the-post electoral system. However, their increase in share was less than that in three other regions: London, the North West (particularly Merseyside) and Yorkshire/Humberside. Nor did they come anywhere near gaining their target from the Conservatives, Stockton South, where the majority went up from the sixth most vulnerable in the country (just 332 votes) to over 5,000. There had been some evidence that James Wharton, the youngest Tory elected in 2010, was safer than it appeared. He had raised his profile during his first term, for example by introducing his Private Member's Bill in 2013 to subject Britain's EU membership to a referendum, which made him very popular among many Conservative backbenchers. Also, Stockton South includes some strong Tory pockets which tend to have a high turnout, such as Yarm, a town which voted in a 2014 local referendum to express its preference to 'defect' from the North East to Yorkshire. It takes a little stretching to see a connection between these two points, but of Wharton's success in 2015 there is no doubt.

Conversely, the North East did not witness a great triumph for the Conservative Party as a whole. They won an overall majority in the election, but that did not involve advancing against Labour in either of their two targets, Darlington or Middlesbrough South & East Cleveland, both covering areas they had gained in the 1980s, when they had previously advanced to a dominant national position. Their one gain was at the expense of the hapless Liberal Democrats, and that in a seat, Berwick-upon-Tweed, where the sitting Member for the past forty-two years (Sir Alan Beith) had retired – so it was not nearly such a surprise or achievement as most of their successes.

The Lib Dems were also odds-on to lose their other seat, Redcar, where not only had their Member also given up the ghost before this election but where they had only won in rather freak circumstances after the mothballing of the local steelworks in February 2010 – after a two-year gap, steel is again being produced in the town. As expected, the Liberal Democrats collapsed after their strong performance in the North East after the 'Clegg surge' during the previous campaign pushed their candidates into strong second places in many seats such as Newcastle North (down from 33 per cent to 9 per cent) and City of Durham (38 per cent to 11 per cent).

One of the reasons none of the older parties really excelled in 2015 was the perhaps surprising fact that this was the best region of all for UKIP. Their share across the North East was 16.7 per cent, half a point higher than the East of England. This has gone largely unremarked because it was so evenly spread that they didn't come close to winning in any seat. Their best performance was in Peter Mandelson's former Hartlepool, where Philip Broughton polled 29 per cent and cut the Labour majority to 3,000; any town that can elect the football club mascot H'Angus the Monkey (Stuart Drummond) as Mayor three times between 2002 and 2009 clearly cannot be taken for granted by any traditional party.

That UKIP was at its strongest in this gritty working-class region certainly gives the lie to any notion that they are merely right-wing Tories in disguise. There are good reasons to believe that overall they may have taken more voters from Labour than from the Conservatives in 2015, and their appeal is not confined to the issues of Europe and immigration, but less specifically represents the frustration and discontent of the unprivileged who feel excluded from the mainstream political process. There are still many such voters (and non-voters – the turnout in the region was well below the national average) in the North East.

Yorkshire and the Humber

As always, the proud and individualistic region of Yorkshire and the Humber (including north Lincolnshire) produced some dramatic and pivotal electoral results in 2015. In the iconic moment of the election that saw the defeat of the last pure Conservative government, in 1997, their leadership hopeful Michael Portillo fell in Enfield Southgate in north London. The equivalent symbol of their achievement of an overall majority after eighteen years was surely the defeat of the Labour shadow

Chancellor Ed Balls in Morley & Outwood in Yorkshire. But this was not just a 'were you still up for' moment, as has been widely observed. When Portillo was beaten, it was already obvious that Tony Blair was well on his way to a huge victory. David Cameron's overall majority had not been predicted by the widely praised (and otherwise accurate) exit polls, and it was Balls's breakfast-time loss that confirmed it. What is more, it was important in that if the Conservatives had not gained those eight seats from Labour, as well as annihilating their junior coalition partners, they would not have won outright – which was Cameron's own yardstick for success in 2015. Morley & Outwood was therefore a much more significant result than Enfield Southgate had been.

Across this vast and disparate region there were many other fascinating changes of hand, and one or two notable places where seats did not fall. Labour did gain one constituency from the Tories, which was, to their utter dismay, nowhere nearly enough. This was Dewsbury, a seat that has seen tension between the white and Asian communities, and where the Muslim Labour MP Shahid Malik had been beaten in 2010. It was recovered by Paula Sherriff, who increased their share by 9.6 per cent, and won by a majority of 1,451 – which was actually the highest of any of the ten Labour gains from the Conservatives, demonstrating that they didn't win any of these easily. However, the Conservatives strengthened their grip on the next closest targets, Pudsey, Keighley, Elmet & Rothwell, and in Cleethorpes and Brigg & Goole in the Humberside section of the region. Labour only just held onto Halifax, where Linda Riordan had retired, to be replaced by a third female MP in succession, Holly Lynch.

The Conservatives did not take any Liberal Democrat seats, but that was because there were no such patterns of contests in Yorkshire and the Humber. The battles between Labour and the Lib Dems were well publicised, though. The supporting contests finished one-all: Labour did easily take the scalp of David Ward in Bradford East, but Greg Mulholland survived as one of the remaining eight Liberal Democrats left in the Commons in Leeds North West. This might rank as something of a surprise in the circumstances, as that seat includes many Leeds University students, and ranked as one of the ten constituencies with the highest proportion of students (28.6 per cent in the 2011 Census, though some of those may well not have been on the electoral roll this time, following the introduction of individual registration in 2014). None of the other top twenty seats on this 'student vote' list returned Liberal Democrats in 2015, compared with four last time. The main bout between Labour and the Lib Dems was one seat not on that list. It attracted the most attention of any constituency in the country. It was, of course, Sheffield Hallam.

There had been speculation for some years that Nick Clegg would lose his own seat. Labour targeted it as part of their own 'decapitation strategy'. However, most Sheffield students are actually in the Central division (where the LD share fell by 31 per cent, the second biggest drop in the country), and the permanent residents of the wards that make up Hallam, the leafy and upmarket south-west sector of the city towards the Peak District, had faithfully elected Lib Dem councillors up to and including 2014. Despite the hyperactivity of the Labour challenger Oliver Coppard, Clegg was always likely to hang on, and he did, by 2,353 votes. It is clear that his survival at constituency level was helped by Conservative tactical voters, as the Tory share fell by almost exactly 10 per cent, one of their worst results in the country. Tories may have saved Clegg's seat, but not his political career or, maybe, his party's future.

One other career that may or may not have come to an end in a Yorkshire result was that of the mercurial George Galloway of the Respect Party. After a stunning gain from Labour in Bradford West in the by-election in 2012, the good folk of West Yorkshire apparently decided that Galloway was not a very good MP, and kicked him out by a thumping margin of 11,420, despite Labour's problems in finding a suitable candidate. It is not clear that George Galloway, having been an MP in Glasgow, Tower Hamlets and Bradford, will not turn up somewhere else in due course, especially if that place is suffering division and discontent.

UKIP had entertained hopes in one seat at least: Great Grimsby, where Austin Mitchell (sometimes styling himself Austin Haddock) had retired after thirty-eight years as a somewhat eccentric Labour MP. The once great port (it boasted the world's largest fishing fleet and the world's largest ice factory) has been through hard times and transformation (it is now Britain's biggest port for importing and exporting cars). One more change this time was the election of its first female MP. Mitchell had railed against the imposition of an all-woman shortlist, but it was the Labour candidate, the locally born Melanie Onn, who won, by over 4,500, with the incomer Victoria Ayling of UKIP back in third place.

Both Yorkshire and Humberside are very proud of their own regional character. It might be going too far to note the defeats of three people who were not born in the region, in Balls, Galloway and Ayling. The ebbs and flows of the multiple patterns of contest are too rich and complex for such simplistic analysis. Yet it is hard not to finish with someone who did win in Yorkshire on 7 May 2015 but lost the country: Ed Miliband, returned as MP for Doncaster North, but metaphorically, and, in due course, perhaps physically, sent packing back to north London.

Wales

Scotland attracted most of the attention in the humiliation of the Labour Party in the 2015 election, but Wales played its part too, and in a way that had not been presaged by months of opinion poll evidence. They made precisely no gains from the Tories, not even in Cardiff North, a constituency with a high proportion of public sector workers, where the Conservatives had a majority of just 194 in 2010 and no incumbent MP this time; in fact, there was a swing of nearly 2 per cent to the right there. Even worse was that the Tories actually took two constituencies from Labour, one in north Wales and one in the south.

The former was the first Conservative gain from Labour on a night when none at all had been expected anywhere in the country, if virtually all the campaign polls were to be believed. It was in the Vale of Clwyd, where Chris Ruane's 2,050 majority vanished on a negative swing of nearly 4 per cent, making this the 'safest' of all the shock Labour losses. The Vale had been No. 55 on the Conservative target list, though hardly anybody had been looking at that list at all, never mind so far down it. In south Wales, there was an equal surprise, as the Tories took Gower, a seat more dominated by Swansea suburbs and even some territory from the ex-coalmining valleys than by the eponymous picturesque peninsula. Gower had never before been won by a Conservative – it had been solidly Labour since 1910 and they first won there in 1906, just six years after the party had been founded – but Byron Davies seized it by a margin of twenty-seven votes, the smallest majority anywhere in the 2015 election. This Davies (all the Conservative gains in Wales were achieved by a Davies) overcame the second-largest Labour lead to fall anywhere, in the Tories' thirty-fourth best chance of a gain in the United Kingdom. As the Conservatives also easily took Brecon & Radnor from the Liberal Democrats, their total number of Welsh seats rose to eleven, their best result since 1983, when Mrs Thatcher won a landslide overall majority of 144. Over Wales as a whole, their share of the vote increased by more than Labour's.

The Liberal Democrats also lost Jenny Willott after ten years' service in Cardiff Central, Labour's only gain in Wales. This was expected because of the high student presence in that seat in the heart of the principality's capital: 33.9 per cent of total residents at the time of the 2011 Census, the third highest in Britain, though the fall in Cardiff Central's electorate from 61,000 to 57,000 between 2010 and 2015 might indicate that some of these may have failed to individually register. Overall, the Lib Dems suffered the indignity of finishing fifth behind Plaid Cymru and even UKIP in the total votes cast in the land of Lloyd George. In Preseli Pembrokeshire they finished in seventh place. They held one seat only, Ceredigion, and that because the main challenger was Plaid Cymru, who also returned a disappointing set of results.

Despite the high profile afforded during the campaign, for example in the leaders' debate, to the Anglophone Leanne Wood, the Party of Wales signally failed to break out of their Welsh-speaking heartlands, merely retaining their existing three seats and gaining just 0.8 per cent overall. Fewer than one in eight voters in Wales chose the nationalist option. The contrast with the results in Scotland is striking. Plaid Cymru even failed to gain Ynys Môn, the island of Anglesey, from Labour – after they had held it with a massive majority in a by-election in 2013 for the National Assembly for Wales after the retirement there of the long-time party leader Ieuan Wyn Jones. It is safe to assume there will be no referendum for *Welsh* separatism, at least, in the foreseeable future.

There is one more problem that will particularly haunt Labour in the coming years up to the next general election in 2020. Wales is heavily over-represented at Westminster in the sense that its constituencies are on average much smaller than those in the rest of the United Kingdom. Their average number of electors is 10,000 less than in Scotland and 15,000 less than England and Northern Ireland. On strictly equal shares, there would be thirty Welsh seats rather than forty at present – and this is what was proposed in the so-called 'zombie review' of constituency boundaries that was never enacted because of Liberal Democrat opposition leading to the Lords voting it down in January 2013. There will be no coalition element to prevent the Conservatives from pushing through a replacement review in time for the next general election. All the parties holding seats will suffer, but none so much as Labour, as they have the most small seats and as many are among the smallest, particularly in the Valleys. Cynon Valley and Blaenau Gwent (historic stronghold of Aneurin Bevan then Michael Foot), for example, have only 51,000 voters each, when the next review is likely to insist on a strict quota approaching 80,000. This means it is almost certain that Wales will contribute even fewer MPs to Labour's attempt to climb the mountain that will be their task in becoming even the largest party next time.

This does not usually happen: the highest proportion of seats to change hands in any region in 2015 was in Northern Ireland, where one sixth of the eighteen constituencies switched party. To some surprise, two of the three gains were achieved by a party that had held no seats at all before the election, the Ulster Unionists, once dominant in the province but denied any representation at Westminster since 2010, when Lady Sylvia Hermon resigned from the party in protest at its alliance with the Conservatives for the general election of that year.

In 2015, Lady Hermon easily retained her North Down seat, still as an Independent, but her former party gained two elsewhere. One was a result of a pact between the UUP and its main rival for the unionist vote, as Tom Elliott overturned Michelle Gildernew's lead (which was fully four votes!) for Sinn Féin in the closely balanced Fermanagh & South Tyrone, where there is a Catholic majority but where there was no such pact on the nationalist/republican side of the political and sectarian cleavage; the SDLP received 2,732 votes. The other UUP win was a straight gain from the DUP, in South Antrim, a constituency that has often swithered between these two parties. On this occasion, Danny Kinahan ousted William McCrea by a margin of just 949 votes. This was the third time that the Reverend McCrea had lost his Westminster seat, uniquely in this election (and most others). The third change of hand in Northern Ireland came in Belfast East, where the only ever Alliance Party MP, Naomi Long, was replaced in the seat she had gained in 2010 from the DUP leader Peter Robinson (following a scandal involving Iris Robinson, then MP for Strangford) back to the same party's Gavin Robinson – no relation to either of the other two Robinsons.

Despite this gain, in general, a small but distinct movement towards the more 'moderate' parties in the complex politics of Northern Ireland can be identified. The non-sectarian Alliance Party increased their share in all the seats they contested bar one (Belfast West, where a People Before Profit candidate hoovered up most of the opposition to Sinn Féin) but including Naomi Long's. Sinn Féin lost a seat, and the Ulster Unionists gained two. Lady Hermon held on easily as an Independent. The SDLP held all their three seats, although in Belfast South this was with a mere 24.5 per cent of the total vote – by far the smallest winning share anywhere in the UK. This result, though extraordinary in this respect, does reflect the splintered politics of the province. No fewer than six parties retained their deposit, and UKIP only missed making it seven by 0.12 per cent. It is still true that no part of the United Kingdom has so many sometimes abstruse and often dramatic and bitter cleavages reflected in the electoral outcomes, in some ways fluid and ever-changing, in others historically entrenched and never-changing.

Table of Regional Shares and Changes in Share of the Vote

	CON	LAB	LD	UKIP	GREEN	SNP	PC	SF	DUP	UUP	SDLP	APNI
SW England	46.5	17.7	15.1	13.6	5.9							
	+3.7	+2.1	-19.6	+9.1	+4.8							
SE England	50.8	18.3	9.4	14.7	5.2							
	+0.9	+2.1	-16.8	+10.6	+3.8							
London	34.9	43.7	7.7	8.1	4.9							
	+0.4	+7.1	-14.4	+6.4	+3.3							
East England	49.0	22.0	8.2	16.2	3.9							
	+1.9	+2.4	-15.9	+11.9	+2.4							
East Midlands	43.5	31.6	5.6	15.8	3.0							
	+2.3	+1.8	-15.2	+12.5	+2.5							
West Midlands	41.8	32.9	5.5	15.7	3.3							
	+2.3	+2.3	-15.0	+11.7	+2.7							
NW England	31.2	44.6	6.5	13.6	3.2							
	-0.5	+5.1	-16.1	+10.4	+2.7							
NE England	25.3	46.9	6.5	16.7	3.6							
	+1.6	+3.3	-17.1	+14.0	+3.3							
Yorkshire/Humber	32.6	39.1	7.1	16.0	3.5							
	+0.1	+4.4	-15.9	+13.2	+2.6							
Scotland	14.9	24.3	7.5	1.6	1.3	50.0						
	-1.7	-17.7	-11.4	+0.9	+0.6	+30.1						
Wales	27.2	36.9	6.5	13.6	2.6		12.1					
	+1.1	+0.7	-13.6	+11.2	+2.2		+0.8					
Northern Ireland								24.5	25.7	16.0	13.9	8.6
								-1.0	+0.7	+0.8	-2.6	+2.3

2015 general election statistics

Compiled by Tim Carr and Robert Waller; commentary by Robert Waller

TOP 50 MARGINALS: ALL PARTIES BY % MAJORITY

	% MAJ	VOTES	CONSTITUENCY	PARTY
1	0.10%	41	Derby North	Con
2	0.10%	27	Gower	Con
3	0.20%	93	City of Chester	Lab
4	0.30%	165	Croydon Central	Con
5	0.50%	274	Ealing Central & Acton	Lab
6	0.60%	328	Berwickshire, Roxburgh & Selkirk	SNP
7	0.70%	237	Vale of Clwyd	Con
8	0.70%	229	Ynys Môn (Anglesey)	Lab
9	0.80%	465	Brentford & Isleworth	Lab
10	0.80%	378	Bury North	Con
11	0.90%	422	Morley & Outwood	Con
12	1.00%	530	Fermanagh & South Tyrone	UUP
13	1.00%	428	Halifax	Lab
14	1.00%	417	Wirral West	Lab
15	1.10%	523	Plymouth Sutton & Devonport	Con
16	1.10%	536	Thurrock	Con

17	1.20%	599	Cambridge	Lab
18	1.20%	589	Ilford North	Lab
19	1.40%	733	Eastbourne	Con
20	1.50%	690	Brighton Kemptown	Con
21	1.50%	798	Dumfriesshire, Clydesdale & Tweeddale	Con
22	1.50%	650	Newcastle-under-Lyme	Lab
23	1.60%	801	Bolton West	Con
24	1.70%	806	Weaver Vale	Con
25	1.80%	795	Barrow & Furness	Lab
26	1.80%	730	Telford	Con
27	2.00%	801	Wolverhampton South West	Lab
28	2.10%	1,138	Hampstead & Kilburn	Lab
29	2.10%	1,083	Lewes	Con
30	2.30%	906	Belfast South	SDLP
31	2.40%	1,097	Bedford	Con
32	2.40%	1,086	Enfield North	Lab
33	2.40%	1,236	Hove	Lab
34	2.40%	1,026	Plymouth Moor View	Con
35	2.60%	949	South Antrim	UUP
36	2.70%	1,451	Dewsbury	Lab
37	3.00%	1,265	Lancaster & Fleetwood	Lab
38	3.00%	1,322	Southport	Lib Dem
39	3.10%	1,443	Lincoln	Con
40	3.10%	1,495	Thornbury & Yate	Con
41	3.20%	1,510	Carshalton & Wallington	Lib Dem
42	3.30%	2,017	Twickenham	Con
43	3.60%	817	Orkney & Shetland	Lib Dem
44	3.90%	1,883	Derbyshire North East	Lab
45	3.90%	2,167	East Dunbartonshire	SNP
46	4.10%	1,925	Peterborough	Con
47	4.20%	2,137	Cardiff North	Con
48	4.20%	2,353	Sheffield Hallam	Lib Dem
49	4.30%	2,412	Corby	Con
50	4.60%	2,750	Warrington South	Con

Note: the swing required is half of the % majority

TOP 50 SEATS: CONSERVATIVE MARGINALS BY % MAJORITY

	% MAJ	VOTES	CONSTITUENCY	2ND PARTY
1	0.10%	41	Derby North	Lab
2	0.10%	27	Gower	Lab
3	0.30%	165	Croydon Central	Lab
4	0.70%	237	Vale of Clwyd	Lab
5	0.80%	378	Bury North	Lab
6	0.90%	422	Morley & Outwood	Lab
7	1.10%	523	Plymouth Sutton & Devonport	Lab
8	1.10%	536	Thurrock	Lab
9	1.40%	733	Eastbourne	Lib Dem
10	1.50%	690	Brighton Kemptown	Lab
11	1.50%	798	Dumfriesshire, Clydesdale & Tweeddale	SNP
12	1.60%	801	Bolton West	Lab
13	1.70%	806	Weaver Vale	Lab
14	1.80%	730	Telford	Lab
15	2.10%	1,083	Lewes	Lib Dem
16	2.40%	1,097	Bedford	Lab
17	2.40%	1,026	Plymouth Moor View	Lab
18	3.10%	1,443	Lincoln	Lab
19	3.10%	1,495	Thornbury & Yate	Lib Dem
20	3.30%	2,017	Twickenham	Lib Dem
21	4.10%	1,925	Peterborough	Lab
22	4.20%	2,137	Cardiff North	Lab
23	4.30%	2,412	Corby	Lab
24	4.60%	2,750	Warrington South	Lab
25	4.60%	2,408	Waveney	Lab
26	4.80%	2,834	Kingston & Surbiton	Lib Dem
27	5.10%	2,469	St Ives	Lib Dem
28	5.20%	2,316	Southampton Itchen	Lab
29	5.70%	2,812	South Thanet	UKIP
30	6.20%	3,053	Keighley	Lab
31	6.30%	2,973	North Warwickshire	Lab
32	6.50%	2,774	Carlisle	Lab
33	6.80%	3,286	Torbay	Lib Dem
34	7.00%	3,082	Halesowen & Rowley Regis	Lab
35	7.30%	3,620	Crewe & Nantwich	Lab
36	7.40%	3,584	Erewash	Lab

37	7.50%	3,724	Hendon	Lab
38	7.70%	3,733	Ipswich	Lab
39	7.90%	3,921	Sutton & Cheam	Lib Dem
40	8.00%	4,287	Broxtowe	Lab
41	8.00%	4,866	Stroud	Lab
42	8.10%	3,833	Bath	Lib Dem
43	8.20%	3,245	Northampton North	Lab
44	8.30%	4,427	Calder Valley	Lab
45	8.50%	3,340	Blackpool North & Cleveleys	Lab
46	8.80%	4,501	Pudsey	Lab
47	9.20%	4,205	Amber Valley	Lab
48	9.20%	4,647	Sherwood	Lab
49	9.30%	5,313	Yeovil	Lib Dem
50	9.40%	4,796	Hastings & Rye	Lab

Note: the swing required is half of the % majority

TOP 100 SEATS: POSSIBLE LABOUR TARGETS (ALL PARTIES) BY % MAJORITY

	% MAJ	VOTES	CONSTITUENCY	INCUMBENT PARTY
1	0.05%	41	Derby North	Con
2	0.05%	27	Gower	Con
3	0.15%	165	Croydon Central	Con
4	0.35%	237	Vale of Clwyd	Con
5	0.40%	378	Bury North	Con
6	0.45%	422	Morley & Outwood	Con
7	0.55%	523	Plymouth Sutton & Devonport	Con
8	0.55%	536	Thurrock	Con
9	0.75%	690	Brighton Kemptown	Con
10	0.80%	801	Bolton West	Con
11	0.85%	806	Weaver Vale	Con
12	0.90%	730	Telford	Con
13	1.20%	1,097	Bedford	Con
14	1.20%	1,026	Plymouth Moor View	Con
15	1.55%	1,443	Lincoln	Con
16	2.05%	1,925	Peterborough	Con
17	2.10%	2,137	Cardiff North	Con
18	2.10%	2,353	Sheffield Hallam	Lib Dem
19	2.15%	2,412	Corby	Con

20	2.30%	2,750	Warrington South	Con
21	2.30%	2,408	Waveney	Con
22	2.60%	2,316	Southampton Itchen	Con
23	3.10%	3,053	Keighley	Con
24	3.15%	2,973	North Warwickshire	Con
25	3.25%	2,774	Carlisle	Con
26	3.30%	3,718	Renfrewshire East	SNP
27	3.35%	2,907	Leeds North West	Lib Dem
28	3.50%	3,082	Halesowen & Rowley Regis	Con
29	3.65%	3,620	Crewe & Nantwich	Con
30	3.70%	3,584	Erewash	Con
31	3.75%	3,724	Hendon	Con
32	3.85%	3,733	Ipswich	Con
33	4.00%	4,287	Broxtowe	Con
34	4.00%	4,866	Stroud	Con
35	4.10%	3,245	Northampton North	Con
36	4.15%	4,427	Calder Valley	Con
37	4.25%	3,340	Blackpool North & Cleveleys	Con
38	4.40%	4,501	Pudsey	Con
39	4.60%	4,205	Amber Valley	Con
40	4.60%	4,647	Sherwood	Con
41	4.70%	4,796	Hastings & Rye	Con
42	4.75%	4,944	Bristol North West	Con
43	4.75%	5,378	Colne Valley	Con
44	4.80%	5,597	Edinburgh North & Leith	SNP
45	4.80%	4,894	High Peak	Con
46	4.85%	4,757	Harrow East	Con
47	4.85%	5,046	Stockton South	Con
48	4.90%	3,793	Northampton South	Con
49	5.10%	4,463	Norwich North	Con
50	5.20%	4,753	Enfield Southgate	Con
51	5.20%	4,955	Stevenage	Con
52	5.25%	4,923	Cannock Chase	Con
53	5.30%	4,590	Morecambe & Lunesdale	Con
54	5.35%	4,882	Nuneaton	Con
55	5.60%	4,270	Dudley South	Con
56	5.60%	5,662	Finchley & Golders Green	Con
57	5.70%	5,945	South Ribble	Con
58	5.70%	5,646	Worcester	Con

59	5.75%	6,803	East Lothian	SNP
60	5.75%	5,654	Rossendale & Darwen	Con
61	5.85%	5,785	South Swindon	Con
62	5.90%	5,184*	Southport	Con / Lab 3rd
63	6.15%	5,684	Paisley & Renfrewshire South	SNP
64	6.15%	5,453	Pendle	Con
65	6.15%	4,969	Preseli Pembrokeshire	Con
66	6.25%	6,294	Dover	Con
67	6.45%	6,520	Reading East	Con
68	6.50%	6,200	Scarborough & Whitby	Con
69	6.55%	6,606	Warwick & Leamington	Con
70	6.65%	3,999	Aberconwy	Con
71	6.70%	6,526	Crawley	Con
72	6.70%	6,880	Vale of Glamorgan	Con
73	6.85%	3,668	Arfon	PC
74	6.85%	6,650	Reading West	Con
75	6.90%	7,241	Gloucester	Con
76	6.90%	6,154	Great Yarmouth	Con
77	7.10%	5,599	Carmarthen East & Dinefwr	PC
78	7.15%	7,098*	South Thanet	Con / Lab 3rd
79	7.20%	7,656	Chipping Barnet	Con
80	7.25%	6,694	Stourbridge	Con
81	7.30%	7,967	Brighton Pavilion	Green
82	7.35%	8,490	Elmet & Rothwell	Con
83	7.35%	8,672	Milton Keynes South	Con
84	7.45%	7,230	Aberdeen South	SNP
85	7.50%	6,054	Carmarthen West & Pembrokeshire South	Con
86	7.65%	7,004	Camborne & Redruth	Con
87	7.65%	6,401*	Portsmouth South	Con / Lab 3rd
88	7.80%	7,938	Battersea	Con
89	7.90%	8,135	Edinburgh South West	SNP
90	8.00%	7,054	Redditch	Con
91	8.35%	8,370	Gravesham	Con
92	8.35%	9,458*	Dumfries & Galloway	SNP / Lab 3rd
93	8.45%	9,753	Milton Keynes North	Con
94	8.65%	9,975	Rutherglen & Hamilton West	SNP
95	8.70%	9,794	Watford	Con
96	8.75%	7,893	Cleethorpes	Con
97	8.80%	10,168	Ochil & South Perthshire	SNP

98	8.85%	6,730	Clwyd West	Con
99	8.85%	9,183	Loughborough	Con
100	8.85%	9,565	Shrewsbury & Atcham	Con

* Winning party lead over Labour in 3rd place; not actual majority

TOP 50 SEATS: LABOUR MARGINALS BY % MAJORITY

	% MAJ	VOTES	CONSTITUENCY	2ND PARTY
1	0.20%	93	City of Chester	Con
2	0.50%	274	Ealing Central & Acton	Con
3	0.70%	229	Ynys Môn (Anglesey)	PC
4	0.80%	465	Brentford & Isleworth	Con
5	1.00%	428	Halifax	Con
6	1.00%	417	Wirral West	Con
7	1.20%	599	Cambridge	Lib Dem
8	1.20%	589	Ilford North	Con
9	1.50%	650	Newcastle-under-Lyme	Con
10	1.80%	795	Barrow & Furness	Con
11	2.00%	801	Wolverhampton South West	Con
12	2.10%	1,138	Hampstead & Kilburn	Con
13	2.40%	1,086	Enfield North	Con
14	2.40%	1,236	Hove	Con
15	2.70%	1,451	Dewsbury	Con
16	3.00%	1,265	Lancaster & Fleetwood	Con
17	3.90%	1,883	Derbyshire North East	Con
18	4.70%	2,208	Harrow West	Con
19	4.90%	1,927	Bridgend	Con
20	5.00%	2,268	Middlesbrough South & East Cleveland	Con
21	5.00%	1,977	Westminster North	Con
22	5.30%	2,842	Tooting	Con
23	5.30%	1,937	Walsall North	Con
24	5.40%	2,637	Edinburgh South	SNP
25	5.60%	1,831	Wrexham	Con
26	5.90%	2,509	Birmingham Northfield	Con
27	6.10%	2,613	Wakefield	Con
28	6.20%	2,693	Eltham	Con
29	6.20%	2,986	Gedling	Con
30	6.50%	2,564	Copeland	Con
31	6.50%	2,539	Stoke-on-Trent South	Con

32	6.60%	2,706	Birmingham Edgbaston	Con
33	6.90%	2,402	Clwyd South	Con
34	7.30%	3,188	Coventry South	Con
35	7.70%	3,158	Darlington	Con
36	7.70%	3,024	Hartlepool	UKIP
37	7.80%	2,930	Delyn	Con
38	8.00%	2,585	Blackpool South	Con
39	8.10%	3,343	Alyn & Deeside	Con
40	8.20%	3,244	Burnley	Lib Dem
41	8.50%	3,134	Scunthorpe	Con
42	8.60%	3,980	Bristol East	Con
43	8.70%	4,489	Bermondsey & Old Southwark	Lib Dem
44	8.70%	3,510	Newport West	Con
45	8.70%	3,810	Southampton Test	Con
46	8.80%	5,673	Bristol West	Green
47	8.80%	4,530	Chorley	Con
48	8.90%	3,508	Bishop Auckland	Con
49	10.00%	4,509	Coventry North West	Con
50	10.10%	4,377	Bolton North East	Con

Note: the swing required is half of the % majority

LIBERAL DEMOCRAT SEATS: BY % MAJORITY

	% MAJ	VOTES	CONSTITUENCY	2ND PARTY
1	3.00%	1,322	Southport	Con
2	3.20%	1,510	Carshalton & Wallington	Con
3	3.60%	817	Orkney & Shetland	SNP
4	4.20%	2,353	Sheffield Hallam	Lab
5	6.70%	2,907	Leeds North West	Lab
6	8.20%	3,067	Ceredigion	PC
7	8.20%	4,043	Norfolk North	Con
8	18.30%	8,949	Westmorland & Lonsdale	Con

TOP 10 SEATS: HIGHEST LIBERAL DEMOCRAT SHARE

	CONSTITUENCY	LIBERAL DEMOCRAT	VOTE SHARE
1	Westmorland & Lonsdale	Tim Farron MP	51.5%
2	Orkney & Shetland	Alistair Carmichael MP	41.4%
3	Sheffield Hallam	Nick Clegg MP	40.0%

4	North Norfolk	Norman Lamb MP	39.1%
5	Eastbourne	Stephen Lloyd defeated	38.2%
6	Twickenham	Vince Cable defeated	38.0%
7	Thornbury & Yate	Steve Webb defeated	37.9%
8	Leeds North West	Greg Mulholland MP	36.8%
9	Dunbartonshire East	Jo Swinson defeated	36.3%
10	Ross, Skye & Lochaber	Charles Kennedy defeated	35.9%

TOP 10 SEATS: LOWEST LIBERAL DEMOCRAT SHARE

	CONSTITUENCY	VOTE SHARE
1	Glasgow East	0.75%
2	Glasgow North East	0.79%
3	Glasgow South West	0.99%
4	Coatbridge, Chryston & Bellshill	1.08%
5	Motherwell & Wishaw	1.25%
6	Dudley North	1.26%
7	Thurrock	1.30%
8	Barking	1.31%
9	Kilmarnock & Loudoun	1.46%
10	Rhondda	1.50%

The Liberal Democrats lost their £500 deposits in 335 seats where they gained less than 5% of the vote.

TOP 20 SEATS: HIGHEST UKIP VOTE SHARE (%)

	UKIP % VOTE	WINNER % VOTE	CONSTITUENCY	WINNER/UKIP
1	44.40%	44.40%	Clacton	UKIP / 1st
2	33.80%	43.80%	Boston & Skegness	Con / 2nd
3	32.40%	38.10%	South Thanet	Con / 2nd
4	32.20%	43.10%	Heywood & Middleton	Lab / 2nd
5	31.70%	33.70%	Thurrock	Con / 3rd
6	31.20%	50.90%	Castle Point	Con / 2nd
7	30.50%	44.10%	Rochester & Strood	Con / 2nd
8	30.20%	52.50%	Rotherham	Lab / 2nd
9	29.80%	41.40%	Dagenham & Rainham	Lab / 2nd
10	28.10%	43.60%	Rother Valley	Lab/ 2nd
11	28.00%	35.60%	Hartlepool	Lab / 2nd
12	26.50%	43.40%	South Basildon & East Thurrock	Con / 2nd
13	25.70%	49.00%	North Thanet	Con / 2nd

14	25.30%	49.00%	Hornchurch & Upminster	Con / 2nd
15	25.20%	47.30%	West Bromwich West	Lab / 2nd
16	25.10%	39.40%	Mansfield	Lab / 3rd
17	25.00%	39.80%	Great Grimsby	Lab / 3rd
18	24.90%	56.90%	Wentworth & Dearne	Lab / 2nd
19	24.80%	49.50%	Sittingbourne & Sheppey	Con / 2nd
20	24.70%	39.90%	Stoke-on-Trent North	Lab / 3rd

TOP 20 SEATS: HIGHEST GREEN VOTE SHARE (%)

	UKIP % VOTE	WINNER % VOTE	CONSTITUENCY	WINNER/GREEN
1	41.80%	41.80%	Brighton Pavilion	Green / 1st
2	26.80%	35.70%	Bristol West	Lab / 2nd
3	15.80%	55.00%	Sheffield Central	Lab / 2nd
4	14.60%	62.90%	Hackney North & Stoke Newington	Lab / 3rd
5	13.90%	39.30%	Norwich South	Lab / 3rd
6	13.80%	64.50%	Buckingham	Con (Speaker) / 3rd
7	13.40%	40.70%	Isle of Wight	Con / 3rd
8	12.80%	52.90%	Holborn & St Pancras	Lab / 3rd
9	12.50%	60.20%	Lewisham Deptford	Lab / 3rd
10	12.10%	67.40%	Liverpool Riverside	Lab / 2nd
11	11.90%	37.80%	Bath	Con / 4th
12	11.60%	64.40%	Hackney South & Shoreditch	Lab / 3rd
13	11.60%	50.00%	Oxford East	Lab / 3rd
14	11.50%	38.40%	Bristol South	Lab / 4th
15	10.30%	53.00%	Totnes	Con / 4th
16	10.20%	60.20%	Islington North	Lab / 3rd
17	10.10%	63.30%	Camberwell & Peckham	Lab / 3rd
18	10.00%	42.40%	York Central	Lab / 4th
19	9.90%	54.60%	Nottingham East	Lab / 4th
20	9.80%	67.10%	Manchester Gorton	Lab / 2nd

TOP 10 SEATS: HIGHEST SNP SHARE

	CONSTITUENCY	VOTE SHARE
1	Dundee West	61.9%
2	Banff & Buchan	60.2%
3	Cumbernauld, Kilsyth & Kirkintilloch East	59.9%
4	Glenrothes	59.8%

5	Dundee East	59.7%
6	West Dunbartonshire	59.1%
7	Glasgow North East	58.1%
8	Falkirk	57.7%
9	Glasgow South West	57.2%
10	Livingston	56.9%

TOP 10 SEATS: HIGHEST PLAID CYMRU SHARE

	CONSTITUENCY	VOTE SHARE	WINNER
1	Arfon	43.9%	PC
2	Dwyfor Meirionnydd	40.9%	PC
3	Carmarthen East & Dinefwr	38.4%	PC
4	Ynys Môn	30.5%	Lab
5	Ceredigion	27.7%	LD
6	Rhondda	27.0%	Lab
7	Llanelli	23.0%	Lab
8	Neath	18.1%	Lab
9	Cynon Valley	16.8%	Lab
10	Caerphilly	14.6%	Lab

TOP 10 SEATS: MPS WITH HIGHEST MAJORITIES BY VOTES

	MP	VOTES
1	George Howarth (Lab, Knowsley)	34,655
2	Stephen Timms (Lab, East Ham)	34,252
3	Ranil Jayawardena (Con, North East Hampshire)	29,916
4	Theresa May (Con, Maidenhead)	29,059
5	Peter Dowd (Lab, Bootle)	28,704
6	Dominic Raab (Con, Esher & Walton)	28,616
7	Jeremy Hunt (Con, South West Surrey)	28,556
8	Lyn Brown (Lab, West Ham)	27,986
9	Steve Rotheram (Lab, Liverpool Walton)	27,777
10	Stephen Twigg (Lab, Liverpool West Derby)	27,367

TOP 10 SEATS: MPS WITH LOWEST MAJORITIES BY VOTES

	MP	VOTES
1	Byron Davies (Con, Gower)	27
2	Amanda Solloway (Con, Derby North)	41
3	Chris Matheson (Lab, City of Chester)	93
4	Gavin Barwell (Con, Croydon Central)	165
5	Albert Owen (Lab, Ynys Môn)	229
6	James Davies (Con, Vale of Clwyd)	237
7	Rupa Huq (Lab, Ealing Central & Acton)	274
8	Calum Kerr (SNP, Berwickshire, Roxburgh & Selkirk)	328
9	David Nuttall (Con, Bury North)	378
10	Margaret Greenwood (Lab, Wirral West)	417

TOP 20 SEATS: HIGHEST CONSERVATIVE SHARE

	CONSTITUENCY	MP	VOTE SHARE
1	North East Hampshire	Ranil Jayawardena	65.9%
2	Maidenhead	Theresa May	65.8%
3	Buckingham	John Bercow	64.4%
4	Windsor	Adam Afriyie	63.4%
5	Beaconsfield	Dominic Grieve	63.2%
6	Chelsea & Fulham	Greg Hands	63.0%
7	Esher & Walton	Dominic Raab	62.9%
8	Meon Valley	George Hollingbery	61.1%
9	Newbury	Richard Benyon	61.0%
10	Arundel & South Downs	Nick Herbert	60.8%
11	East Hampshire	Damian Hinds	60.7%
12	Mole Valley	Sir Paul Beresford	60.6%
13	Maldon	John Whittingdale	60.6%
14	Witney	David Cameron	60.2%
15	Northamptonshire South	Andrea Leadsom	60.2%
16	New Forest West	Desmond Swayne	60.0%
17	South West Surrey	Jeremy Hunt	59.9%
18	Surrey Heath	Michael Gove	59.9%
19	Runnymede & Weybridge	Philip Hammond	59.7%
20	Penrith & The Border	Rory Stewart	59.7%

TOP 20 SEATS: HIGHEST LABOUR SHARE

	CONSTITUENCY	MP	VOTE SHARE
1	Liverpool Walton	Steve Rotheram	81.3%
2	Knowsley	George Howarth	78.1%
3	East Ham	Stephen Timms	77.6%
4	Liverpool West Derby	Stephen Twigg	75.2%
5	Bootle	Peter Dowd	74.5%
6	Birmingham Ladywood	Shabana Mahmood	73.6%
7	Liverpool Wavertree	Luciana Berger	69.3%
8	Garston & Halewood	Maria Eagle	69.1%
9	Walthamstow	Stella Creasy	68.9%
10	West Ham	Lyn Brown	68.4%
11	Birmingham Hodge Hill	Liam Byrne	68.4%
12	Birkenhead	Frank Field	67.6%
13	Liverpool Riverside	Louise Ellman	67.4%
14	Tottenham	David Lammy	67.3%
15	Manchester Gorton	Sir Gerald Kaufman	67.1%
16	Ealing Southall	Virendra Sharma	65.0%
17	Hackney South & Shoreditch	Meg Hillier	64.4%
18	Ilford South	Mike Gapes	64.0%
19	Camberwell & Peckham	Harriet Harman	63.3%
20	Hackney North & Stoke Newington	Diane Abbott	62.9%

TOP 10 SEATS: LOWEST WINNING PARTY VOTE SHARE (%)

	VOTES	CONSTITUENCY	WINNER
1	24.50%	Belfast South	SDLP
2	31.00%	Southport	Lib Dem
3	31.10%	Ynys Môn (Anglesey)	Lab
4	32.70%	South Antrim	UUP
5	32.70%	Upper Bann	DUP
6	33.70%	Thurrock	Con
7	34.80%	Portsmouth South	Con from Lib Dems
8	34.90%	Carshalton & Wallington	Lib Dem
9	35.60%	Hartlepool	Lab
10	35.70%	Bristol West	Lab from Lib Dems

TOP 10 SEATS: LOWEST LABOUR SHARE

	CONSTITUENCY	VOTE SHARE
1	Aberdeenshire West & Kincardine	4.5%
2	Ross, Skye & Lochaber	4.9%
3	Berwickshire, Roxburgh & Selkirk	4.9%
4	North Cornwall	5.4%
5	Westmorland & Lonsdale	5.4%
6	Montgomeryshire	5.6%
7	Banff & Buchan	5.8%
8	Gordon	5.9%
9	Mid Dorset & North Poole	6.0%
10	Wells	6.6%

Eight of these seats had Liberal Democrat MPs before the 2015 election; only one afterwards.

TOP 10 SEATS: LOWEST CONSERVATIVE VOTE SHARE IN BRITAIN (OUTSIDE NORTHERN IRELAND)

	CONSTITUENCY	VOTE SHARE
1	Glasgow North East	4.7%
2	Liverpool Walton	4.7%
3	Glasgow South West	5.0%
4	Inverness, Nairn, Badenoch & Strathspey	5.9%
5	Glasgow East	6.0%
6	Glasgow Central	6.0%
7	Ross, Skye & Lochaber	6.2%
8	Coatbridge, Chryston & Bellshill	6.3%
9	Liverpool West Derby	6.6%
10	Knowsley	6.6%

Seven in Scotland, and three in Merseyside – clearly the weakest regions for the Conservative Party in recent decades.

TOP 10 SEATS: BIGGEST RISES IN LABOUR VOTE

	CONSTITUENCY	INCREASE IN VOTE SHARE
1	Birmingham Hall Green	26.91%
2	Brent Central	20.90%
3	Sheffield Hallam	19.71%
4	Poplar & Limehouse	18.55%
5	Bethnal Green & Bow	18.25%

6	Birmingham Ladywood	17.95%
7	Walthamstow	17.01%
8	Manchester Gorton	16.96%
9	Hornsey & Wood Green	16.90%
10	Birmingham Hodge Hill	16.42%

All these seats are safely Labour, but they piled up votes where they did not really need them, except for Hornsey & Wood Green, where they managed a gain from the Liberal Democrat Lynne Featherstone, and Sheffield Hallam, where despite their third-largest increase they failed to 'decapitate' Nick Clegg.

TOP 10 SEATS: BIGGEST FALLS IN LABOUR VOTE

	CONSTITUENCY	FALL IN VOTE SHARE
1	Glasgow North East	-34.66%
2	Coatbridge, Chryston & Bellshill	-32.68%
3	Glenrothes	-31.74%
4	Kirkcaldy & Cowdenbeath	-31.16%
5	West Dunbartonshire	-29.95%
6	Glasgow South West	-29.66%
7	Motherwell & Wishaw	-29.24%
8	Glasgow East	-29.18%
9	Cumbernauld, Kilsyth & Kirkintilloch East	-27.22%
10	Inverclyde	-25.65%

All these ten dramatic collapses resulted in gains for the SNP. The fourth largest was in the seat of the retiring former Labour leader and Prime Minister Gordon Brown (Kirkcaldy & Cowdenbeath).

TOP 10 SEATS: BIGGEST RISES IN CONSERVATIVE VOTE

	CONSTITUENCY	INCREASE IN VOTE SHARE
1	Bromsgrove	10.16%
2	Hampstead & Kilburn	9.59%
3	Yeovil	9.57%
4	Hexham	9.46%
5	Brent Central	9.16%
6	City of Durham	8.95%
7	Watford	8.51%
8	North East Somerset	8.51%
9	Richmond Park	8.50%
10	Somerton & Frome	8.49%

Yeovil and Somerton & Frome were gains from the Liberal Democrats. Bromsgrove, top of the list, is the seat of a rising star of the Cabinet, Sajid Javid. The MP for North East Somerset is the eccentric but active Jacob Rees-Mogg. In Hampstead & Kilburn, the Tories' second-best rise anywhere was still not enough to take the seat of the retiring Labour MP Glenda Jackson, as Tulip Siddiq benefited from an even larger rise in the Labour share following the collapse of the LD vote in what had previously been a tight three-way marginal.

TOP 10 SEATS: BIGGEST FALLS IN CONSERVATIVE VOTE

	CONSTITUENCY	FALL IN VOTE SHARE
1	Clacton	-16.37%
2	Bradford West	-15.86%
3	Bradford East	-15.54%
4	Richmond (Yorkshire)	-11.42%
5	Edinburgh West	-10.91%
6	Dagenham & Rainham	-9.95%
7	Sheffield Hallam	-9.95%
8	Cambridge	-9.91%
9	South Thanet	-9.86%
10	Argyll & Bute	-9.12%

Clacton is UKIP's one seat, where the change of share takes no account of the impact of Douglas Carswell's by-election victory, and South Thanet reflects the high-profile candidature of Nigel Farage. In the two Bradford seats, the Conservative decline demonstrates the return of Muslim voters to their traditional Labour allegiance after other parties took those seats in 2010. In Richmond (Yorkshire), William Hague had retired as candidate to be replaced by an incomer, Rishi Sunak. In Sheffield Hallam there appears to have been a Tory tactical vote to help save their former coalition partner Nick Clegg against a Labour onslaught. The same may have been the case in Cambridge and in Edinburgh West and Argyll & Bute, where unionists recognised that the SNP were the challengers.

TOP 10 SEATS: BIGGEST RISES IN SNP VOTE

	CONSTITUENCY	INCREASE IN VOTE SHARE
1	Glasgow North East	43.91
2	Glasgow North	41.19
3	Glasgow South West	40.82
4	Coatbridge, Chryston & Bellshill	39.76
5	Dunfermline & West Fife	39.64
6	Glasgow North West	39.26
7	West Dunbartonshire	38.94
8	Motherwell & Wishaw	38.39
9	Glenrothes	38.06
10	Kirkcaldy & Cowdenbeath	37.93

It is interesting that the three largest SNP rises are all in Glasgow, where a majority was recorded for 'Yes' in the 2014 referendum.

TOP 10 SEATS: BIGGEST FALLS IN LIBERAL DEMOCRAT VOTE

	CONSTITUENCY	FALL IN VOTE SHARE
1	Brent Central	-35.81%
2	Sheffield Central	-31.25%
3	Dunfermline & West Fife	-31.08%
4	Hereford & South Herefordshire	-30.52%
5	Edinburgh South	-30.32%
6	Edinburgh North & Leith	-29.28%
7	Bristol West	-29.20%
8	Weston-super-Mare	-28.76%
9	Glasgow North	-28.61%
10	Manchester Gorton	-28.40%

TOP 10 SEATS: HIGHEST 3RD PARTY VOTE SHARE (%)

	VOTES	CONSTITUENCY	PARTY
1	31.70%	Thurrock	UKIP
2	25.20%	South Basildon & East Thurrock	Lab
3	25.10%	Mansfield	UKIP
4	25.00%	Great Grimsby	UKIP
5	24.70%	Dumfries & Galloway	Lab
6	24.70%	Stoke-on-Trent North	UKIP
7	24.60%	Upper Bann	SF
8	24.40%	Dagenham & Rainham	Con
9	24.10%	Bradford South	UKIP
10	24.10%	Newry & Armagh	SDLP

TOP 10 SEATS: HIGHEST TURNOUTS 2015

	CONSTITUENCY	TURNOUT	WINNER
1	East Dunbartonshire	81.9%	SNP gain from LD
2	East Renfrewshire	81.1%	SNP gain from Lab
3	Stirling	77.5%	SNP gain from Lab
4	Twickenham	77.3%	Con gain from LD
5	Ross, Skye & Lochaber	77.2%	SNP gain from LD

6	Edinburgh West	76.5%	SNP gain from LD
7	Richmond Park	76.5%	Con
8	Monmouth	76.2%	Con
9	Paisley & Renfrewshire North	76.2%	SNP gain from Lab
10	Dumfriesshire, Clydesdale & Tweeddale	76.1%	Con

Seven of the ten highest turnouts were in Scotland. The highest two of all were in the seats where Jo Swinson of the Liberal Democrats tried to hold on against the SNP surge and where the Scottish Labour leader Jim Murphy was relatively narrowly beaten. Vince Cable's former Twickenham seat was the highest in England.

The biggest turnout rise was Thirsk & Malton (+17.70) but that is a special case as it was a postponed poll in 2010 due to the death of a candidate. The contest was held three weeks later on 27 May, and understandably the turnout at 50.0% was 15% below the national average for 6 May 2010.

It is followed by Inverclyde (+11.80), Caithness, Sutherland & Easter Ross (+11.01), Falkirk (+10.35), Liverpool Riverside (+10.33), Motherwell & Wishaw (+10.18), Paisley & Renfrewshire South (+10.07) and Dundee East (+10.00) – all in Scotland.

TOP 10 SEATS: LOWEST TURNOUTS 2015

	CONSTITUENCY	TURNOUT	WINNER
1	Stoke-On-Trent Central	51.3%	Lab
2	Blackley & Broughton	51.6%	Lab
3	East Londonderry	51.9%	DUP
4	Manchester Central	52.7%	Lab
5	Birmingham Ladywood	52.7%	Lab
6	Strangford	52.8%	DUP
7	Foyle	52.8%	SDLP
8	Middlesbrough	52.9%	Lab
9	Birmingham Erdington	53.3%	Lab
10	East Antrim	53.3%	DUP

Four of the ten lowest turnouts were in Northern Ireland, where rules to check the identity of voters have been tightened since the years when it was felt that impersonation was a problem. However, all the seats in this list were safely held by the incumbent parties.

The biggest turnout fall was Halesowen & Rowley Regis (-10.00), followed by South Staffordshire (-9.43) then North East Cambridgeshire (-8.71), Rugby (-7.28) and Rossendale & Darwen (-6.00).

The editors would like to thank the following for their invaluable help in compiling some of these tables: David Boothroyd, Andrea Parma, Andrew Stidwill and Anthony Wells.

The demographics of the new House of Commons

Compiled by Robert Waller

Oldest MPs

CONSERVATIVE

Sir Alan Haselhurst	Jun 1937
Bill Cash	May 1940
Kenneth Clarke	Jul 1940
Angela Watkinson	Nov 1941
Roger Gale	Aug 1943
Peter Lilley	Aug 1943
Glyn Davies	Feb 1944
Peter Bottomley	Jul 1944
Sir Paul Beresford	Apr 1946
Christopher Chope	May 1947
Gerald Howarth	Sep 1947
Gordon Henderson	Jan 1948
Nicholas Soames	Feb 1948
Pauline Latham	Feb 1948
David Davis	Dec 1948
Keith Simpson	Mar 1949

Sir Greg Knight	Apr 1949
David Evennett	Jun 1949
Bob Stewart	Jul 1949

LABOUR

Sir Gerald Kaufman	Jun 1930
Dennis Skinner	Feb 1932
David Winnick	Jun 1933
Paul Flynn	Feb 1935
Ann Clwyd	Mar 1937
Geoffrey Robinson	May 1938
Michael Meacher	Nov 1939
Barry Sheerman	Aug 1940
Jim Cunningham	Feb 1941
Kelvin Hopkins	Aug 1941
Frank Field	Jul 1942
Margaret Beckett	Jan 1943
Ronnie Campbell	Aug 1943
Margaret Hodge	Sep 1944
Louise Ellman	Nov 1945
Adrian Bailey	Dec 1945
Roger Godsiff	Jun 1946
Kate Hoey	Jun 1946
David Crausby	Jun 1946
Ann Coffey	Aug 1946
Sir Kevin Barron	Oct 1946
Virendra Sharma	Apr 1947
Marie Rimmer	Apr 1947
John Spellar	Aug 1947
Stephen Pound	Jul 1948
Jack Dromey	Sep 1948
Jeremy Corbyn	May 1949
George Howarth	Jun 1949
Alan Meale	Jul 1949

OTHERS

Pat Doherty	Jul 1945

Roger Mullin		Mar 1948
John Pugh		Jun 1948
Marion Fellows		May 1949
Alasdair McDonnell		Sep 1949
George Kerevan		Sep 1949

Longest-serving MPs

Sir Gerald Kaufman	Lab	1970
Kenneth Clarke	Con	1970
Michael Meacher	Lab	1970
Dennis Skinner	Lab	1970
Peter Bottomley	Con	1975
Geoffrey Robinson	Lab	1976
Sir Alan Haselhurst	Con	1977
David Winnick	Lab	1979
Barry Sheerman	Lab	1979
Frank Field	Lab	1979
Harriet Harman	Lab	1982
Margaret Beckett	Lab	1983
Edward Leigh	Con	1983
Peter Lilley	Con	1983
Jeremy Corbyn	Lab	1983
Nick Brown	Lab	1983
Sir Kevin Barron	Lab	1983
David Amess	Con	1983
Nicholas Soames	Con	1983
Roger Gale	Con	1983
Ann Clwyd	Lab	1984M
Bill Cash	Con	1984M
Patrick McLoughlin	Con	1986M
George Howarth	Lab	1986N
Diane Abbott	Lab	1987
Graham Allen	Lab	1987
Julian Brazier	Con	1987
Simon Burns	Con	1987
Ronnie Campbell	Lab	1987
Paul Flynn	Lab	1987

Alan Meale	Lab	1987
John Redwood	Con	1987
Andrew Smith	Lab	1987
David Tredinnick	Con	1987
Keith Vaz	Lab	1987

Youngest MPs

Mhairi Black (Paisley & Renfrewshire South)	12 September 1994
Stuart Donaldson (West Aberdeenshire & Kincardine)	5 September 1991
Tom Pursglove (Corby)	5 November 1988
William Wragg (Hazel Grove)	11 December 1987
Louise Haigh (Sheffield Heeley)	22 July 1987
Angela Crawley (Lanark & Hamilton East)	3 June 1987
Holly Walker-Lynch (Halifax)	8 October 1986
Ranil Jayawardena (North East Hampshire)	3 September 1986
Stewart McDonald (Glasgow South)	24 August 1986
Ben Howlett (Bath)	21 August 1986
Luke Hall (Thornbury & Yate)	8 July 1986
Kirsty Blackman (Aberdeen North)	20 March 1986
Neil Gray (Airdrie & Shotts)	16 March 1986
Cat Smith (Lancaster & Fleetwood)	16 June 1985
Craig Williams (Cardiff North)	7 June 1985
Callum McCaig (Aberdeen South)	6 January 1985
Gavin Robinson (Belfast East)	November 1984
Conor McGinn (St Helens North)	31 July 1984
Michelle Donelan (Chippenham)	8 April 1984
James Wharton (Stockton South)	16 February 1984

Twenty constituencies with highest proportion of voters over 65

		%	PARTY HOLDING SEAT
1	Christchurch	36.0	Con
2	Clacton	35.0	UKIP gain from Con
3	North Norfolk	34.1	LD
4	New Forest West	33.9	Con
5	East Devon	31.7	Con

6	Bexhill & Battle	31.3	Con
7	West Dorset	31.1	Con
8	Totnes	30.9	Con
9	Louth & Horncastle	30.5	Con
10	Worthing West	30.1	Con
11	Dwyfor Meirionnydd	30.0	Plaid Cymru
12	Suffolk Coastal	29.7	Con
13	Tiverton & Honiton	29.2	Con
14	Chichester	28.9	Con
15	Westmorland & Lonsdale	28.8	LD
16	Lewes	28.6	Con gain from LD
17	West Worcestershire	28.5	Con
18	Aberconwy	28.4	Con
19	Arundel & South Downs	28.3	Con
20	Brecon & Radnorshire	28.2	Con gain from LD

The Ipsos MORI analysis of the 2015 election suggests that UKIP did best among the over-65 age group, in which they scored 17%, compared with their national share of 12.6%.

They also say that there was a swing of no less than 5.5% from Labour to Conservative in this high-turnout group. Ipsos MORI estimate 78% of pensioners voted compared with the national average of 66.1%. This represents yet another reason why Labour failed to advance at all overall, and Ed Miliband fell so far short of entering Downing Street.

Ten constituencies with highest proportion born in Africa

		%	PARTY HOLDING SEAT
1	Camberwell & Peckham	16.6	Lab
2	Erith & Thamesmead	14.4	Lab
3	Harrow East	13.9	Con
4	Leicester East	13.3	Lab
5	Edmonton	12.5	Lab
6	West Ham	12.0	Lab
7	Brent North	11.5	Lab
8	Brent Central	11.4	Lab gain from LD
9	Greenwich & Woolwich	11.4	Lab
10	Croydon North	11.3	Lab

In general, the seats with the highest proportion of residents born in Africa voted very strongly for Labour in 2015 – for example, in Brent Central there was a 28% swing from Liberal Democrat to Labour as Dawn Butler regained the seat of the retiring Sarah Teather, and in West Ham, Lyn Brown increased her majority to 27,986. The exception is Harrow East, where the Conservative Bob Blackman actually increased his vote and share to win a second term.

This list includes two distinct groups – those in the London boroughs of Hendon and Brent and in Leicester (where Keith Vaz increased his share by 7.4%) includes many of South Asian ancestry who came to Britain after being expelled from Kenya and Uganda in the 1960s and 1970s. Those in seats in south and east London and Edmonton (where Labour's new MP Kate Osamor – whose mother Martha, also a political activist, was born in Nigeria – advanced by nearly 8%) are mainly more recent Afro-Caribbean immigrants from West Africa and Somalia. Commonwealth citizens can vote in general elections.

Twenty constituencies with highest proportion of black residents

		%	PARTY HOLDING SEAT
1	Camberwell & Peckham	37.4	Lab
2	Croydon North	31.5	Lab
3	Lewisham Deptford	28.9	Lab
4	Edmonton	27.3	Lab
5	Hackney South & Shoreditch	26.9	Lab
6	Tottenham	26.7	Lab
7	Lewisham East	25.8	Lab
8	Erith & Thamesmead	25.7	Lab
9	Brent Central	25.5	Lab gain from LD
10	Dulwich & West Norwood	25.0	Lab
11	Vauxhall	24.7	Lab
12	Streatham	24.3	Lab
13	West Ham	23.1	Lab
14	Birmingham Ladywood	22.6	Lab
15	Lewisham West & Penge	22.4	Lab
16	Barking	20.2	Lab
17	Bermondsey & Old Southwark	20.1	Lab gain from LD
18	Greenwich & Woolwich	20.1	Lab

| 19 | Hackney North & Stoke Newington | 19.6 | Lab |
| 20 | Walthamstow | 18.9 | Lab |

Some interesting features:

- All the top 20 seats are held by Labour, having gained two from the Liberal Democrats – after Sarah Teather's retirement in Brent Central and the defeat of Simon Hughes in Bermondsey.

- 19 of the 20 seats are within the boundaries of Greater London – the only exception is Birmingham Ladywood.

- There are no constituencies with a black majority, whereas there are six with an Asian majority.

- There are no Conservative seats in the top 20; the highest in the list is Enfield North (15.5%) at No. 25.

- Only four of the top 20 have black MPs at present: Tottenham (David Lammy), Streatham (Chuka Umunna) and Hackney North (Diane Abbott) being joined in 2015 by Kate Osamor of Edmonton.

Twenty constituencies with lowest proportion of white residents

		%	PARTY HOLDING SEAT
1	East Ham	23.1	Lab
2	Ilford South	24.2	Lab
3	Brent North	26.6	Lab
4	Birmingham Ladywood	27.3	Lab
5	Ealing Southall	30.4	Lab
6	Leicester East	31.4	Lab
7	West Ham	34.5	Lab
8	Croydon North	35.2	Lab
9	Birmingham Hall Green	35.5	Lab
10	Birmingham Hodge Hill	35.7	Lab
11	Bradford West	37.1	Lab gain from Respect
12	Brent Central	38.8	Lab gain from LD
13	Harrow East	39.2	Con

14	Birmingham Perry Barr	39.7	Lab
15	Harrow West	40.1	Lab
16	Hayes & Harlington	43.4	Lab
17	Poplar & Limehouse	43.5	Lab
18	Camberwell & Peckham	44.8	Lab
19	Feltham & Heston	44.9	Lab
20	Slough	45.1	Lab

Some interesting features:

- Seven of the 20 now have black and ethnic minority MPs, up two in the 2015 general election due to the Labour gains in Bradford West and Brent Central.

- Although boundary changes make exact comparisons impossible, it is fairly clear that the percentage of white residents dropped in every one of the above constituencies between the 2001 and 2011 Censuses.

- In 2001 there were 10 seats with a white minority; in 2011 there were 27.

- The greatest fall, of over 20%, was in Ilford South – as recently as 1992 a highly marginal seat, gained then by Labour from the Conservatives by only 402 votes. In 2015, Labour increased their share of the vote in this constituency by a further 14.6%.

- Four out of the five highest rises in Labour share of the vote in 2015 were in these 20 seats.

Twenty constituencies with highest proportion of Asian residents

		%	PARTY HOLDING SEAT
1	Leicester East	58.1	Lab
2	Ilford South	57.2	Lab
3	Bradford West	54.5	Lab gain from Respect
4	East Ham	53.8	Lab
5	Brent North	52.4	Lab
6	Ealing Southall	50.7	Lab
7	Birmingham Hodge Hill	49.8	Lab

8	Birmingham Hall Green	49.5	Lab
9	Harrow East	45.7	Con
10	Harrow West	42.9	Lab
11	Poplar & Limehouse	42.2	Lab
12	Feltham & Heston	40.8	Lab
13	Birmingham Ladywood	40.5	Lab
14	Slough	40.3	Lab
15	Bethnal Green & Bow	40.0	Lab
16	Bradford East	39.3	Lab gain from LD
17	Birmingham Perry Barr	38.8	Lab
18	Blackburn	37.5	Lab
19	Leicester South	37.4	Lab
20	Hayes & Harlington	36.4	Lab

Some interesting features:

- The number of the top 20 Asian seats with an MP of Asian origin is still only eight. In 2015 it went up by just two when George Galloway (Respect) was beaten by Labour's Naseem Shah in Bradford West, and David Ward (Liberal Democrat) lost to Imran Hussain (Labour) in Bradford East.

- Labour now holds 19 of the 20, with the only exception being the Conservative Bob Blackman's Harrow East.

- The British Asian population is much more spread out than the Afro-Caribbean population, with just half of the 20 seats above being located in Greater London.

Twenty constituencies with highest proportion of Muslim residents

		%	PARTY HOLDING SEAT
1	Birmingham Hodge Hill	52.1	Lab
2	Bradford West	51.3	Lab gain from Respect
3	Birmingham Hall Green	46.6	Lab
4	East Ham	37.4	Lab
5	Bradford East	36.9	Lab gain from LD

6	Blackburn	36.3	Lab
7	Bethnal Green & Bow	35.4	Lab
8	Birmingham Ladywood	35.2	Lab
9	Ilford South	34.9	Lab
10	Poplar & Limehouse	33.6	Lab
11	Manchester Gorton	28.8	Lab
12	Leicester South	27.8	Lab
13	West Ham	26.8	Lab
14	Walthamstow	25.4	Lab
15	Luton South	25.3	Lab
16	Oldham West & Royton	24.6	Lab
17	Edmonton	24.5	Lab
18	Slough	23.8	Lab
19	Rochdale	23.6	Lab
20	Birmingham Perry Barr	22.7	Lab

- After the 2015 election, all 20 seats now have a Labour MP, as Muslims appeared to have much reduced their support for George Galloway (Respect) in Bradford West after his dramatic 2012 by-election victory, and for the Liberal Democrats in Bradford East, and returned to their previous solid pattern of Labour support. This is confirmed by huge increases in the Labour share in other seats high on the list such as Birmingham Hodge Hill (up 16.4%), Bethnal Green & Bow (up 18.25%) and the seat with the highest Labour rise anywhere, Birmingham Hall Green (a mighty 26.9%). Seven of the 10 seats with the largest Labour increases in share in 2015 are also on this list of the top 20 Muslim seats.

- However, only five of the top 20 in the list currently have Muslim MPs, and this figure increased by just two after the 2015 election, with the retiring Jack Straw being replaced with another non-Muslim Labour candidate in Blackburn (Kate Hollern). Labour's new Muslim MP in Bradford West, Naz Shah, has a very interesting history as the daughter of a woman imprisoned for killing her violently abusive partner, and who herself was subjected to an arranged marriage in Pakistan.

- The Conservative-held seat highest on the list in 2010, the marginal Dewsbury (18.5% Muslim), which was placed at No. 32, was one of Labour's very disappointing haul of gains (ten in all) from the Conservatives in the 2015 election.

- The 2011 Census revealed for the first time that there are now two seats with a majority of Muslim residents (though not necessarily voters, due to the younger age profile among this group). After 2001, there were only three seats over 30% Muslim, compared with ten now, and nine over 20% compared with 26 ten years later.

Twenty constituencies with highest proportion of voters with degrees

		%	PARTY HOLDING SEAT
1	Battersea	57.4	Con
2	Richmond Park	55.2	Con
3	Cities of London & Westminster	54.5	Con
4	Wimbledon	54.4	Con
5	Hampstead & Kilburn	54.0	Lab
6	Chelsea & Fulham	53.7	Con
7	Kensington	52.2	Con
8	Hornsey & Wood Green	52.0	Lab gain from LD
9	Putney	51.6	Con
10	Tooting	51.4	Lab
11	Twickenham	49.5	Con gain from LD
12	Islington North	48.8	Lab
13	Vauxhall	48.7	Lab
14	Ealing Central & Acton	48.5	Lab gain from Con
15	Dulwich & West Norwood	47.6	Lab
16	Hammersmith	47.5	Lab
17	Islington South & Finsbury	47.4	Lab
18	Westminster North	47.3	Lab
19	Bristol West	47.2	Lab gain from LD
20	Edinburgh South	46.9	Lab

Some interesting features in the 2015 election were that Labour made a much higher proportion of gains in this 'most highly educated' set of constituencies than they did in the country as a whole. Not only did they wipe out the Liberal Democrats in their two seats, the university-influenced Bristol West and Hornsey & Wood Green in north London, but the second most difficult Conservative seat they gained is Ealing Central & Acton.

Twenty constituencies with highest proportion of full-time students

		%	PARTY HOLDING SEAT
1	Sheffield Central	38.1	Lab
2	Nottingham South	34.5	Lab
3	Cardiff Central	33.9	Lab gain from LD
4	Newcastle upon Tyne East	31.4	Lab
5	Liverpool Riverside	30.9	Lab
6	Manchester Central	29.1	Lab
7	Leeds North West	28.6	LD
8	Oxford East	27.7	Lab
9	Cambridge	27.5	Lab gain from LD
10	Manchester Gorton	26.3	Lab
11	Glasgow Central	25.2	SNP gain from Lab
12	Glasgow North	25.0	SNP gain from Lab
13	Leeds Central	24.9	Lab
14	Leicester South	24.8	Lab
15	Swansea West	24.7	Lab
16	Bristol West	24.3	Lab gain from LD
17	Portsmouth South	24.2	Con gain from LD
18	Coventry South	24.2	Lab
19	Canterbury	24.0	Con
20	Birmingham Ladywood	23.3	Lab

Some interesting features:

- Following Nick Clegg's perceived change of position on student fee increases, it was often said that the Liberal Democrats, who have done well in recent elections in constituencies influenced by universities, would suffer greatly at the 2015 election. In 2010, five of the top 20 seats by proportion of full-time students aged 16–24 were won by Liberal Democrats (including Portsmouth South, where Mike Hancock was suspended then resigned the whip in 2014). The prediction did indeed come to pass, with only Greg Mulholland holding on for the Lib Dems in a top 20 student seat.

- Some Lib Dem seats widely predicted to fall to Labour because of the 'student swing', notably Sheffield Hallam (Nick Clegg), Manchester

Withington and Norwich South, are not in fact on this top 20 list. The latter two were still gained by Labour, though.

- It was thought likely that there might be a dramatic increase in the Green Party vote in seats with many students. The Greens did finish a strong second in Bristol West with 17,237 votes (26.8%, their second best share after Caroline Lucas's Brighton Pavilion), and a distant second in Sheffield Central (15.8%), but otherwise just a few per cent better than average in the others on the list.

- On average, according to Ipsos MORI, the Greens did about twice as well (8%) among 18–24-year-olds as a whole (not distinguishing students separately) as their average share of 3.8%.

- Labour also performed at their strongest among the 18–24 age group, with a 7.5% swing from the Conservatives – but this had little effect as the turnout was very poor – 43% compared with over 66% across the country as a whole. There is clearly still a major problem in interesting and engaging young, mainly first-time, voters – at least outside Scotland.

Twenty constituencies with lowest proportion of voters with degrees

		%	PARTY HOLDING SEAT
1	Birmingham Hodge Hill	12.1	Lab
2	Walsall North	12.2	Lab
3	Kingston upon Hull East	12.7	Lab
4	Glasgow East	12.7	SNP gain from Lab
5	West Bromwich West	13.1	Lab
6	Nottingham North	13.3	Lab
7	Liverpool Walton	13.3	Lab
8	Clacton	13.4	UKIP gain from Con
9	Stoke-on-Trent North	13.7	Lab
10	Wolverhampton South East	13.9	Lab
11	Rhondda	14.0	Lab
12	Great Yarmouth	14.2	Con
13	Knowsley	14.3	Lab
14	Rotherham	14.3	Lab

15	Doncaster North	14.3	Lab
16	Boston & Skegness	14.6	Con
17	Great Grimsby	14.6	Lab
18	Blackpool South	14.6	Lab
19	Castle Point	14.6	Con
20	Ashfield	14.6	Lab

The most interesting theme running through this surprisingly disparate list is: the United Kingdom Independence Party.

As well as the perhaps expected selection of very safe Labour industrial seats, including that of party leader Ed Miliband in Doncaster North, there are four Conservative seats on the east coast where UKIP did exceptionally well in local and European elections in 2013–14, including some touted as candidates for a possible Westminster gain in 2015 – such as Great Yarmouth, where they won most of the seats in recent council elections, and Boston & Skegness, with its high rate of Eastern European immigration. It might also be remembered that Castle Point may have a claim to have been UKIP's first seat, as Bob Spink briefly defected from the Conservatives in 2008 before standing in 2010 as an Independent Green Belt candidate.

In 2015, Douglas Carswell did of course hold on to his 2014 by-election gain to be UKIP's only MP after the election. Boston & Skegness and Castle Point returned among their five highest shares, and in all UKIP were second in nine of the seats in the top 20 list – half of those in England.

There does, therefore, appear to be a correlation between some of UKIP's best performances and those seats with the fewest voters with degrees.

Twenty constituencies with highest proportion of single parents

		%	PARTY HOLDING SEAT
1	Belfast West	19.1	Sinn Féin
2	Edmonton	15.3	Lab
3	Barking	14.6	Lab
4	Foyle	14.5	SDLP
5	Croydon North	14.5	Lab
6	Nottingham North	14.2	Lab
7	Belfast North	13.8	DUP
8	Tottenham	13.6	Lab

9	Liverpool Walton	13.0	Lab
10	Enfield North	12.8	Con
11	Erith & Thamesmead	12.7	Lab
12	Knowsley	12.7	Lab
13	Birmingham Hodge Hill	12.6	Lab
14	Glasgow East	12.5	SNP gain from Lab
15	Croydon Central	12.2	Con
16	Birmingham Erdington	12.2	Lab
17	Liverpool West Derby	12.2	Lab
18	Camberwell & Peckham	12.1	Lab
19	Dagenham & Rainham	12.1	Lab
20	Birkenhead	12.0	Lab

An interesting mixture of types of seat: predominantly white, working-class areas, such as those in Nottingham and Merseyside; those with a substantial Afro-Caribbean population, such as Edmonton, Tottenham and Erith & Thamesmead; and seats in Northern Ireland and Scotland.

The two Conservative marginals on this list, Enfield North and Croydon Central, moved up the rank order significantly between the 2001 and 2011 Censuses, and this suggested social changes that would make them very difficult to hold in 2015, especially given Labour's strong performance in London boroughs and the European election in the capital in 2014. Indeed, Enfield North was one of Labour's ten gains from the Tories, as Joan Ryan recaptured the seat she lost to Nick de Bois in 2010, but it does emphasise how well Gavin Barwell did to cling on in Croydon Central by the narrow margin of 165 votes.

Twenty constituencies with highest proportion of social rented housing

		%	PARTY HOLDING SEAT
1	Camberwell & Peckham	50.6	Lab
2	Hackney South & Shoreditch	50.1	Lab
3	Glasgow North East	49.0	SNP gain from Lab
4	Islington South & Finsbury	43.7	Lab
5	Bermondsey & Old Southwark	43.5	Lab gain from LD
6	Glasgow East	43.3	SNP gain from Lab
7	Bethnal Green & Bow	42.7	Lab

8	Holborn & St Pancras	41.8	Lab
9	Vauxhall	41.2	Lab
10	Glasgow South West	39.8	SNP gain from Lab
11	Greenwich & Woolwich	39.3	Lab
12	Birmingham Ladywood	38.2	Lab
13	Motherwell & Wishaw	37.6	SNP gain from Lab
14	Sheffield Brightside & Hillsborough	37.5	Lab
15	Hackney North & Stoke Newington	37.3	Lab
16	Blackley & Broughton	37.3	Lab
17	West Dunbartonshire	37.3	SNP gain from Lab
18	Glasgow North West	36.9	SNP gain from Lab
19	Nottingham North	36.8	Lab
20	Poplar & Limehouse	36.8	Lab

In the 2015 general election, according to Ipsos MORI, who jointly produced the very accurate exit poll on 7 May, voters living in the social rented housing sector swung from Conservative to Labour by 4.5% (Labour up three points to 50%, Conservative down six to 18%) – enough, if replicated across the country, to produce a very different result and deny David Cameron his chance of a second term. However, it might also be noted that UKIP performed well above average too, with an 18% share – actually level with the Conservatives, while the Liberal Democrats slumped dramatically from 19% to 3%.

Therefore it is no surprise that almost all of the constituencies on this list in England were won by the Labour Party, including their gain in Bermondsey, which, with some boundary changes, Simon Hughes had managed to hold for the Liberal Democrats and their predecessors for over thirty-two years since his initial by-election victory in February 1983.

However, council housing has for many decades been generally more prevalent in Scotland, and the SNP had no problem gaining the six Scottish seats on the list, including their biggest swing anywhere in taking the former Labour stronghold of Glasgow North East with a swing of no less than 39.3% – the highest in a general election in documented electoral history. Indeed, on average the swings in these six constituencies were even higher than the astonishing level achieved by the SNP across Scotland. Therefore, it cannot be said that Labour can rely on the votes of the social renters, especially as according to the Ipsos MORI figures, at 56% they were 10 per cent less likely to turn out than the national average.

Twenty constituencies with highest proportion of owner-occupied housing

		%	PARTY HOLDING SEAT
1	East Dunbartonshire	85.8	SNP gain from LD
2	Sefton Central	85.5	Lab
3	Rayleigh & Wickford	84.5	Con
4	Cheadle	83.7	Con gain from LD
5	Wyre & Preston North	83.5	Con
6	Castle Point	82.6	Con
7	Haltemprice & Howden	82.4	Con
8	East Renfrewshire	82.0	SNP gain from Lab
9	Charnwood	81.6	Con
10	York Outer	81.5	Con
11	Mid Derbyshire	80.7	Con
12	Old Bexley & Sidcup	79.8	Con
13	Orpington	79.7	Con
14	Staffordshire Moorlands	79.7	Con
15	Solihull	79.6	Con gain from LD
16	South Leicestershire	79.6	Con
17	Bromsgrove	79.5	Con
18	Sutton Coldfield	79.4	Con
19	Thornbury & Yate	79.4	Con gain from LD
20	Old Bexley & Sidcup	81.3	Con

Some interesting features:

- While high owner occupation is usually a positive feature for Conservatism (remember Mrs Thatcher's sale of council housing), the table shows that this is not universally so. Four seats won in 2015 by other parties appear in the top 20, including No. 1 and 2 in this category. The point is that these are all in regions where the Conservative Party has become unpopular – Merseyside (where Labour won two) and Scotland (taken by the SNP, of course). Region can trump housing tenure as a determinant of political preference.

- Only two of the seats above are in Greater London – Old Bexley & Sidcup, the linear descendant of the constituency held by Edward Heath from 1950 to 2001, and Orpington, famously won by the

Liberals in a by-election in the 1960s. The Liberal Democrats lost all four of their seats in this category in 2015, even though they had sitting MPs.

- According to the Ipsos MORI data released after the election, there was actually a small swing from Labour to Conservative among voters in the owner-occupied sector in the 2015 election.

Ten constituencies with highest proportion in same-sex civil partnerships

		%	PARTY HOLDING SEAT
1	Bermondsey & Old Southwark	3.2	Lab gain from LD
2	Brighton Kemptown	3.2	Con
3	Cities of London & Westminster	3.0	Con
4	Brighton Pavilion	2.9	Green
5	Islington South & Finsbury	2.7	Lab
6	Holborn & St Pancras	2.6	Lab
7	Lewisham Deptford	2.6	Lab
8	Camberwell & Peckham	2.6	Lab
9	Hove	2.4	Lab gain from Con
10	Dulwich & West Norwood	2.4	Lab

These figures are from reported returns from the 2011 Census, so predate the institution of same-sex marriage. They also should not be taken as an indicator of 'percentage gay/lesbian', which would include many not in same-sex civil partnerships or not reporting to the official government Census.

However, the list does still have political interest, as probably including the greatest variety of constituency patterns of contest of any of our lists. It includes the only Green seat (where Caroline Lucas greatly increased her majority to nearly 8,000 in Brighton Pavilion); two Conservative seats vulnerable to Labour – one gained, Hove, and one retained, Brighton Kemptown; a safe Tory stronghold, the Cities of London & Westminster; several safe Labour constituencies in London; and finally the seat of the Liberal Democrat Simon Hughes, who was also the only gay MP for any of the top 10 seats in this category before the election but lost to Labour – who did better in this category of seats than most others in 2015. However, there is still one openly gay MP – Peter Kyle, the Labour victor in Hove.

The seats with the lowest percentage of civil partnerships recorded in England and Wales are at 0.4%: Castle Point in Essex, which includes Canvey Island (safe Conservative, but with a strong UKIP presence in second place); Harrow East (a Conservative seat where they held off a Labour challenge); and Thornbury & Yate in Gloucestershire, which the Liberal Democrats lost to the Conservatives.

Twenty constituencies with highest proportion of higher professional and managerial workers

		%	PARTY HOLDING SEAT
1	Wimbledon	24.0	Con
2	Cities of London & Westminster	23.8	Con
3	Battersea	23.4	Con
4	Richmond Park	23.3	Con
5	Chelsea & Fulham	22.6	Con
6	Hampstead & Kilburn	21.2	Lab
7	Kensington	20.7	Con
8	Wokingham	20.5	Con
9	Putney	20.4	Con
10	Twickenham	20.2	Con gain from LD
11	South Cambridgeshire	19.9	Con
12	St Albans	19.8	Con
13	Hitchin & Harpenden	19.8	Con
14	Esher & Walton	19.8	Con
15	North East Hampshire	19.5	Con
16	Sheffield Hallam	19.2	LD
17	Islington South & Finsbury	19.1	Lab
18	Maidenhead	19.1	Con
19	Westminster North	18.9	Lab
20	Altrincham & Sale West	18.8	Con

Class has for many decades been regarded as the strongest single predictor of voting patterns and, although class-based voting has been in decline in Britain since about 1960, that still holds true. However, it is by no means the be-all-and-end-all as far as constituencies are concerned, as shown by the presence in the above list of three Labour seats inclined to the left – and also by the fact that Wimbledon, Putney, Battersea and St Albans were all won by Labour in 1997 and 2001.

Besides the presence of one current Liberal Democrat seat, that of Nick Clegg, Vince Cable's Twickenham was only lost in 2015 and Richmond Park was also theirs until lost in 2010. So it can be said that having a very high percentage of senior managers and professionals is not necessarily a sign of strong Conservatism.

Twenty constituencies with lowest proportion of higher professional and managerial workers

		%	PARTY HOLDING SEAT
1	Birmingham Hodge Hill	2.9	Lab
2	Liverpool Walton	3.6	Lab
3	Glasgow East	3.8	SNP gain from Lab
4	Rhondda	3.8	Lab
5	Belfast West	3.9	Sinn Féin
6	Nottingham North	4.0	Lab
7	Blaenau Gwent	4.0	Lab
8	Middlesbrough	4.1	Lab
9	Hull East	4.1	Lab
10	Great Grimsby	4.1	Lab
11	Wolverhampton South East	4.2	Lab
12	Glasgow North East	4.3	SNP gain from Lab
13	West Bromwich West	4.3	Lab
14	Walsall North	4.3	Lab
15	Glenrothes	4.4	SNP gain from Lab
16	Wolverhampton North East	4.4	Lab
17	Glasgow South West	4.4	SNP gain from Lab
18	Blackpool South	4.5	Lab
19	Merthyr Tydfil & Rhymney	4.5	Lab
20	Knowsley	4.5	Lab

The list of seats with the lowest proportion of senior managers and professionals in Britain has in general been strongly correlated with great Labour strength, but in 2015 they lost the four in Scotland with even higher than average swings to the SNP, who recorded among their five highest shares of the vote anywhere in Glasgow North East and Glenrothes. Labour did hold on to Blackpool South, which was on the Conservative target list, and Great Grimsby, which was regarded as one of UKIP's best chances.

Generally, the constituencies are in the category of 'white working class', as those with more recent patterns of immigration tend also to have more aspirational characteristics, with more educational qualifications, and often in large cities which themselves host more professionals and managers. However, right at the top of this list, as of others, is Birmingham Hodge Hill, which has a Muslim and Asian majority and very high unemployment, as well as other indices of social and economic deprivation.

The new intake of 2015

Tim Carr

The class of 2015 has contributed significantly to what is considered the most diverse parliament ever. The House of Commons now has a record number of women MPs, of MPs from a BME background, reportedly more gay MPs than any other parliament in the world and the youngest MP since 1667. While all of these achievements will be broadly celebrated, the House of Commons still has some way to go before it will truly be more representative of the general population.

The 2015 general election saw a large intake of 182 newly elected MPs entering the House of Commons, 177 of whom had not been elected previously. The five returning MPs are Dawn Butler, Boris Johnson, Rob Marris, Joan Ryan and Alex Salmond.

Both the Conservative and Labour parliamentary parties now have a remarkably similar proportion of new Members: 22–23% of MPs. Most striking, of course, is the mass intake of 50 new Scottish National Party MPs, who will account for the vast majority (89%) of the parliamentary party.

ALL MPS/NEW MPS

	ALL MPS	NEW MPS	% OF NEW PARLIAMENTARY PARTY
Conservative	331	74	22%
Labour	232	53	23%
SNP	56	50	89%
Lib Dems	8	0	0%

DUP	8	1	12.5%
Sinn Féin	4	1	25%
Plaid Cymru	3	1	33%
SDLP	3	0	0%
UUP	2	2	100%
UKIP	1	0	0%
Green	1	0	0%
Ind (NI)	1	0	0%
	650	182	

SNP: Scottish National Party

DUP: Democratic Unionist Party

SDLP: Social Democratic & Labour Party

UUP: Ulster Unionist Party

Gender

A record number of 191 women were elected at the 2015 election, comprising 29% of MPs, and continuing the recent trend. Until 1997, women had never held more than 10% of seats in the Commons. The 2015 total comfortably beat the previous record of 143 (23%) elected in 2010 and the 120 elected in 1997. Altogether 44.5% (81) of the newly elected MPs were women. This compares to 72 newly elected female MPs (31%) in the class of 2010.

More than half (52%) of the women MPs in the Commons are Labour, 36% are Conservative and 10% are SNP. Labour also has the highest proportion (42.7%) of women, with gender parity potentially in sight within the next one or two general elections. Proponents of the all-women shortlist process in winnable seats, or safe seats where the MP was retiring, will see this advance as a vindication of the policy, which has at times been highly controversial with constituency associations.

As a proportion of the Conservative parliamentary party, women MPs now make up 20.5%, up from 16% in 2010. The SNP now has 20 female MPs (36%), 19 of whom were elected in 2015. Ten female former MPs were defeated by the SNP at the polls, providing a net gain of ten. The Liberal Democrats lost seven female MPs, and of the eight Liberal Democrat MPs re-elected, none are women.

A similar proportion (1,033 or 26%) of the 3,971 candidates who stood at the general election were women, composed of 36% of SNP candidates,

34% of Labour candidates, 26% of Conservatives and 26% of Liberal Democrats.

Internationally, our substantive increase in women MPs has meant that in the UN 2014 rankings of female representation, the UK has leapt from 64th position (out of 148) to around 37th. The UK is still behind countries such as Rwanda (63.8%), Sweden (45.0%), Belgium (41.3%), Spain (39.7%), Germany (36.6%), Austria (33.3%) and Italy (31.4%), but ahead of France (26.2%), Australia (26.0%), Canada (25.1%) and the USA (18.3%) based upon the UN figures.

WOMEN NEW MPS/NEW PARLIAMENT

	ALL MPS	NEW MPS	ALL MPS (WOMEN)		NEW MPS (WOMEN)	
Conservative	331	74	68	20.5%	27	36.5%
Labour	232	53	99	42.7%	34	64%
SNP	56	50	20	35.7%	19	38%
Lib Dems	8	0	0	0%	0	0%
DUP	8	1	0	0%	0	0%
Sinn Féin	4	1	0	0%	0	0%
Plaid Cymru	3	1	1	33%	1	100%
SDLP	3	0	1	33%	0	0%
UUP	2	2	0	0%	0	0%
UKIP	1	1	0	0%	0	0%
Green	1	0	1	100%	0	0%
Ind (NI)	1	0	1	100%	0	0%
	650	182	191		81	

SNP: Scottish National Party

DUP: Democratic Unionist Party

SDLP: Social Democratic & Labour Party

UUP: Ulster Unionist Party

Age

Prior to the election, the average (mean) MP was 51 years old. The common perception is that MPs are becoming younger, but historically the average age of MPs elected has remained around 50 years since 1918. Despite a number of young MPs having been elected, the early indication is that the 2015 general election is unlikely to have changed the average age of MPs and that it will remain around 50–51 years of age. With newly elected MPs in their 40s being the largest group, it does appear that this age provides the optimum time to either allow prior careers before entering politics or sufficient time to gather political experience and solicit political support in order to be selected to safe or winnable seats.

Of the 106 new MPs whose year of birth was known prior to the election, they were on average born in 1970, making them approximately 45 years old. In 2010, 5% of the new intake were in their 20s, 34% were in their 30s, 41% were in the 40s, 17% were in their 50s and 4% were in their 60s. In 2015, 8% of the new intake are in their 20s, 29% are in their 30s, 32% are in their 40s, 22% are in their 50s and 7% in their 60s.

The new intake includes Mhairi Black, SNP MP for Paisley & Renfrewshire South, who, at 20 years of age, is the new youngest MP in the House of Commons. She becomes the youngest MP since 1667 and the youngest elected MP since 1832.

Historically, Conservative MPs have tended to be marginally younger (by three to four years) and, on the basis of the figures in the table below, this trend looks set to continue.

As a percentage of their intake, the SNP has a noticeably larger number of young people in their 20s than the other parties. 14% (seven) of the new SNP MPs are in their 20s.

AGE OF NEW MPS (% OF NEW INTAKE BY PARTY IN EACH AGE BRACKET)

	NEW MPS	20–29		30–39		40–49		50–59		60–69		UNCONFIRMED	
All	182	14	8%	53	29%	58	32%	40	22%	13	7%	4	2%
Conservative	74	5	7%	27	36%	25	34%	13	18%	2	3%	2	3%
Labour	53	2	4%	16	30%	19	36%	11	21%	5	9%		
SNP	50	7	14%	9	18%	14	28%	13	26%	5	10%	2	4%
UUP	2							2	100%				
DUP	1			1	100%								
Sinn Féin	1									1	100%		
Plaid Cymru	1							1	100%				
			182		191		80					4	

% may not add to 100%

Ethnicity

A record number of 41 BME MPs (6.3% of the Commons versus 13% of the population) were elected in 2015, an increase from 27 at the last election (25 of whom retained their seats). University College London (UCL) suggest that there are 42 BME MPs, which would increase the proportion to nearer 6.5%. Labour's Anas Sarwar was defeated in Glasgow Central and the Conservatives' Paul Uppal in Wolverhampton South West. Uppal's defeat means that the House of Commons will not contain any British Sikh MPs for the first time since 1997.

Sixteen of the BME MPs were newly elected in 2015. This reflects an accelerating trend of BME MPs elected in recent elections with non-white candidates being selected in winnable or safe retirement seats. It is also worth noting that BME MPs are not restricted to ethnically diverse seats but, noticeably in 2015, were elected in Conservative-held seats with a predominantly white electorate.

Labour has the highest number of non-white MPs at 23, but the Conservatives are not far behind with 17. The SNP is the only party outside the two largest parties to have a (single) non-white MP.

Alan Mak, the Conservative MP for Havant, born and raised in York, became the UK's first MP of Chinese background.

The new Labour MPs are: Dawn Butler (Brent Central, also a former MP), Thangam Debbonaire (Bristol West), Dr Rupa Huq (Ealing Central & Acton), Imran Hussain (Bradford East), Clive Lewis (Norwich South), Kate Osamor (Edmonton), Naz Shah (Bradford West) and Tulip Siddiq (Hampstead & Kilburn). Six of the eight were elected in target seats. Dawn Butler was the first black female MP to be appointed a government minister (in 2009).

The new Conservative MPs are: James Cleverly (Braintree), Suella Fernandes (Fareham), Nusrat Ghani (Wealden), Ranil Jayawardena (Hampshire North East), Seema Kennedy (South Ribble), Alan Mak (Havant) and Rishi Sunak (Richmond Yorkshire). It is noticeable that all the Conservatives were elected in Conservative-held seats where the previous MP retired.

The new SNP MP is Tasmina Ahmed-Sheikh, elected in Ochil & South Perthshire.

A record number of BME candidates stood at the general election, including 55 (9%) Conservatives and 53 (8%) Labour prospective parliamentary candidates. It is estimated that the Greens had the lowest number and percentage of BME candidates at the election.

	MPS	NEW MPS	% OF NEW PARLIAMENTARY PARTY
Conservative	17	7	22%
Labour	23	8	23%
SNP	1	1	89%
	41	16	

Lesbian, Gay, Bisexual and Transgender (LGBT)

The UK has led the way in publicly declared LGBT politicians. One study from the University of North Carolina suggests that of the 214 declared LGBT politicians around the world since the first in 1976, the UK has claimed 36 of them. The 26 LGBT MPs in the last parliament was already the highest number in the world.

After 2015 the number has increased to 32 openly gay, lesbian or transgender MPs, including one new LGBT Conservative MP, four Labour and seven SNP, accounting for most of the increase and 12.5% of SNP MPs. Noticeably, the number of women LGBT MPs remains small, only six out of the 32 open LGBT MPs.

LGBT MPS

	MPS	MPS (MALE)	MPS (FEMALE)	NEW MPS	% OF NEW PARLIAMENTARY PARTY
Conservative	12	11	1	1	3.6%
Labour	13	11	2	4	5.6%
SNP	7	4	3	7	12.5%
	32	26	6	12	

Education

Historically, the long-term trends of the educational background of MPs are of a decline in privately educated and Oxbridge-educated MPs and an increase in non-Oxbridge university-educated MPs.[1] This broadly looks to be the picture in 2015, although there are gaps in the available information,

---

1   David Butler, Dennis Kavanagh and others, *The British General Election of...* (1951–2010)

and final figures may not be known for some time. Various academics and charitable organisations have also produced differing information.

According to Butler and Kavanagh, the source used by the House of Commons Library, in 1951, 338 MPs from the three main parties (Conservative, Labour and Liberals) attended university, including 229 who went to Oxford or Cambridge. In comparison, 478 MPs elected at the 2010 general election had been to university, of whom 165 had been to Oxbridge.

In 1951, 75% of Conservative MPs had been educated privately (81% in 1966), but this had declined to 54% in 2010. Over the same period, all university attendance had increased from 65% to 80%, but Oxbridge attendance had declined from 52% (a high of 57% in 1966) of those attending university to 34% in 2010.

The Social Mobility and Child Poverty Commission 'Elitist Britain' report of 2014 suggested that 33% of the 2010–15 MPs were privately educated, with a party breakdown of 52% of Conservatives and 10% of Labour MPs (and 41% of Liberal Democrats).

For Labour, 20% of MPs were privately educated in 1951 (reaching a high of 22% in 1955), falling to 12% in 2010 (from 18% in 2005). University attendance increased by half over the same period, from 41% in 1951 to 61% in 2010, while Oxbridge attendance had fallen slightly from 19% in 1951 (a high of 25% in 1974) to 15% in 2010.

Looking at the whole of the new House of Commons (650 MPs), the education and social mobility charity the Sutton Trust suggests that 32% of UK-educated MPs were educated privately, with 49% going to comprehensive schools and 19% to state grammar schools. By party, the Sutton Trust suggests that 48% of all Conservative MPs and 17% of Labour are privately educated.

It reports that 89% of MPs are graduates; 26% went to Oxford or Cambridge, 28% went to other Russell Group universities and the remaining 35% went to other universities in the UK or overseas. UCL suggests that the Oxbridge figure is higher at 31% of MPs and general university attendance lower at 66%.

The class of 2015 appears to broadly follow these trends, although there are significant gaps in the research. It is not yet known where 35% of the new MPs were educated at secondary school level.

Among the 118 new MPs, where their education details are known, 33 (28% of the known sample) attended at least one independent school (25 Conservatives, six Labour, one SNP and one Ulster Unionist). As a proportion of those details known, this equates to 62% of Conservatives (53 of 74 known), 18% of Labour (34 of 53) and 2% SNP (29 of 50). This might suggest an increase in the levels of private education for both the Conservatives and Labour, but it would be safer to defer judgement until more details are known.

For the record, research from Byron Criddle shows that the percentage of Old Etonian Conservative MPs has fallen from 24% in 1951 to 6.5% in 2010. There were 19 Old Etonian Conservative MPs (plus one Liberal Democrat) in the 2010–15 parliament (17 between 2005 and 2010), but two stood down at the election (Sir George Young and James Arbuthnot). There appears to have been only one 'new' MP educated at Eton – Boris Johnson. So the decline in numbers appears to have continued, albeit very marginally.

More is known about the higher education achievements of the new intake. 15% of the new intake of MPs holds a degree from either Oxford or Cambridge universities, suggesting a further long-term decline. Nearly 26% of Conservatives attended Oxbridge, but none of the 50 new SNP MPs, who were predominantly educated at one of the Scottish universities, did so.

Nearly 80% of the new MPs have studied at a higher education establishment – and the figure could be significantly higher, as it is not known whether or not 14% attended further/higher education. The 80% attendance rate is consistent across all the three main parties.

At least nine of the new MPs (six Labour and three Conservatives) were the first member of their family to attend university.

HIGHER EDUCATION

	OXBRIDGE		OTHER RUSSELL GROUP		OTHER		INTERNATIONAL		NONE OR UNKNOWN		DID NOT ATTEND	
All new MPs	28	15.4%	53	29.1%	62	34.1%	2	1.1%	26	14.3%	11	6.0%
Conservative	19	25.7%	24	32.4%	16	21.6%	0	0.0%	8	10.8%	7	9.5%
Labour	9	17.0%	12	22.6%	20	37.7%	1	1.9%	8	15.1%	3	5.7%
SNP	0	0.0%	15	30.0%	24	48.0%	1	2.0%	9	18.0%	1	2.0%
DUP			1	100%								
Sinn Féin									1	100%		
Plaid Cymru					1	100%						
UUP			1	50%	1	50%						

SNP: Scottish National Party

DUP: Democratic Unionist Party

SDLP: Social Democratic & Labour Party

UUP: Ulster Unionist Party

The figures above are based on attendance at an educational establishment for first degree only, not postgraduate study

Work and occupations

One thing that the new class of 2015 makes clear is that the working lives of politicians, and probably the wider population, has changed substantially in recent decades. There was a time when most people had one chosen profession or occupation for most of their working lives and could be classified as such. While this may remain the case for some professionals, the backgrounds of the new MPs suggest that this is no longer the norm in modern Britain. People are now far more likely to move several times both between jobs and also, increasingly, between different professions as they pass through their working lives.

Most of the new intake of MPs in 2015 have had at least two distinct careers (politics frequently being one of them), with some having as many as four. Focusing any analysis on one 'main' profession or occupation is potentially subjective and risks missing some interesting trends and details. It is more useful to talk in terms of whether one of the new MPs has 'experience' in a particular area.

As an example of some varying careers, Lucy Allan (Conservative, Telford) has been a chartered accountant, an investment manager, a lawyer and the founder of a charity. David Warburton (Conservative, Somerton & Frome) had various unskilled jobs, was a music teacher and composer, and more recently has founded several companies.

The occupational backgrounds of MPs have changed substantially over time. According to the House of Commons Library, in 1951, 18% of MPs from the three main parties were formerly manual workers, compared to only 4% in 2010. Very few of the class of 2015 have been manual workers: Scott Mann (Conservative, Cornwall North) was a postman; Derek Thomas (Conservative, St Ives) was a Cornish stone mason; John McNally (SNP, Falkirk) was a barber; and Harry Harpham (Labour, Sheffield Brightside & Hillsborough) was a Nottinghamshire miner.

Similarly, there has been a general decline in the professions. From a high of 16% in 1959, the proportion of MPs who are barristers had fallen to 6% in 2010, and for teachers it peaked at around 20% in 1997 but declined to 8% in 2010. As the table below shows, 7% of the 2015 intake are qualified barristers and 6% have been either primary or secondary school teachers. Three of the new intake (Joanna Cherry, Lucy Frazer and Sir Keir Starmer) are QCs.

As might be expected, there are substantial differences between the three main parties (Conservative, Labour and SNP). The professions or occupations highest among the Conservatives (excluding politics) are business (43% of new Conservatives), law (18%), consultancy (18%) and finance (16%), although charity work (12%) and the media (12%) are worth highlighting.

For Labour, the top occupations are charity work (28%), business (23%), public sector (20%), consultancy (17%), trade unions (17%), law (15%) and health (13%). For the new SNP MPs, business and finance feature surprisingly highly, perhaps illustrating the importance of the financial sector in Scotland: business (40%), finance (16%), education (16%), public sector (16%), charity (14%), consultancy (10%) and the media (10%).

A majority (71%) of the new intake has some experience of working in the private sector: 82% of the new Conservative MPs, 57% of Labour and 70% of the new SNP MPs.

WORK AND OCCUPATIONS

	ALL NEW MPS (182)		CONSERVATIVE (74 NEW MPS)		LABOUR (53 NEW MPS)		SNP (50 NEW MPS)	
Agriculture	3	2%	2	3%	0	0%	0	0%
Armed forces	9	5%	6	8%	1	2%	0	0%
Arts	8	4%	2	3%	1	2%	3	6%
Business	64	35%	32	43%	12	23%	20	40%
Charity/NGO	32	18%	9	12%	15	28%	7	14%
Consultant[1]	27	15%	13	18%	9	17%	5	10%
Education	19	10%	4	5%	6	11%	8	16%
– Teacher	10	6%	3	4%	4	8%	3	6%
Finance	20	11%	12	16%	0	0%	8	16%
IT	5	3%	0	0%	2	4%	3	6%
Law[2]	26	14%	13	18%	8	15%	4	8%
– Barrister	12	7%	9	12%	4	8%	1	2%
Media	17	9%	9	12%	2	4%	5	10%
Health[3]	12	7%	4	5%	7	13%	2	4%
– Primary care	8	4%	3	4%	3	6%	2	4%
Misc.[4]	12	7%	2	3%	5	9%	5	10%
Politics[5]	41	23%	13	18%	13	25%	11	22%
Former MP	5	3%	1	1%	3	6%	1	2%
Elected rep[6]	9	5%	5	7%	0	0%	0	0%
Special adviser	4	2%	1	1%	2	4%	1	2%
Political researcher[7]	43	24%	12	16%	18	34%	13	26%
Public sector[8]	24	13%	5	6%	11	20%	8	16%
Sport	3	2%	0	0%	3	6%	0	0%

F/t trade unionist	10	5%	0	0%	9	17%	1	2%
Private sector experience	129	71%	61	82%	30	57%	35	70%

1. Consultant, including public affairs, communications, lobbyist, self-employed business consultant

2. Solicitor, corporate lawyer, barrister; separate figures for barristers

3. Medicine, health worker, community care

4. Miscellaneous roles, including manual and non- or semi-skilled labour

5. Party worker, full-time councillor, think tank

6. Current or former member of a devolved assembly/Parliament or the London Assembly, but not including the House of Commons

7. Political researcher/adviser/office manager/constituency worker for MP, peer, MEP or devolved assembly member/parliamentarian

8. Includes central government civil servant, non-ministerial departments, agencies and other public bodies, and local authorities

Note: as with all the figures and categories, a single MP may appear in several of the politics, former MP, elected rep, special adviser and political researcher figures; see the political class table for an overview of the new MPs' political experience.

One interesting sector that has risen in prominence is the arts. Andrea Jenkyns (Conservative, Morley & Outwood) has been a semi-professional singer, David Warburton (Conservative, Somerton & Frome) has been a composer and Michelle Thomson (SNP, Edinburgh West) was a professional pianist. Labour's Jeff Smith (Manchester Withington) was an events manager and DJ. Danny Kinahan (UUP, Antrim South) has worked for Christie's and is an art dealer. The SNP's Deidre Brock (Edinburgh North & Leith) was an actor for ten years in her native Australia, and Tasmina Ahmed-Sheikh (Ochil & South Perthshire) starred in several highly successful Asian television shows directed by her husband.

Below are some of the more unusual background details from the new intake:

- Neil Gray (SNP, Airdrie & Shotts) competed for Scotland in the 400 metres until injury cut short his athletics career

- Sir Keir Starmer (Labour, Holborn & St Pancras) was named after former Labour Party leader Keir Hardie

- Conor McGinn (Labour, St Helens North) is the son of a former Sinn Féin councillor

- Craig Mackinlay (Conservative, South Thanet) is a former leader and deputy leader of UKIP – and beat Nigel Farage in the election

- Gavin Robinson (DUP, Belfast East) was Mayor of Belfast at the age of 27

- Christina Rees (Labour, Neath) was a professional squash player (Welsh No. 1) and coach

- Tasmina Ahmed-Sheikh (SNP, Ochil & South Perthshire) has been a member of both the Conservatives and Labour

- Royston Smith (Conservative, Southampton Itchen) is a George Medal winner for bravery

The political class

Much has been written in recent years about the apparent growth of a political class of MP. This appears to be confirmed by the new intake of 2015 with high levels of direct political involvement prior to becoming an MP, particularly among the new Labour MPs. 45% (82) of the new intake have had a job working directly in politics, as an elected political representative, a party worker or a researcher/adviser for an MP, MEP, peer or devolved assembly member – 60% (32) of Labour, 34% (25) of Conservatives and 42% (21) of SNP.

This figure rises to 75% to include those who have been politically active, either as a councillor or having previously stood for election. This encompasses 77% of the Labour intake, 81% of Conservatives and 62% of SNP.

Only 25% of the new MPs are apparently relatively new to politics and have not previously stood for election, been active in local government or worked directly in politics (23% of Labour, 19% of Conservatives and 38% of SNP).

	NEW MPS	DIRECT POLITICAL JOBS[1]		POLITICAL EXPERIENCE ONLY[2]		NEW TO POLITICS?	
All	182	82	45%	55	30%	45	25%
Conservative	74	25	34%	35	47%	14	19%
Labour	53	32	60%	9	17%	12	23%
SNP	50	21	42%	10	20%	19	38%

1. Elected political representative, party worker, political researcher/adviser, public policy think tank

2. Councillor, previously stood for election to Parliament, a devolved assembly/Parliament or as a Police and Crime Commissioner

30% (54) of the new intake have previously stood for election to Parliament, including Labour's Daniel Zeichner (Cambridge), who was elected on his fifth attempt, having first stood (in Mid Norfolk) in 1997, and the SNP's Roger Mullin (Kirkcaldy & Cowdenbeath), who has previously stood in four general elections, one Westminster by-election and one Scottish election. Perhaps surprisingly, only 12 of those MPs elected in 2015 stood for election in the same seat at the 2010 general election.

Experience in local government is still a common route to the House of Commons, with just over half (92 or 51%) of the new intake having been elected councillors (44 or 59% of the Conservatives, 25 or 47% of Labour, 19 or 38% of SNP, and four others). Only a modest 10% (18) have been a councillor in London. Twelve of the new MPs have been leaders of their council: Julie Cooper, Peter Dowd, Peter Grant, Drew Hendry, Kate Hollern, David Mackintosh, Justin Madders, Callum McCaig, Marie Rimmer, Royston Smith, Owen Thompson and Catherine West.

There are four former special advisers:

- Oliver Dowden (Conservative, Hertsmere) – former deputy chief of staff to David Cameron, the Prime Minister

- Stephen Gethins (SNP, Fife North East) – former special adviser to Alex Salmond as First Minister

- Dr Peter Kyle (Labour, Hove) – former special adviser to Hilary Armstrong MP at the Cabinet Office

- Anna Turley (Labour, Redcar) – former special adviser to Hilary Armstrong and David Blunkett

There are five former MPs who have been re-elected to the House of Commons:

- Dawn Butler (Labour, Brent Central) – former MP for Brent South

- Boris Johnson (Conservative, Uxbridge & Ruislip South) – former MP for Henley

- Rob Marris (Labour, Wolverhampton South West) – former MP for the same constituency

- Joan Ryan (Labour, Enfield North) – former MP for the same constituency

- Alex Salmond (SNP, Gordon) – former MP for Banff & Buchan

Ten of the new intake are or have been a member of another legislative assembly or other elected position:

- Victoria Borwick (Conservative, Kensington) – member of the London Assembly

- Mickey Brady (Sinn Féin, Newry & Armagh) – member of the Northern Ireland Assembly

- James Cleverly (Conservative, Braintree) – member of the London Assembly

- Byron Davies (Conservative, Gower) – former member of the National Assembly for Wales

- Tom Elliott (Ulster Unionist, Fermanagh & South Tyrone) – member of the Northern Ireland Assembly

- Boris Johnson (Conservative, Uxbridge & Ruislip South) – elected Mayor of London

- Kit Malthouse (Conservative, Hampshire North West) – member of the London Assembly

- Anne McLoughlin (SNP, Glasgow North East) – former member of the Scottish Parliament

- Gavin Robinson (Democratic Unionist, Belfast East) – member of the Northern Ireland Assembly

- Antoinette Sandbach (Conservative, Eddisbury) – former member of the National Assembly for Wales

Ten of the new intake have family political connections:

- Victoria Atkins (Conservative, Louth & Horncastle) is the daughter of former MP and MEP Sir Robert Atkins

- Victoria Borwick (Conservative, Kensington) is married to peer Lord Borwick

- Richard Burgon (Labour, Leeds East) is the nephew of former Elmet MP Colin Burgon

- James Cartlidge (Conservative, Suffolk South) is married to the daughter of Sir Gerald Howarth MP

- Stuart Donaldson (SNP, Aberdeenshire West & Kincardine) is the son of Scottish Public Health Minister Maureen Watt

- Patricia Gibson (SNP, Ayrshire North & Arran) is married to Kenneth Gibson MSP

- Stephen Kinnock (Labour, Aberavon) is the son of Neil and Glenys Kinnock and is married to Danish Prime Minister Helle Thorning-Schmidt

- Natalie McGarry (SNP, Glasgow East) is the niece of Tricia Marwick, MSP and the Presiding Officer (Speaker) of the Scottish Parliament

- Victoria Prentis (Conservative, Banbury) is the daughter of former Conservative MP and now peer Tim Boswell

- Christina Rees (Labour, Neath) is the ex-wife of former MP and Secretary of State for Wales Ron Davies

Index of new MPs

Index of new MPs by surname

Name	Party	Constituency
Tasmina Ahmed-Sheikh OBE	SNP	Ochil & South Perthshire
Lucy Allan	Con	Telford
Heidi Allen	Con	Cambridgeshire South
Caroline Ansell	Con	Eastbourne
Edward Argar	Con	Charnwood
Richard Arkless	SNP	Dumfries & Galloway
Victoria Atkins	Con	Louth & Horncastle
Hannah Bardell	SNP	Livingston
James Berry	Con	Kingston & Surbiton
Mhairi Black	SNP	Paisley & Renfrewshire South
Ian Blackford	SNP	Ross, Skye & Lochaber
Kirsty Blackman	SNP	Aberdeen North
Victoria Borwick	Con	Kensington
Phil Boswell	SNP	Coatbridge, Chryston & Bellshill
Mickey Brady	SF	Newry & Armagh
Deidre Brock	SNP	Edinburgh North & Leith
Alan Brown	SNP	Kilmarnock & Loudoun
Richard Burgon	Lab	Leeds East
Dawn Butler	Lab	Brent Central
Ruth Cadbury	Lab	Brentford & Isleworth
Dr Lisa Cameron	SNP	East Kilbride, Strathaven & Lesmahagow
James Cartlidge	Con	Suffolk South
Maria Caulfield	Con	Lewes
Alex Chalk	Con	Cheltenham

Douglas Chapman	SNP	Dunfermline & Fife West
Joanna Cherry QC	SNP	Edinburgh South West
Jo Churchill	Con	Bury St Edmunds
James Cleverly	Con	Braintree
Julie Cooper	Lab	Burnley
Alberto Costa	Con	Leicestershire South
Ronnie Cowan	SNP	Inverclyde
Jo Cox	Lab	Batley & Spen
Neil Coyle	Lab	Bermondsey & Old Southwark
Angela Crawley	SNP	Lanark & Hamilton East
Judith Cummins	Lab	Bradford South
Chris Davies	Con	Brecon & Radnorshire
Dr James Davies	Con	Vale of Clwyd
Mims Davies	Con	Eastleigh
Byron Davies	Con	Gower
Martyn Day	SNP	Linlithgow & Falkirk East
Thangam Debbonaire	Lab	Bristol West
Martin Docherty	SNP	Dunbartonshire West
Stuart Donaldson	SNP	Aberdeenshire West & Kincardine
Michelle Donelan	Con	Chippenham
Steve Double	Con	St Austell & Newquay
Peter Dowd	Lab	Bootle
Oliver Dowden	Con	Hertsmere
Flick Drummond	Con	Portsmouth South
Tom Elliott	UUP	Fermanagh & South Tyrone
Marion Fellows	SNP	Motherwell & Wishaw
Suella Fernandes	Con	Fareham
Margaret Ferrier	SNP	Rutherglen & Hamilton West
Colleen Fletcher	Lab	Coventry North East
Kevin Foster	Con	Torbay
Vicky Foxcroft	Lab	Lewisham Deptford
Lucy Frazer QC	Con	Cambridgeshire South East
Marcus Fysh	Con	Yeovil
Stephen Gethins	SNP	Fife North East
Nusrat Ghani	Con	Wealden
Patricia Gibson	SNP	Ayrshire North & Arran
Patrick Grady	SNP	Glasgow North
Peter Grant	SNP	Glenrothes
Neil Gray	SNP	Airdrie & Shotts

Christopher Green	Con	Bolton West
Margaret Greenwood	Lab	Wirral West
Louise Haigh	Lab	Sheffield Heeley
Luke Hall	Con	Thornbury & Yate
Harry Harpham	Lab	Sheffield Brightside & Hillsborough
Carolyn Harris	Lab	Swansea East
Helen Hayes	Lab	Dulwich & West Norwood
Sue Hayman	Lab	Workington
James Heappey	Con	Wells
Peter Heaton-Jones	Con	Devon North
Drew Hendry	SNP	Inverness, Nairn, Badenoch & Strathspey
Simon Hoare	Con	Dorset North
Kate Hollern	Lab	Blackburn
Kevin Hollinrake	Con	Thirsk & Malton
Ben Howlett	Con	Bath
Nigel Huddleston	Con	Worcestershire Mid
Dr Rupa Huq	Lab	Ealing Central & Acton
Imran Hussain	Lab	Bradford East
Ranil Jayawardena	Con	Hampshire North East
Andrea Jenkyns	Con	Morley & Outwood
Boris Johnson	Con	Uxbridge & Ruislip South
Gerald Jones	Lab	Merthyr Tydfil & Rhymney
Seema Kennedy	Con	South Ribble
George Kerevan	SNP	East Lothian
Calum Kerr	SNP	Berwickshire, Roxburgh & Selkirk
Danny Kinahan	UUP	Antrim South
Stephen Kinnock	Lab	Aberavon
Julian Knight	Con	Solihull
Dr Peter Kyle	Lab	Hove
Chris Law	SNP	Dundee West
Clive Lewis	Lab	Norwich South
Rebecca Long-Bailey	Lab	Salford & Eccles
Holly Lynch	Lab	Halifax
Craig Mackinlay	Con	South Thanet
David Mackintosh	Con	Northampton South
Justin Madders	Lab	Ellesmere Port & Neston
Alan Mak	Con	Havant
Kit Malthouse	Con	Hampshire North West
Scott Mann	Con	Cornwall North

Rob Marris	Lab	Wolverhampton South West
Rachael Maskell	Lab	York Central
Chris Matheson	Lab	Chester, City of
Dr Tania Mathias	Con	Twickenham
Callum McCaig	SNP	Aberdeen South
Stewart McDonald	SNP	Glasgow South
Stuart McDonald	SNP	Cumbernauld, Kilsyth & Kirkintilloch East
Natalie McGarry	SNP	Glasgow East
Conor McGinn	Lab	St Helens North
Anne McLaughlin	SNP	Glasgow North East
John McNally	SNP	Falkirk
Johnny Mercer	Con	Plymouth Moor View
Huw Merriman	Con	Bexhill & Battle
Amanda Milling	Con	Cannock Chase
Carol Monaghan	SNP	Glasgow North West
Dr Paul Monaghan	SNP	Caithness, Sutherland & Easter Ross
Wendy Morton	Con	Aldridge-Brownhills
Professor Roger Mullin	SNP	Kirkcaldy & Cowdenbeath
Gavin Newlands	SNP	Paisley & Renfrewshire North
John Nicolson	SNP	Dunbartonshire East
Brendan O'Hara	SNP	Argyll & Bute
Melanie Onn	Lab	Great Grimsby
Kate Osamor	Lab	Edmonton
Kirsten Oswald	SNP	Renfrewshire East
Steven Paterson	SNP	Stirling
Matthew Pennycook	Lab	Greenwich & Woolwich
Jess Phillips	Lab	Birmingham Yardley
Chris Philp	Con	Croydon South
Rebecca Pow	Con	Taunton Deane
Victoria Prentis	Con	Banbury
Tom Pursglove	Con	Corby
Jeremy Quin	Con	Horsham
Will Quince	Con	Colchester
Angela Rayner	Lab	Ashton-under-Lyne
Christina Rees	Lab	Neath
Marie Rimmer CBE	Lab	St Helens South & Whiston
Gavin Robinson	DUP	Belfast East
Mary Robinson	Con	Cheadle
Joan Ryan	Lab	Enfield North

Alex Salmond	SNP	Gordon
Antoinette Sandbach	Con	Eddisbury
Liz Saville-Roberts	PC	Dwyfor Meirionnydd
Paul Scully	Con	Sutton & Cheam
Naz Shah	Lab	Bradford West
Tommy Sheppard	SNP	Edinburgh East
Paula Sherriff	Lab	Dewsbury
Tulip Siddiq	Lab	Hampstead & Kilburn
Ruth Smeeth	Lab	Stoke-on-Trent North
Cat Smith	Lab	Lancaster & Fleetwood
Jeff Smith	Lab	Manchester Withington
Royston Smith	Con	Southampton Itchen
Karin Smyth	Lab	Bristol South
Amanda Solloway	Con	Derby North
Sir Keir Starmer KCB QC	Lab	Holborn & St Pancras
Chris Stephens	SNP	Glasgow South West
Jo Stevens	Lab	Cardiff Central
Wes Streeting	Lab	Ilford North
Rishi Sunak	Con	Richmond Yorkshire
Alison Thewliss	SNP	Glasgow Central
Derek Thomas	Con	St Ives
Nick Thomas-Symonds	Lab	Torfaen
Owen Thompson	SNP	Midlothian
Michelle Thomson	SNP	Edinburgh West
Maggie Throup	Con	Erewash
Kelly Tolhurst	Con	Rochester & Strood
Michael Tomlinson	Con	Dorset Mid & Poole North
Craig Tracey	Con	Warwickshire North
Anne-Marie Trevelyan	Con	Berwick upon Tweed
Thomas Tugendhat MBE	Con	Tonbridge & Malling
Anna Turley	Lab	Redcar
David Warburton	Con	Somerton & Frome
Matt Warman	Con	Boston & Skegness
Catherine West	Lab	Hornsey & Wood Green
Helen Whately	Con	Faversham & Kent Mid
Philippa Whitford	SNP	Ayrshire Central
Craig Williams	Con	Cardiff North
Corri Wilson	SNP	Ayr, Carrick & Cumnock
Mike Wood	Con	Dudley South

| William Wragg | Con | Hazel Grove |
| Daniel Zeichner | Lab | Cambridge |

Abbreviations:

Con: Conservative

DUP: Democratic Unionist Party

Lab: Labour

PC: Plaid Cymru

SNP: Scottish National Party

SF: Sinn Féin

UUP: Ulster Unionist Party

Index of new MPs by party

Conservative (74)

Lucy Allan	Telford
Heidi Allen	Cambridgeshire South
Caroline Ansell	Eastbourne
Edward Argar	Charnwood
Victoria Atkins	Louth & Horncastle
James Berry	Kingston & Surbiton
Victoria Borwick	Kensington
James Cartlidge	Suffolk South
Maria Caulfield	Lewes
Alex Chalk	Cheltenham
Jo Churchill	Bury St Edmunds
James Cleverly	Braintree
Alberto Costa	Leicestershire South
Chris Davies	Brecon & Radnorshire
Dr James Davies	Vale of Clwyd
Mims Davies	Eastleigh
Byron Davies	Gower
Michelle Donelan	Chippenham
Steve Double	St Austell & Newquay
Oliver Dowden	Hertsmere
Flick Drummond	Portsmouth South

Suella Fernandes	Fareham
Kevin Foster	Torbay
Lucy Frazer QC	Cambridgeshire South East
Marcus Fysh	Yeovil
Nusrat Ghani	Wealden
Christopher Green	Bolton West
Luke Hall	Thornbury & Yate
James Heappey	Wells
Peter Heaton-Jones	Devon North
Simon Hoare	Dorset North
Kevin Hollinrake	Thirsk & Malton
Ben Howlett	Bath
Nigel Huddleston	Worcestershire Mid
Ranil Jayawardena	Hampshire North East
Andrea Jenkyns	Morley & Outwood
Boris Johnson	Uxbridge & Ruislip South
Seema Kennedy	South Ribble
Julian Knight	Solihull
Craig Mackinlay	South Thanet
David Mackintosh	Northampton South
Alan Mak	Havant
Kit Malthouse	Hampshire North West
Scott Mann	Cornwall North
Dr Tania Mathias	Twickenham
Johnny Mercer	Plymouth Moor View
Huw Merriman	Bexhill & Battle
Amanda Milling	Cannock Chase
Wendy Morton	Aldridge-Brownhills
Chris Philp	Croydon South
Rebecca Pow	Taunton Deane
Victoria Prentis	Banbury
Tom Pursglove	Corby
Jeremy Quin	Horsham
Will Quince	Colchester
Mary Robinson	Cheadle
Antoinette Sandbach	Eddisbury
Paul Scully	Sutton & Cheam
Royston Smith	Southampton Itchen
Amanda Solloway	Derby North

Rishi Sunak	Richmond Yorkshire
Derek Thomas	St Ives
Maggie Throup	Erewash
Kelly Tolhurst	Rochester & Strood
Michael Tomlinson	Dorset Mid & Poole North
Craig Tracey	Warwickshire North
Anne-Marie Trevelyan	Berwick upon Tweed
Thomas Tugendhat MBE	Tonbridge & Malling
David Warburton	Somerton & Frome
Matt Warman	Boston & Skegness
Helen Whately	Faversham & Kent Mid
Craig Williams	Cardiff North
Mike Wood	Dudley South
William Wragg	Hazel Grove

Labour (53)

Richard Burgon	Leeds East
Dawn Butler	Brent Central
Ruth Cadbury	Brentford & Isleworth
Julie Cooper	Burnley
Jo Cox	Batley & Spen
Neil Coyle	Bermondsey & Old Southwark
Judith Cummins	Bradford South
Thangam Debbonaire	Bristol West
Peter Dowd	Bootle
Colleen Fletcher	Coventry North East
Vicky Foxcroft	Lewisham Deptford
Margaret Greenwood	Wirral West
Louise Haigh	Sheffield Heeley
Harry Harpham	Sheffield Brightside & Hillsborough
Carolyn Harris	Swansea East
Helen Hayes	Dulwich & West Norwood
Sue Hayman	Workington
Kate Hollern	Blackburn
Dr Rupa Huq	Ealing Central & Acton
Imran Hussain	Bradford East
Gerald Jones	Merthyr Tydfil & Rhymney
Stephen Kinnock	Aberavon

Dr Peter Kyle	Hove
Clive Lewis	Norwich South
Rebecca Long Bailey	Salford & Eccles
Holly Lynch	Halifax
Justin Madders	Ellesmere Port & Neston
Rob Marris	Wolverhampton South West
Rachael Maskell	York Central
Chris Matheson	Chester, City of
Conor McGinn	St Helens North
Melanie Onn	Great Grimsby
Kate Osamor	Edmonton
Matthew Pennycook	Greenwich & Woolwich
Jess Phillips	Birmingham Yardley
Angela Rayner	Ashton-under-Lyne
Christina Rees	Neath
Marie Rimmer CBE	St Helens South & Whiston
Joan Ryan	Enfield North
Naz Shah	Bradford West
Paula Sherriff	Dewsbury
Tulip Siddiq	Hampstead & Kilburn
Ruth Smeeth	Stoke-on-Trent North
Cat Smith	Lancaster & Fleetwood
Jeff Smith	Manchester Withington
Karin Smyth	Bristol South
Sir Keir Starmer KCB QC	Holborn & St Pancras
Jo Stevens	Cardiff Central
Wes Streeting	Ilford North
Nick Thomas-Symonds	Torfaen
Anna Turley	Redcar
Catherine West	Hornsey & Wood Green
Daniel Zeichner	Cambridge

Scottish National Party (50)

Richard Arkless	Dumfries & Galloway
Hannah Bardell	Livingston
Mhairi Black	Paisley & Renfrewshire South
Ian Blackford	Ross, Skye & Lochaber
Kirsty Blackman	Aberdeen North

Phil Boswell	Coatbridge, Chryston & Bellshill
Deidre Brock	Edinburgh North & Leith
Alan Brown	Kilmarnock & Loudoun
Dr Lisa Cameron	East Kilbride, Strathaven & Lesmahagow
Doug Chapman	Dunfermline & Fife West
Joanna Cherry QC	Edinburgh South West
Ronnie Cowan	Inverclyde
Angela Crawley	Lanark & Hamilton East
Martyn Day	Linlithgow & Falkirk East
Martin Docherty	Dunbartonshire West
Stuart Donaldson	Aberdeenshire West & Kincardine
Marion Fellows	Motherwell & Wishaw
Margaret Ferrier	Rutherglen & Hamilton West
Stephen Gethins	Fife North East
Patricia Gibson	Ayrshire North & Arran
Patrick Grady	Glasgow North
Peter Grant	Glenrothes
Neil Gray	Airdrie & Shotts
Drew Hendry	Inverness, Nairn, Badenoch & Strathspey
George Kerevan	East Lothian
Calum Kerr	Berwickshire, Roxburgh & Selkirk
Chris Law	Dundee West
Callum McCaig	Aberdeen South
Stewart McDonald	Glasgow South
Stuart McDonald	Cumbernauld, Kilsyth & Kirkintilloch East
Natalie McGarry	Glasgow East
Anne McLaughlin	Glasgow North East
John McNally	Falkirk
Carol Monaghan	Glasgow North West
Dr Paul Monaghan	Caithness, Sutherland & Easter Ross
Professor Roger Mullin	Kirkcaldy & Cowdenbeath
Gavin Newlands	Paisley & Renfrewshire North
John Nicolson	Dunbartonshire East
Brendan O'Hara	Argyll & Bute
Kirsten Oswald	Renfrewshire East
Steven Paterson	Stirling
Alex Salmond	Gordon
Tasmina Ahmed-Sheikh OBE	Ochil & South Perthshire
Tommy Sheppard	Edinburgh East

Chris Stephens	Glasgow South West
Alison Thewliss	Glasgow Central
Owen Thompson	Midlothian
Michelle Thomson	Edinburgh West
Philippa Whitford	Ayrshire Central
Corri Wilson	Ayr, Carrick & Cumnock

Ulster Unionist Party (2)

Tom Elliott	Fermanagh & South Tyrone
Danny Kinahan	Antrim South

Democratic Unionist Party (1)

Gavin Robinson	Belfast East

Plaid Cymru (1)

Liz Saville-Roberts	Dwyfor Meirionnydd

Sinn Féin (1)

Mickey Brady	Newry & Armagh

Index of new MPs by constituency

Constituency	Name	Party
Aberavon	Stephen Kinnock	Lab
Aberdeen North	Kirsty Blackman	SNP
Aberdeen South	Callum McCaig	SNP
Aberdeenshire West & Kincardine	Stuart Donaldson	SNP
Airdrie & Shotts	Neil Gray	SNP
Aldridge-Brownhills	Wendy Morton	Con
Antrim South	Danny Kinahan	UUP
Argyll & Bute	Brendan O'Hara	SNP
Ashton-under-Lyne	Angela Rayner	Lab

Ayr, Carrick & Cumnock	Corri Wilson	SNP
Ayrshire Central	Philippa Whitford	SNP
Ayrshire North & Arran	Patricia Gibson	SNP
Banbury	Victoria Prentis	Con
Bath	Ben Howlett	Con
Batley & Spen	Jo Cox	Lab
Belfast East	Gavin Robinson	DUP
Bermondsey & Old Southwark	Neil Coyle	Lab
Berwick upon Tweed	Anne-Marie Trevelyan	Con
Berwickshire, Roxburgh & Selkirk	Calum Kerr	SNP
Bexhill & Battle	Huw Merriman	Con
Birmingham Yardley	Jess Phillips	Lab
Blackburn	Kate Hollern	Lab
Bolton West	Christopher Green	Con
Bootle	Peter Dowd	Lab
Boston & Skegness	Matt Warman	Con
Bradford East	Imran Hussain	Lab
Bradford South	Judith Cummins	Lab
Bradford West	Naz Shah	Lab
Braintree	James Cleverly	Con
Brecon & Radnorshire	Chris Davies	Con
Brent Central	Dawn Butler	Lab
Brentford & Isleworth	Ruth Cadbury	Lab
Bristol South	Karin Smyth	Lab
Bristol West	Thangam Debbonaire	Lab
Burnley	Julie Cooper	Lab
Bury St Edmunds	Jo Churchill	Con
Caithness, Sutherland & Easter Ross	Dr Paul Monaghan	SNP
Cambridge	Daniel Zeichner	Lab
Cambridgeshire South	Heidi Allen	Con
Cambridgeshire South East	Lucy Frazer QC	Con
Cannock Chase	Amanda Milling	Con
Cardiff Central	Jo Stevens	Lab
Cardiff North	Craig Williams	Con
Charnwood	Edward Argar	Con
Cheadle	Mary Robinson	Con
Cheltenham	Alex Chalk	Con
Chester, City of	Chris Matheson	Lab
Chippenham	Michelle Donelan	Con

Coatbridge, Chryston & Bellshill	Phil Boswell	SNP
Colchester	Will Quince	Con
Corby	Tom Pursglove	Con
Cornwall North	Scott Mann	Con
Coventry North East	Colleen Fletcher	Lab
Croydon South	Chris Philp	Con
Cumbernauld, Kilsyth & Kirkintilloch East	Stuart McDonald	SNP
Derby North	Amanda Solloway	Con
Devon North	Peter Heaton-Jones	Con
Dewsbury	Paula Sherriff	Lab
Dorset Mid & Poole North	Michael Tomlinson	Con
Dorset North	Simon Hoare	Con
Dudley South	Mike Wood	Con
Dulwich & West Norwood	Helen Hayes	Lab
Dumfries & Galloway	Richard Arkless	SNP
Dunbartonshire East	John Nicolson	SNP
Dunbartonshire West	Martin Docherty	SNP
Dundee West	Chris Law	SNP
Dunfermline & Fife West	Douglas Chapman	SNP
Dwyfor Meirionnydd	Liz Saville-Roberts	PC
Ealing Central & Acton	Dr Rupa Huq	Lab
East Kilbride, Strathaven & Lesmahagow	Dr Lisa Cameron	SNP
East Lothian	George Kerevan	SNP
Eastbourne	Caroline Ansell	Con
Eastleigh	Mims Davies	Con
Eddisbury	Antoinette Sandbach	Con
Edinburgh East	Tommy Sheppard	SNP
Edinburgh North & Leith	Deidre Brock	SNP
Edinburgh South West	Joanna Cherry QC	SNP
Edinburgh West	Michelle Thomson	SNP
Edmonton	Kate Osamor	Lab
Ellesmere Port & Neston	Justin Madders	Lab
Enfield North	Joan Ryan	Lab
Erewash	Maggie Throup	Con
Falkirk	John McNally	SNP
Fareham	Suella Fernandes	Con
Faversham & Kent Mid	Helen Whately	Con
Fermanagh & South Tyrone	Tom Elliott	UUP
Fife North East	Stephen Gethins	SNP

Glasgow Central	Alison Thewliss	SNP
Glasgow East	Natalie McGarry	SNP
Glasgow North	Patrick Grady	SNP
Glasgow North East	Anne McLaughlin	SNP
Glasgow North West	Carol Monaghan	SNP
Glasgow South	Stewart McDonald	SNP
Glasgow South West	Chris Stephens	SNP
Glenrothes	Peter Grant	SNP
Gordon	Alex Salmond	SNP
Gower	Byron Davies	Con
Great Grimsby	Melanie Onn	Lab
Greenwich & Woolwich	Matthew Pennycook	Lab
Halifax	Holly Lynch	Lab
Hampshire North East	Ranil Jayawardena	Con
Hampshire North West	Kit Malthouse	Con
Hampstead & Kilburn	Tulip Siddiq	Lab
Havant	Alan Mak	Con
Hazel Grove	William Wragg	Con
Hertsmere	Oliver Dowden	Con
Holborn & St Pancras	Sir Keir Starmer KCB QC	Lab
Hornsey & Wood Green	Catherine West	Lab
Horsham	Jeremy Quin	Con
Hove	Dr Peter Kyle	Lab
Ilford North	Wes Streeting	Lab
Inverclyde	Ronnie Cowan	SNP
Inverness, Nairn, Badenoch & Strathspey	Drew Hendry	SNP
Kensington	Victoria Borwick	Con
Kilmarnock & Loudoun	Alan Brown	SNP
Kingston & Surbiton	James Berry	Con
Kirkcaldy & Cowdenbeath	Professor Roger Mullin	SNP
Lanark & Hamilton East	Angela Crawley	SNP
Lancaster & Fleetwood	Cat Smith	Lab
Leeds East	Richard Burgon	Lab
Leicestershire South	Alberto Costa	Con
Lewes	Maria Caulfield	Con
Lewisham Deptford	Vicky Foxcroft	Lab
Linlithgow & Falkirk East	Martyn Day	SNP
Livingston	Hannah Bardell	SNP
Louth & Horncastle	Victoria Atkins	Con

Manchester Withington	Jeff Smith	Lab
Merthyr Tydfil & Rhymney	Gerald Jones	Lab
Midlothian	Owen Thompson	SNP
Morley & Outwood	Andrea Jenkyns	Con
Motherwell & Wishaw	Marion Fellows	SNP
Neath	Christina Rees	Lab
Newry & Armagh	Mickey Brady	SF
Northampton South	David Mackintosh	Con
Norwich South	Clive Lewis	Lab
Ochil & South Perthshire	Tasmina Ahmed-Sheikh OBE	SNP
Paisley & Renfrewshire North	Gavin Newlands	SNP
Paisley & Renfrewshire South	Mhairi Black	SNP
Plymouth Moor View	Johnny Mercer	Con
Portsmouth South	Flick Drummond	Con
Redcar	Anna Turley	Lab
Renfrewshire East	Kirsten Oswald	SNP
Richmond Yorkshire	Rishi Sunak	Con
Rochester & Strood	Kelly Tolhurst	Con
Ross, Skye & Lochaber	Ian Blackford	SNP
Rutherglen & Hamilton West	Margaret Ferrier	SNP
St Austell & Newquay	Steve Double	Con
St Helens North	Conor McGinn	Lab
St Helens South & Whiston	Marie Rimmer CBE	Lab
St Ives	Derek Thomas	Con
Salford & Eccles	Rebecca Long-Bailey	Lab
Sheffield Brightside & Hillsborough	Harry Harpham	Lab
Sheffield Heeley	Louise Haigh	Lab
Solihull	Julian Knight	Con
Somerton & Frome	David Warburton	Con
South Ribble	Seema Kennedy	Con
South Thanet	Craig Mackinlay	Con
Southampton Itchen	Royston Smith	Con
Stirling	Steven Paterson	SNP
Stoke-on-Trent North	Ruth Smeeth	Lab
Suffolk South	James Cartlidge	Con
Sutton & Cheam	Paul Scully	Con
Swansea East	Carolyn Harris	Lab
Taunton Deane	Rebecca Pow	Con
Telford	Lucy Allan	Con

Thirsk & Malton	Kevin Hollinrake	Con
Thornbury & Yate	Luke Hall	Con
Tonbridge & Malling	Thomas Tugendhat MBE	Con
Torbay	Kevin Foster	Con
Torfaen	Nick Thomas-Symonds	Lab
Twickenham	Dr Tania Mathias	Con
Uxbridge & Ruislip South	Boris Johnson	Con
Vale of Clwyd	James Davies	Con
Warwickshire North	Craig Tracey	Con
Wealden	Nusrat Ghani	Con
Wells	James Heappey	Con
Wirral West	Margaret Greenwood	Lab
Wolverhampton South West	Rob Marris	Lab
Worcestershire Mid	Nigel Huddleston	Con
Workington	Sue Hayman	Lab
Yeovil	Marcus Fysh	Con
York Central	Rachael Maskell	Lab

Abbreviations:

Con: Conservative

DUP: Democratic Unionist Party

Lab: Labour

PC: Plaid Cymru

SNP: Scottish National Party

SF: Sinn Féin

UUP: Ulster Unionist Party

Index of new MPs by region

East Midlands (8)

Boston & Skegness	Matt Warman	Con
Charnwood	Edward Argar	Con
Corby	Tom Pursglove	Con
Derby North	Amanda Solloway	Con
Erewash	Maggie Throup	Con
Leicestershire South	Alberto Costa	Con

Louth & Horncastle	Victoria Atkins	Con
Northampton South	David Mackintosh	Con

East of England (9)

Braintree	James Cleverly	Con
Bury St Edmunds	Jo Churchill	Con
Cambridge	Daniel Zeichner	Lab
Cambridgeshire South	Heidi Allen	Con
Cambridgeshire South East	Lucy Frazer QC	Con
Colchester	Will Quince	Con
Hertsmere	Oliver Dowden	Con
Norwich South	Clive Lewis	Lab
Suffolk South	James Cartlidge	Con

London (19)

Bermondsey & Old Southwark	Neil Coyle	Lab
Brent Central	Dawn Butler	Lab
Brentford & Isleworth	Ruth Cadbury	Lab
Croydon South	Chris Philp	Con
Dulwich & West Norwood	Helen Hayes	Lab
Ealing Central & Acton	Dr Rupa Huq	Lab
Edmonton	Kate Osamor	Lab
Enfield North	Joan Ryan	Lab
Greenwich & Woolwich	Matthew Pennycook	Lab
Hampstead & Kilburn	Tulip Siddiq	Lab
Holborn & St Pancras	Sir Keir Starmer KCB QC	Lab
Hornsey & Wood Green	Catherine West	Lab
Ilford North	Wes Streeting	Lab
Kensington	Victoria Borwick	Con
Kingston & Surbiton	James Berry	Con
Lewisham Deptford	Vicky Foxcroft	Lab
Sutton & Cheam	Paul Scully	Con
Twickenham	Dr Tania Mathias	Con
Uxbridge & Ruislip South	Boris Johnson	Con

North East (2)

Berwick upon Tweed	Anne-Marie Trevelyan	Con
Redcar	Anna Turley	Lab

North West (18)

Ashton-under-Lyne	Angela Rayner	Lab
Blackburn	Kate Hollern	Lab
Bolton West	Christopher Green	Con
Bootle	Peter Dowd	Lab
Burnley	Julie Cooper	Lab
Cheadle	Mary Robinson	Con
Chester, City of	Chris Matheson	Lab
Eddisbury	Antoinette Sandbach	Con
Ellesmere Port & Neston	Justin Madders	Lab
Hazel Grove	William Wragg	Con
Lancaster & Fleetwood	Cat Smith	Lab
Manchester Withington	Jeff Smith	Lab
Salford & Eccles	Rebecca Long-Bailey	Lab
South Ribble	Seema Kennedy	Con
St Helens North	Conor McGinn	Lab
St Helens South & Whiston	Marie Rimmer CBE	Lab
Wirral West	Margaret Greenwood	Lab
Workington	Sue Hayman	Lab

Northern Ireland (4)

Antrim South	Danny Kinahan	UUP
Belfast East	Gavin Robinson	DUP
Fermanagh & South Tyrone	Tom Elliott	UUP
Newry & Armagh	Mickey Brady	SF

Scotland (50)

Aberdeen North	Kirsty Blackman	SNP
Aberdeen South	Callum McCaig	SNP
Aberdeenshire West & Kincardine	Stuart Donaldson	SNP
Airdrie & Shotts	Neil Gray	SNP
Argyll & Bute	Brendan O'Hara	SNP

Ayr, Carrick & Cumnock	Corri Wilson	SNP
Ayrshire Central	Philippa Whitford	SNP
Ayrshire North & Arran	Patricia Gibson	SNP
Berwickshire, Roxburgh & Selkirk	Calum Kerr	SNP
Caithness, Sutherland & Easter Ross	Dr Paul Monaghan	SNP
Coatbridge, Chryston & Bellshill	Phil Boswell	SNP
Cumbernauld, Kilsyth & Kirkintilloch East	Stuart McDonald	SNP
Dumfries & Galloway	Richard Arkless	SNP
Dunbartonshire East	John Nicolson	SNP
Dunbartonshire West	Martin Docherty	SNP
Dundee West	Chris Law	SNP
Dunfermline & Fife West	Douglas Chapman	SNP
East Kilbride, Strathaven & Lesmahagow	Dr Lisa Cameron	SNP
East Lothian	George Kerevan	SNP
Edinburgh East	Tommy Sheppard	SNP
Edinburgh North & Leith	Deidre Brock	SNP
Edinburgh South West	Joanna Cherry QC	SNP
Edinburgh West	Michelle Thomson	SNP
Falkirk	John McNally	SNP
Fife North East	Stephen Gethins	SNP
Glasgow Central	Alison Thewliss	SNP
Glasgow East	Natalie McGarry	SNP
Glasgow North	Patrick Grady	SNP
Glasgow North East	Anne McLaughlin	SNP
Glasgow North West	Carol Monaghan	SNP
Glasgow South	Stewart McDonald	SNP
Glasgow South West	Chris Stephens	SNP
Glenrothes	Peter Grant	SNP
Gordon	Alex Salmond	SNP
Inverclyde	Ronnie Cowan	SNP
Inverness, Nairn, Badenoch & Strathspey	Drew Hendry	SNP
Kilmarnock & Loudoun	Alan Brown	SNP
Kirkcaldy & Cowdenbeath	Professor Roger Mullin	SNP
Lanark & Hamilton East	Angela Crawley	SNP
Linlithgow & Falkirk East	Martyn Day	SNP
Livingston	Hannah Bardell	SNP
Midlothian	Owen Thompson	SNP
Motherwell & Wishaw	Marion Fellows	SNP
Ochil & South Perthshire	Tasmina Ahmed-Sheikh OBE	SNP

Paisley & Renfrewshire North	Gavin Newlands	SNP
Paisley & Renfrewshire South	Mhairi Black	SNP
Renfrewshire East	Kirsten Oswald	SNP
Ross, Skye & Lochaber	Ian Blackford	SNP
Rutherglen & Hamilton West	Margaret Ferrier	SNP
Stirling	Steven Paterson	SNP

South East (18)

Banbury	Victoria Prentis	Con
Bexhill & Battle	Huw Merriman	Con
Eastbourne	Caroline Ansell	Con
Eastleigh	Mims Davies	Con
Fareham	Suella Fernandes	Con
Faversham & Kent Mid	Helen Whately	Con
Hampshire North East	Ranil Jayawardena	Con
Hampshire North West	Kit Malthouse	Con
Havant	Alan Mak	Con
Horsham	Jeremy Quin	Con
Hove	Dr Peter Kyle	Lab
Lewes	Maria Caulfield	Con
Portsmouth South	Flick Drummond	Con
Rochester & Strood	Kelly Tolhurst	Con
South Thanet	Craig Mackinlay	Con
Southampton Itchen	Royston Smith	Con
Tonbridge & Malling	Thomas Tugendhat MBE	Con
Wealden	Nusrat Ghani	Con

South West (18)

Bath	Ben Howlett	Con
Bristol South	Karin Smyth	Lab
Bristol West	Thangam Debbonaire	Lab
Cheltenham	Alex Chalk	Con
Chippenham	Michelle Donelan	Con
Cornwall North	Scott Mann	Con
Devon North	Peter Heaton-Jones	Con
Dorset Mid & Poole North	Michael Tomlinson	Con
Dorset North	Simon Hoare	Con

Plymouth Moor View	Johnny Mercer	Con
St Austell & Newquay	Steve Double	Con
St Ives	Derek Thomas	Con
Somerton & Frome	David Warburton	Con
Taunton Deane	Rebecca Pow	Con
Thornbury & Yate	Luke Hall	Con
Torbay	Kevin Foster	Con
Wells	James Heappey	Con
Yeovil	Marcus Fysh	Con

Wales (11)

Aberavon	Stephen Kinnock	Lab
Brecon & Radnorshire	Chris Davies	Con
Cardiff Central	Jo Stevens	Lab
Cardiff North	Craig Williams	Con
Dwyfor Meirionnydd	Liz Saville-Roberts	PC
Gower	Byron Davies	Con
Merthyr Tydfil & Rhymney	Gerald Jones	Lab
Neath	Christina Rees	Lab
Swansea East	Carolyn Harris	Lab
Torfaen	Nick Thomas-Symonds	Lab
Vale of Clwyd	Dr James Davies	Con

West Midlands (11)

Aldridge-Brownhills	Wendy Morton	Con
Birmingham Yardley	Jess Phillips	Lab
Cannock Chase	Amanda Milling	Con
Coventry North East	Colleen Fletcher	Lab
Dudley South	Mike Wood	Con
Solihull	Julian Knight	Con
Stoke-on-Trent North	Ruth Smeeth	Lab
Telford	Lucy Allan	Con
Warwickshire North	Craig Tracey	Con
Wolverhampton South West	Rob Marris	Lab
Worcestershire Mid	Nigel Huddleston	Con

Yorkshire and The Humber (14)

Batley & Spen	Jo Cox	Lab
Bradford East	Imran Hussain	Lab
Bradford South	Judith Cummins	Lab
Bradford West	Naz Shah	Lab
Dewsbury	Paula Sherriff	Lab
Great Grimsby	Melanie Onn	Lab
Halifax	Holly Lynch	Lab
Leeds East	Richard Burgon	Lab
Morley & Outwood	Andrea Jenkyns	Con
Richmond Yorkshire	Rishi Sunak	Con
Sheffield Brightside & Hillsborough	Harry Harpham	Lab
Sheffield Heeley	Louise Haigh	Lab
Thirsk & Malton	Kevin Hollinrake	Con
York Central	Rachael Maskell	Lab

New women MPs (81) by party

Labour (34)

Dawn Butler	Brent Central
Ruth Cadbury	Brentford & Isleworth
Julie Cooper	Burnley
Jo Cox	Batley & Spen
Judith Cummins	Bradford South
Thangam Debbonaire	Bristol West
Colleen Fletcher	Coventry North East
Vicky Foxcroft	Lewisham Deptford
Margaret Greenwood	Wirral West
Louise Haigh	Sheffield Heeley
Carolyn Harris	Swansea East
Helen Hayes	Dulwich & West Norwood
Sue Hayman	Workington
Kate Hollern	Blackburn
Dr Rupa Huq	Ealing Central & Acton
Rebecca Long-Bailey	Salford & Eccles
Holly Lynch	Halifax
Rachael Maskell	York Central
Melanie Onn	Great Grimsby
Kate Osamor	Edmonton
Jess Phillips	Birmingham Yardley
Angela Rayner	Ashton-under-Lyne
Christina Rees	Neath
Marie Rimmer CBE	St Helens South & Whiston

Joan Ryan	Enfield North
Naz Shah	Bradford West
Paula Sherriff	Dewsbury
Tulip Siddiq	Hampstead & Kilburn
Ruth Smeeth	Stoke-on-Trent North
Cat Smith	Lancaster & Fleetwood
Karin Smyth	Bristol South
Jo Stevens	Cardiff Central
Anna Turley	Redcar
Catherine West	Hornsey & Wood Green

Conservative (27)

Lucy Allan	Telford
Heidi Allen	Cambridgeshire South
Caroline Ansell	Eastbourne
Victoria Atkins	Louth & Horncastle
Victoria Borwick	Kensington
Maria Caulfield	Lewes
Jo Churchill	Bury St Edmunds
Mims Davies	Eastleigh
Michelle Donelan	Chippenham
Flick Drummond	Portsmouth South
Suella Fernandes	Fareham
Lucy Frazer QC	Cambridgeshire South East
Nusrat Ghani	Wealden
Andrea Jenkyns	Morley & Outwood
Seema Kennedy	South Ribble
Dr Tania Mathias	Twickenham
Amanda Milling	Cannock Chase
Wendy Morton	Aldridge-Brownhills
Rebecca Pow	Taunton Deane
Victoria Prentis	Banbury
Mary Robinson	Cheadle
Antoinette Sandbach	Eddisbury
Amanda Solloway	Derby North
Maggie Throup	Erewash
Kelly Tolhurst	Rochester & Strood
Anne-Marie Trevelyan	Berwick upon Tweed

Helen Whately   Faversham & Kent Mid

Scottish National Party (19)

Hannah Bardell	Livingston
Mhairi Black	Paisley & Renfrewshire South
Kirsty Blackman	Aberdeen North
Deidre Brock	Edinburgh North & Leith
Dr Lisa Cameron	East Kilbride, Strathaven & Lesmahagow
Joanna Cherry QC	Edinburgh South West
Angela Crawley	Lanark & Hamilton East
Marion Fellows	Motherwell & Wishaw
Margaret Ferrier	Rutherglen & Hamilton West
Patricia Gibson	Ayrshire North & Arran
Natalie McGarry	Glasgow East
Anne McLaughlin	Glasgow North East
Carol Monaghan	Glasgow North West
Kirsten Oswald	Renfrewshire East
Tasmina Ahmed-Sheikh OBE	Ochil & South Perthshire
Alison Thewliss	Glasgow Central
Michelle Thomson	Edinburgh West
Philippa Whitford	Ayrshire Central
Corri Wilson	Ayr, Carrick & Cumnock

Plaid Cymru (1)

Liz Saville-Roberts   Dwyfor Meirionnydd

New BME MPs (16) by party

Labour (8)

Dawn Butler	Lab	Brent Central
Thangam Debbonaire	Lab	Bristol West
Dr Rupa Huq	Lab	Ealing Central & Acton
Imran Hussain	Lab	Bradford East
Clive Lewis	Lab	Norwich South
Kate Osamor	Lab	Edmonton
Naz Shah	Lab	Bradford West
Tulip Siddiq	Lab	Hampstead & Kilburn

Conservative (7)

James Cleverly	Con	Braintree
Suella Fernandes	Con	Fareham
Nusrat Ghani	Con	Wealden
Ranil Jayawardena	Con	Hampshire North East
Seema Kennedy	Con	South Ribble
Alan Mak	Con	Havant
Rishi Sunak	Con	Richmond Yorkshire

Scottish National Party (1)

Tasmina Ahmed-Sheikh OBE	SNP	Ochil & South Perthshire

Defeated MPs

Labour (39)

Douglas Alexander	Paisley & Renfrewshire South
Willie Bain	Glasgow North East
Ed Balls	Morley & Outwood
Gordon Banks	Ochil & South Perthshire
Anne Begg	Aberdeen South
Russell Brown	Dumfries & Galloway
Katy Clark	Ayrshire North & Arran
Tom Clarke	Coatbridge, Chryston & Bellshill
Michael Connarty	Linlithgow & Falkirk East
Margaret Curran	Glasgow East
Ian Davidson	Glasgow South West
James Davies	Vale of Clwyd
Thomas Docherty	Dunfermline & Fife West
Brian Donohoe	Ayrshire Central
Gemma Doyle	Dunbartonshire West
Sheila Gilmore	Edinburgh East
Tom Greatrex	Rutherglen & Hamilton West
Tom Harris	Glasgow South
Julie Hilling	Bolton West
Jim Hood	Lanark & Hamilton East
Cathy Jamieson	Kilmarnock & Loudoun
Mark Lazarowicz	Edinburgh North & Leith
Michael McCann	East Kilbride, Strathaven & Lesmahagow
Dr Gregg McClymont	Cumbernauld, Kilsyth & Kirkintilloch East
Ann McKechin	Glasgow North
Iain McKenzie	Inverclyde
Graeme Morrice	Livingston

Jim Murphy	Renfrewshire East
Pamela Nash	Airdrie & Shotts
Fiona O'Donnell	East Lothian
Sandra Osborne	Ayr, Carrick & Cumnock
John Robertson	Glasgow North West
Frank Roy	Motherwell & Wishaw
Anas Sarwar	Glasgow Central
Andy Sawford	Corby
Alison Seabeck	Plymouth Moor View
Jim Sheridan	Paisley & Renfrewshire North
Chris Williamson	Derby North
David Wright	Telford

Liberal Democrat (38)

Danny Alexander	Inverness, Nairn, Badenoch & Strathspey
Norman Baker	Lewes
Gordon Birtwistle	Burnley
Paul Burstow	Sutton & Cheam
Lorely Burt	Solihull
Dr Vince Cable	Twickenham
Mike Crockart	Edinburgh West
Ed Davey	Kingston & Surbiton
Lynne Featherstone	Hornsey & Wood Green
Andrew George	St Ives
Stephen Gilbert	St Austell & Newquay
Duncan Hames	Chippenham
Sir Nick Harvey	Devon North
John Hemming	Birmingham Yardley
Martin Horwood	Cheltenham
Simon Hughes	Bermondsey & Old Southwark
Mark Hunter	Cheadle
Dr Julian Huppert	Cambridge
Charles Kennedy	Ross, Skye & Lochaber
David Laws	Yeovil
John Leech	Manchester Withington
Stephen Lloyd	Eastbourne
Michael Moore	Berwickshire, Roxburgh & Selkirk
Tessa Munt	Wells

Alan Reid	Argyll & Bute
Dan Rogerson	Cornwall North
Sir Bob Russell	Colchester
Adrian Sanders	Torbay
Sir Robert Smith	Aberdeenshire West & Kincardine
Jo Swinson	Dunbartonshire East
Mike Thornton	Eastleigh
John Thurso	Caithness, Sutherland & Easter Ross
David Ward	Bradford East
Steve Webb	Thornbury & Yate
Roger Williams	Brecon & Radnorshire
Stephen Williams	Bristol West
Jenny Willott	Cardiff Central
Simon Wright	Norwich South

Conservative (9)

Angie Bray	Ealing Central & Acton
Nick de Bois	Enfield North
Mary Macleod	Brentford & Isleworth
Esther McVey	Wirral West
Stephen Mosley	City of Chester
Eric Ollerenshaw	Lancaster & Fleetwood
Simon Reevell	Dewsbury
Lee Scott	Ilford North
Paul Uppal	Wolverhampton South West

Others (6)

George Galloway (Respect)	Bradford West
Michelle Gildernew (Sinn Féin)	Fermanagh & South Tyrone
Mike Hancock (Independent)*	Portsmouth South
Naomi Long (Alliance)	Belfast East
Dr William McCrea (DUP)	Antrim South
Mark Reckless (UKIP)	Rochester & Strood

* Resigned from the Liberal Democrats in September 2014 and stood as an Independent candidate in 2015

Retired or de-selected MPs

Labour (39)

Rt Hon Bob Ainsworth	Coventry North East
Hugh Bayley	York Central
Joe Benton	Bootle
Rt Hon Hazel Blears	Salford & Eccles
Rt Hon David Blunkett	Sheffield Brightside & Hillsborough
Rt Hon Gordon Brown	Kirkcaldy & Cowdenbeath
Martin Caton	Gower
Sir Tony Cunningham	Workington
Rt Hon Alistair Darling	Edinburgh South West
Rt Hon John Denham	Southampton Itchen
Rt Hon Frank Dobson	Holborn & St Pancras
Frank Doran	Aberdeen North
Dr Hywel Francis	Aberavon
Rt Hon Peter Hain	Neath
David Hamilton	Midlothian
Dai Havard	Merthyr Tydfil & Rhymney
David Heyes	Ashton-under-Lyne
Glenda Jackson CBE	Hampstead & Kilburn
Siân James	Swansea East
Rt Hon Dame Tessa Jowell DBE	Dulwich & West Norwood
Andy Love	Edmonton
Jim McGovern	Dundee West
Rt Hon Dame Anne McGuire	Stirling
Andrew Miller	Ellesmere Port & Neston

Austin Mitchell	Great Grimsby
George Mudie	Leeds East
Meg Munn	Sheffield Heeley
Rt Hon Paul Murphy	Torfaen
Rt Hon Dame Dawn Primarolo	Bristol South
Rt Hon Nick Raynsford	Greenwich & Woolwich
Linda Riordan	Halifax
Lindsay Roy	Glenrothes
Rt Hon Dame Joan Ruddock DBE	Lewisham Deptford
Gerry Sutcliffe	Bradford South
Joan Walley	Stoke-on-Trent North
Dave Watts	St Helens North
Mike Wood	Batley & Spen
Rt Hon Shaun Woodward	St Helens South & Whiston
Rt Hon Jack Straw	Blackburn

Conservative (38)

Rt Hon James Arbuthnot	Hampshire North East
Rt Hon Sir Tony Baldry	Banbury
Rt Hon Greg Barker	Bexhill & Battle
Brian Binley	Northampton South
Aiden Burley	Cannock Chase
Dan Byles	Warwickshire North
James Clappison	Hertsmere
Rt Hon Stephen Dorrell	Charnwood
Jonathan Evans	Cardiff North
Lorraine Fullbrook	South Ribble
Rt Hon William Hague	Richmond Yorkshire
Rt Hon Charles Hendry	Wealden
Mark Hoban	Fareham
Chris Kelly	Dudley South
Rt Hon Andrew Lansley CBE	Cambridgeshire South
Jessica Lee	Erewash
Sir Peter Luff	Worcestershire Mid
Rt Hon Francis Maude	Horsham
Anne McIntosh *	Thirsk & Malton
Brooks Newmark	Braintree
Stephen O'Brien	Eddisbury

Rt Hon Sir Richard Ottaway	Croydon South
Sir James Paice	Cambridgeshire South East
Rt Hon Sir John Randall	Uxbridge & Ruislip South
Rt Hon Sir Malcolm Rifkind KCMG	Kensington
Rt Hon Andrew Robathan	Leicestershire South
Rt Hon Hugh Robertson	Faversham & Kent Mid
David Ruffley	Bury St Edmunds
Laura Sandys	South Thanet
Sir Richard Shepherd	Aldridge-Brownhills
Mark Simmonds	Boston & Skegness
Rt Hon Sir John Stanley	Tonbridge & Malling
Rt Hon Sir Peter Tapsell	Louth & Horncastle
Bob Walter	Dorset North
Mike Weatherley	Hove
Rt Hon David Willetts	Havant
Tim Yeo*	Suffolk South
Rt Hon Sir George Young CH	Hampshire North West

* De-selected by their constituency parties

Liberal Democrat (10)

Rt Hon Sir Alan Beith	Berwick upon Tweed
Rt Hon Annette Brooke OBE	Dorset Mid & Poole North
Jeremy Browne	Taunton Deane
Rt Hon Sir Malcolm Bruce	Gordon
Rt Hon Sir Menzies Campbell CH CBE QC	Fife North East
Don Foster	Bath
Rt Hon David Heath CBE	Somerton & Frome
Rt Hon Sir Andrew Stunell OBE	Hazel Grove
Ian Swales	Redcar
Sarah Teather	Brent Central

Others (3)

Eric Joyce (Indie)	Falkirk
Elfyn Llwyd (PC)	Dwyfor Meirionnydd
Conor Murphy (SF)	Newry & Armagh

The class of 2015

Lucy Allan

CONSERVATIVE MP FOR TELFORD

FORMER MP	David Wright, Labour, defeated
MAJORITY	730 (1.8%)
VOTE SHARE	39.6%
CHANGE	+3.3%
2ND PLACE	Lab

www.lucyallan.com   @lucyallan

LUCY ALLAN IS a qualified lawyer, accountant and family rights campaigner. Born in October 1964 in Cheltenham, she studied Anthropology at Durham University. She spent her first seventeen years of work as a chartered accountant with PwC, joining as a graduate trainee in 1987, in time developing a specialism in business turnaround. In 1994 she moved into investment management, reaching director. In 2004 she took a Master's degree in Law at Kingston Law School and set up an advice service for employees, Workplace Law Ltd. She also became a non-executive director of Wandsworth NHS in 2009 and served as a judicial office holder for the Ministry of Justice from 2008 until 2013.

In 2006 she was elected onto Wandsworth Borough Council, serving as chair of the Transport and Leisure & Environment Committees. During her time as a councillor she sat on fostering and adoption panels, served as a school governor in Wandsworth and was chairwoman of the local pupil referral unit. She was also a trustee of Women's Aid Federation of England, a domestic violence charity supporting children from violent homes. She stood down from the council in 2011 and from Wandsworth NHS, and set up the Family First Group, a campaign group dedicated to reducing the number of children in state care. She is married to Robin and they have one son. ▪

Heidi Allen

CONSERVATIVE MP FOR CAMBRIDGESHIRE SOUTH

FORMER MP	Andrew Lansley, Conservative, stood down
MAJORITY	20,594 (33.5%)
VOTE SHARE	51.1%
CHANGE	+3.7%
2ND PLACE	Lab

www.heidiallen.co.uk @heidiallen75

HEIDI-SUZANNE ALLEN WAS born in 1975 in a rural village in Yorkshire. She studied Astrophysics at University College London from 1993 before going on to work as a senior manager in organisations such as Royal, Tubelines, Esso and Churchill Insurance Group. She is managing director of the family manufacturing business, RS Bike Paint Ltd, which was founded in 1978, and has been a company secretary and a director since 2008. Her husband, Phil, whom she married in 2009, also works for the business.

She was elected as a councillor on St Albans City and District Council in 2012, representing the South Marshalswick ward. She is an executive member of the London Colney Conservative branch and an ambassador of Hertfordshire Society for the Blind. Controversially, she was not selected as the Conservative candidate for South East Cambridgeshire following a mix-up that potentially deprived her of the selection. ∎

Caroline Ansell

CONSERVATIVE MP FOR EASTBOURNE

FORMER MP	Stephen Lloyd, Liberal Democrat, defeated
MAJORITY	733 (1.4%)
VOTE SHARE	39.6%
CHANGE	-1.1%
2ND PLACE	Lib Dem

www.carolineansell.co.uk   @Caroline_Ansell

CAROLINE ANSELL IS a 43-year-old teacher and school inspector. Educated at Beresford House School, she studied for a degree at London University, a Master's at Sussex University and her teaching training at Canterbury. She also did a graduate year at business school in France, learning to speak French fluently. She has taught French, English and drama for most of her career and has been a school inspector for four years.

She unsuccessfully stood for election in the Hampden Park ward of Eastbourne Borough Council in the 2011 elections but was successfully elected to represent the Meads ward a year later. She was the opposition deputy leader and portfolio holder for Financial Services. She served as the local authority governor of Langney Primary School and is a school governor at Ocklynge and at Seaford Head Community College. She lives in the Old Town area of Eastbourne, is married to Nick, a PE teacher, and is the mother of three pre-teen boys. A committed Christian, she has said that politics is a way of expressing her faith. ▪

Edward Argar

CONSERVATIVE MP FOR CHARNWOOD

FORMER MP	Stephen Dorrell, Conservative, stood down
MAJORITY	16,931 (32.4%)
VOTE SHARE	54.3%
CHANGE	+4.7%
2ND PLACE	Lab

www.edwardargar.org.uk

EDWARD ARGAR WAS born in 1977 and grew up on the Kent–East Sussex border. His parents were teachers and he is the grandson of sheep and hop farmers and a Kent army family. Having attended local state schools, he studied History at Oriel College, Oxford, after taking a year out working in a local shop to help pay for his studying. After leaving Oxford, he worked as an adviser to the Conservative deputy leader and shadow Foreign Secretary Michael Ancram. Since 2005 he has had a number of corporate and commercial roles in businesses, including at Hedra, Serco and Mouchel. He worked as a self-employed management and communications consultant before his election.

He has served as a Westminster councillor since 2006, representing the Warwick ward, and has been a cabinet member for City Management, Transport and Environment since 2008. He was a board member of the local NHS Trust until 2010 and is a commissioner/member of the London Waterways Commission. He is also a trustee of environmental charity Groundwork London, and a school governor. He stood in Oxford East in 2010 and, before his selection to Charnwood, had been a finalist in Wealden, Mid Worcestershire, Newark and Tonbridge & Malling. ∎

Richard Arkless

SCOTTISH NATIONAL PARTY (SNP) MP FOR
DUMFRIES & GALLOWAY

FORMER MP	Russell Brown, Labour, defeated
MAJORITY	6,514 (11.5%)
VOTE SHARE	41.4%
CHANGE	+29.1%
2ND PLACE	Con

@ArklessRichard

BORN IN STRANRAER in 1975, Richard Arkless was raised in east London before his family returned home to Scotland when he was nine, when they bought a small hotel. He was educated at Stranraer Academy before going on to study at Glasgow Caledonian University, graduating in 1998 with a degree in Financial Services & Risk Management. After working for six years, he attended Strathclyde University, gaining an LLB Law degree in 2006, and then went on to Glasgow Graduate School of Law, completing a diploma in Legal Practice. He joined Morton Fraser in Edinburgh in 2007 as a trainee solicitor, then joined a legal firm in Cheshire, ULL (Ultimate Law) in 2009, specialising in consumer and commercial litigation.

In 2013 he postponed his legal career to start his own business with his wife Anne: LED Warehouse UK, an independent online retailer of LED lights, based in south-west Scotland. New to active political involvement, he was a leading member of Business for Scotland during the referendum campaign. ∎

Victoria Atkins

CONSERVATIVE MP FOR LOUTH & HORNCASTLE

FORMER MP	Sir Peter Tapsell, Conservative, stood down
MAJORITY	14,977 (29.8%)
VOTE SHARE	51.2%
CHANGE	+1.5%
2ND PLACE	UKIP

www.victoriaatkins.org.uk   @vmatkins

THE DAUGHTER OF Sir Robert Atkins, former minister, MP and MEP, Victoria Atkins is one of two children, born in London in the late 1970s but raised in Lancashire in her father's constituency of Preston North & South Ribble. Having attended Cambridge University to read Law, she returned to London to practise as a barrister, which she has done since 1998. A leading member of the Red Lion Chambers, she is one of only thirty advocates in England and Wales to be appointed to the Attorney General and Serious Fraud Office's list of specialist fraud prosecutors. She is a member of the Association of Regulatory and Disciplinary Lawyers, the Criminal Bar Association and the South Eastern Circuit.

She sought selection in 2010 and was shortlisted for the safe Conservative seat of Salisbury, but was beaten to the nomination by John Glen. In 2012 she unsuccessfully stood as the Conservative candidate in Gloucestershire's Police and Crime Commissioner election. She was selected for Louth & Horncastle following an open primary process, the fourth time she has taken part in an open primary. Before her selection, she lived in the Cotswolds with her husband, Paul, who is managing director of a food company, and their son Monty. ▪

Hannah Bardell

SCOTTISH NATIONAL PARTY (SNP) MP FOR LIVINGSTON

FORMER MP	Graeme Morrice, Labour, defeated
MAJORITY	16,843 (29.3%)
VOTE SHARE	56.9%
CHANGE	+31.0%
2ND PLACE	Lab

@HannahB4LiviMP @HBardell

BORN IN JUNE 1983 in Craigshill, Livingston, Hannah Bardell won the Pushkin Prize at the age of thirteen for a story about a family being moved off their land as part of the Highland Clearances. She attended Broxburn Academy and graduated from the University of Stirling with a degree in Film & Media, Politics and English in 2005. After eighteen months working as a researcher/assistant producer on the political *Sunday Programme* for STV Glasgow and GMTV, she became office manager in 2007 to Alex Salmond MP and Ian Hudghton MEP. In 2010 she joined the American Consulate of the US State Department in Edinburgh as protocol executive and events co-ordinator. In 2012 she became communications manager for Subsea 7, an oil and gas company, and in 2013 was appointed head of communications and marketing (UK & Africa) for Stork Technical Services, another oil and gas company, both in Aberdeen.

She is a former member of the Grampian Chamber of Commerce Policy Committee and of Business for Scotland and she sits on the Aberdeen Performing Arts Development Committee. She also stood for selection as a candidate in Aberdeen South, before being selected for Livingston, the seat in which her mother, Lis Bardell, stood at the 2010 general election. ∎

James Berry

CONSERVATIVE MP FOR KINGSTON & SURBITON

FORMER MP	Ed Davey, Liberal Democrat, defeated
MAJORITY	2,834 (4.8%)
VOTE SHARE	39.2%
CHANGE	+2.7%
2ND PLACE	Lib Dem

www.votejamesberry.com   @votejamesberry

THE SON OF a college principal and a special needs primary school teacher, James Berry was born and raised in Canterbury, Kent. He studied law at University College London and was awarded a scholarship to Harvard Law School, where he met his wife, Nehali, a fellow lawyer, on the first day studying together. Working as a barrister in London, he has specialised in healthcare and police issues and was involved in the high-profile Raoul Moat inquest and the Leveson Inquiry. He is editor of the UK Police Law blog, and a school governor. ∎

Mhairi Black

SCOTTISH NATIONAL PARTY (SNP) MP FOR PAISLEY & RENFREWSHIRE SOUTH

FORMER MP	Douglas Alexander, Labour, defeated
MAJORITY	5,684 (12.3%)
VOTE SHARE	50.9%
CHANGE	+32.9%
2ND PLACE	Lab

@mhairi1921

TWENTY-YEAR-OLD MHAIRI BLACK was born in Paisley and has lived there all her life. She is currently in her final year at Glasgow University studying Politics and Public Policy, and is returning after the general election to take her final-year exams. She is the campaign officer for Glasgow University Scottish Nationalist Association and also women's officer for Paisley SNP. She has volunteered for Oxfam and in her spare time supports Partick Thistle Football Club.

She is the youngest elected MP since the Reform Act of 1832 and the youngest MP since 1667. The previous youngest elected MP was Liberal James Dickson, who, when elected in 1880, was twenty-one years old. ■

Ian Blackford

SCOTTISH NATIONAL PARTY (SNP) MP FOR ROSS,
SKYE & LOCHABER

FORMER MP	Charles Kennedy, Liberal Democrat, defeated
MAJORITY	5,124 (12.3%)
VOTE SHARE	48.1%
CHANGE	+33.0%
2ND PLACE	Lib Dem

@IBlackfordSkye

BORN IN 1961, Ian Blackford attended Royal High School until 1979. A banker by profession, he has worked with the Bankers Trust, UBS Philips and Nat-West Markets. Until 2002 he was head of Dutch equities and head of Scotland for Deutsche Bank AG. He was then head of investor relations for Dutch-listed CSM from 2005 until 2012. Working as an investor relations consultant, he has remained as an adviser to CSM. He is non-executive chairman of the telecommunications firm Commsworld, and since 2008 has been a trustee at the Golden Charter Trust. He was also a non-executive director of Edinburgh Bicycle Co-operative between 2008 and 2013, and was previously the chairman of the Glendale Trust, an organisation responsible for a community-owned estate on Skye. He owns and runs two former crofter cottages on the Isle of Skye as holiday cottages, where he lives with his wife Ann, who comes from Skye.

A former treasurer to the SNP, he had a public falling-out with Alex Salmond and the SNP executive in 2010 over party finances, when he resigned briefly. He is a former member of the shadow SNP Cabinet with responsibility for Social Security and Pensions and is chair of the SNP Currency Commission. He stood as a candidate in the Paisley 1997 by-election and in Ayr at the 1997 general election. ▪

Kirsty Blackman

SCOTTISH NATIONAL PARTY (SNP) MP FOR
ABERDEEN NORTH

FORMER MP	Frank Doran, Labour, stood down
MAJORITY	13,396 (30.5%)
VOTE SHARE	56.4%
CHANGE	+34.2%
2ND PLACE	Lab

@AbdnNorthKirsty

BORN IN ABERDEEN in 1986, Kirsty Blackman (née West) was educated at the independent Robert Gordon's College. Having been a member of the SNP's youth wing, Young Scots for Independence, she joined the SNP in 2005. A former branch secretary, she has been parliamentary assistant to Brian Adam MSP, Nigel Don MSP and Mark McDonald MSP at various times over the last eight or so years. Since 2013 she has been self-employed in her business CosyBosies, selling handmade items.

She was elected as an Aberdeen city councillor, representing Hilton, Woodside and Stockethill, in 2007 and was re-elected in 2012. She was the convenor of the SNP group on the council and was formerly the council's spokesperson for education. She has served on various bodies and organisations, including the Aberdeen Endowment Trust, the Aberdeen Exhibition and Conference Centre (until 2013) and the Aberdeen International Football Festival (until 2012), and remains a member of several community groups. She is married to Luke and is the mother of a young son and baby daughter. ∎

Victoria Borwick AM

CONSERVATIVE MP FOR KENSINGTON

FORMER MP	Sir Malcom Rifkind, Conservative, stood down
MAJORITY	7,361 (21.1%)
VOTE SHARE	52.3%
CHANGE	+2.2%
2ND PLACE	Lab

http://victoriaborwick.london   @DepMayorLondon

LADY VICTORIA BORWICK was born in April 1956. Educated at Wispers School, Haslemere, she has been in events management for most of her working life, serving as group director of Clarion Events, a subsidiary of the P&O Group, between 1979 and 2002. In 1999 she was picked by London mayoral hopeful Steve Norris as his running mate and potential Deputy Mayor. She stood herself for the Conservative nomination in 2004 and 2008, coming second to Boris Johnson in 2008. Elected to Kensington & Chelsea London Borough Council in May 2002 in the Abingdon ward, she became the Conservative Party's director of fundraising later that year. In 2008 she was elected to

the London Assembly, and Boris Johnson appointed her as Deputy Mayor in 2012. She serves on the Transport Committee and the Police and Crime Committee and is a member of the Metropolitan Police Authority.

She is a member of the advisory council of the Open Europe think tank and a governor of the Royal Brompton and Harefield Hospitals. In 1981 she married Jamie Borwick, who succeeded to the peerage as Baron Borwick in 2007 and was elected to the House of Lords in 2013. They have three sons and a daughter. ▪

Phil Boswell

SCOTTISH NATIONAL PARTY (SNP) MP FOR
COATBRIDGE, CHRYSTON & BELLSHILL

FORMER MP	Tom Clarke, Labour, defeated
MAJORITY	11,501 (22.7%)
VOTE SHARE	56.6%
CHANGE	+39.8%
2ND PLACE	Lab

@PhilBoswellSNP

PHIL BOSWELL IS an oil industry engineer from Coatbridge and has worked in Aberdeen, London, the Humber and Qatar. Educated at Glasgow Caledonian University, graduating in 1989 with a degree in Quantity Surveying, he has undertaken a variety of contracts. He was a senior contracts engineer for Qatar Petroleum between 2003 and 2006, working in Doha. He has worked for BP and Shell in Aberdeen, Rio Tinto and Premier Oil in London, and Phillips 66 in Grimsby. He also studied for a diploma in Arbitration at the University of Reading between 2005 and 2007 and is a Fellow of the Chartered Institute of Arbitrators. An SNP activist from West Aberdeenshire, he was Yes campaign manager for all Aberdeenshire during the referendum campaign. ∎

Mickey Brady

SINN FÉIN MP FOR NEWRY & ARMAGH

FORMER MP	Conor Murphy, Sinn Féin, stood down
MAJORITY	4,176 (8.4%)
VOTE SHARE	41.1%
CHANGE	-0.9%
2ND PLACE	UUP

@MickeyBradyMLA

BORN IN BALLYBOT, County Armagh, in October 1950, Mickey Brady has worked for the Newry welfare rights centre for over twenty-five years. First elected to the Northern Ireland Assembly in 2007, representing Newry & Armagh, he was re-elected in 2011. He is a member of the Health, Social Development and Standards and Privileges Committees and is the Sinn Féin spokesperson for Welfare and Older People. He is a board member of Confederation of Community Groups and a member of the board of governors of St Colman's Abbey Primary School. ▪

Deidre Brock

SCOTTISH NATIONAL PARTY (SNP) MP FOR
EDINBURGH NORTH & LEITH

FORMER MP	Mark Lazarowicz, Labour, defeated
MAJORITY	5,597 (9.6%)
VOTE SHARE	40.9%
CHANGE	+31.3%
2ND PLACE	Lab

@DeidreBrock

BORN IN PERTH, Australia, in 1961, Deidre Brock studied English at John Curtin University before gaining a diploma in Performing Arts at the Western Australian Academy of Performing Arts. Moving to Sydney, she spent the next ten years working as an actor, supported by a variety of retail, sales and marketing jobs. Visiting Scotland in 1995, she took the decision to move there permanently in 1996, becoming personal assistant to the managing director of a South African wine club based in Edinburgh. In 2004 she worked as parliamentary assistant to Rob Gibson MSP in the Scottish Parliament.

She successfully stood for election to Edinburgh Council for the first time in 2007, representing the Leith Walk ward. Between 2007 and 2012 she was convenor of the Culture and Leisure Committee on the council, and after her re-election in 2012 she was appointed Deputy Lord Provost. Most recently, she has sat on the Planning, Transport and Environment, and Children and Families Committees. She has sat on the boards of many art and cultural organisations including the Edinburgh International Festival, the Centre for the Moving Image (Edinburgh International Film Festival and Filmhouse) and Creative Edinburgh. She met her partner in her adopted Scotland and the couple have two girls. ▪

Alan Brown

SCOTTISH NATIONAL PARTY (SNP) MP FOR
KILMARNOCK & LOUDOUN

FORMER MP	Cathy Jamieson, Labour, defeated
MAJORITY	13,638 (25.3%)
VOTE SHARE	55.7%
CHANGE	+29.7%
2ND PLACE	Lab

www.alanbrownsnp.org   @AlanBrownSNP

BORN IN AUGUST 1970, Alan Brown attended a local primary school and Loudoun Academy and graduated from Glasgow University with a degree in Civil Engineering. He has been a civil engineer for twenty-one years, most recently as a principal civil engineer for Grontmij (consulting and engineering) in Glasgow. A councillor in East Ayrshire representing Irvine Valley since May 2007, he is a former spokesperson for planning and is currently a member of the cabinet with responsibility for planning, management, resources and equality. He is a director of the Newmilns Snow and Sports Complex (charitable status) and of the Irvine Valley Regeneration Partnership. He has served as the council representative to the Convention of Scottish Local Authorities (CoSLA), Kilmarnock Leisure Centre Trust and Scotland Excel, and is a trustee of East Ayrshire Leisure Trust Board. He is married to Cyndi and father to two teenage boys. ▪

Richard Burgon

LABOUR MP FOR LEEDS EAST

FORMER MP	George Mudie, Labour, stood down
MAJORITY	12,533 (32.8%)
VOTE SHARE	53.7%
CHANGE	+3.4%
2ND PLACE	Con

www.richardburgon.com   @RichardBurgon

RICHARD BURGON WAS born, bred and has worked in Leeds for most of his life. With an Irish family heritage, he was educated at Cardinal Heenan Roman Catholic High School and was the first person in his family to attend university, studying Law at St John's College at Cambridge University. While at Cambridge he was chair of the Cambridge University Labour Club between 2001 and 2002. Qualifying as a lawyer in 2006, he returned to Leeds as a trade union lawyer, working for Thompsons on employment law and personal injury from the firm's Leeds office. The nephew of former Elmet MP Colin Burgon, he unsuccessfully stood for election to the National Policy Forum in 2012 and previously sought selection in Rotherham and Barnsley Central. He has also been a research associate for the Catalyst think tank. ∎

Dawn Butler

LABOUR MP FOR BRENT CENTRAL

FORMER MP	Sarah Teather, Liberal Democrat, stood down
MAJORITY	19,649 (41.8%)
VOTE SHARE	62.1%
CHANGE	+20.9%
2ND PLACE	Con

www.dawnbutler.org.uk   @DawnButlerBrent

BORN IN FOREST Gate in east London in 1969 to Jamaican immigrant parents, Dawn Butler worked as an officer of the GMB Union, including time as a national race and equality officer. She was also an adviser to Mayor of London Ken Livingstone on employment and social issues. Following Paul Boateng's appointment as British High Commissioner to South Africa, she was elected as the MP for Brent South in 2005. She was briefly a parliamentary private secretary and was appointed a government whip in 2008 and a Minister for Young Citizens and Youth Engagement in the Cabinet Office in 2009. She was the first black female MP to be appointed a minister. After her seat was abolished in boundary changes, she stood as a candidate for the new Brent Central constituency, which she lost narrowly to Liberal Democrat Sarah Teather.

Since 2010 she has worked as a freelance training consultant, a political commentator for the *Voice* newspaper, and a community, events and political consultant for the Jamaican National Building Society. She is a trustee of Brent Citizens Advice Bureau and a board member of the Jamaican 2012 Committee for the Jamaican High Commission. ▪

Ruth Cadbury

LABOUR MP FOR BRENTFORD & ISLEWORTH

FORMER MP	Mary Macleod, Conservative, defeated
MAJORITY	465 (0.8%)
VOTE SHARE	43.8%
CHANGE	+10.2%
2ND PLACE	Con

www.ruth2015win.com   @RuthCadbury

RUTH CADBURY WAS born and brought up in Birmingham, a member of the famous Cadbury family. She continues to be a trustee of the Barrow Cadbury Trust, a social justice foundation founded by her great-grandparents. Since studying Geography at Salford University, she has been a town planner working for Planning Aid for London, Richmond upon Thames Council and Sustrans, the cycling charity, as a policy adviser. As a freelance consultant she advised the Improvement and Development Agency's leadership programme.

Having joined the Labour Party in 1981, she has been a Hounslow borough councillor almost continually since 1986, serving as deputy leader and the cabinet lead on Regeneration and Economic Development. She also chaired the London Council's Olympics group before and after London won the bid. Most recently, she has chaired the Planning Committee. Living close to Heathrow Airport, she is a member of HACAN Clear Skies and of BAA's Community Building Noise Insulation Fund Board. She sits on the executive of the Labour group of councillors, is a member of Labour's National Policy Forum and advises the national party on local government matters. A committed Quaker, she has lived in Brentford for thirty years with her husband Nick, a non-executive director of nearby West Middlesex university hospital, and their two sons. ∎

Dr Lisa Cameron

SCOTTISH NATIONAL PARTY (SNP) MP FOR
EAST KILBRIDE, STRATHAVEN & LESMAHAGOW

FORMER MP	Michael McCann, Labour, defeated
MAJORITY	16,527 (27.3%)
VOTE SHARE	55.6%
CHANGE	+32.6%
2ND PLACE	Lab

@lisacameronsnp

BORN IN APRIL 1972, Dr Lisa Cameron grew up in the Westwood area of East Kilbride, where she went to school. She graduated from Strathclyde University, the University of Stirling and finally Glasgow University with a doctorate in Clinical Psychology. She is an NHS consultant working with clients who have mental health problems and learning difficulties. She has worked at Hairmyres Hospital, Wishaw General Hospital, Dykebar Hospital and the State Hospital. She is an accredited risk assessor for the Risk Management Authority and has worked as an expert witness in cases of childhood sexual abuse and domestic violence.

She has been a Unite the Union representative since 2001, serving on several committees and groups. She lives in South Lanarkshire with her husband Mark and their two daughters. ▪

James Cartlidge

CONSERVATIVE MP FOR SUFFOLK SOUTH

FORMER MP	Tim Yeo, Conservative, de-selected
MAJORITY	17,545 (33.8%)
VOTE SHARE	53.1%
CHANGE	+5.3%
2ND PLACE	Lab

www.jamescartlidge.com   @jc4southsuffolk

JAMES CARTLIDGE WAS born in London and went to Queen Elizabeth's Grammar School for Boys in Barnet before studying Economics at Manchester University. Leaving university with a first-class degree, he joined Conservative campaign headquarters as a researcher. He then became a freelance journalist, writing leader articles for the *Daily Telegraph* and opinion pieces for *The Guardian* and *The Spectator*, before setting up his own social housing business, Share to Buy, in 2004, which he has run since.

He represents Bures St Mary on Babergh District Council since winning a by-election in 2013, sitting on the Audit Committee and a housing policy group. He stood against Joan Ruddock in Lewisham Deptford at the 2005 general election, finishing third. He is a volunteer business adviser to homeless charity Broadway Homelessness and Support. He is married to Emily and the couple live in Assington near Sudbury with their four children including young twins. His father-in-law is Aldershot Conservative MP Sir Gerald Howarth. The couple survived the 2004 Asian tsunami while on honeymoon in Sri Lanka when their hotel was the only one in the resort to remain standing. In his spare time he plays the drums for a local band, Tequila Mockingbird. ∎

Maria Caulfield

CONSERVATIVE MP FOR LEWES

FORMER MP	Norman Baker, Liberal Democrat, defeated
MAJORITY	1,083 (2.1%)
VOTE SHARE	38.0%
CHANGE	+1.3%
2ND PLACE	Lib Dem

www.mariacaulfield.co.uk   @mariacaulfield

BORN IN 1973, the daughter of Irish immigrant farmers, Maria Caulfield grew up in south London. She is a Cancer Research UK research sister (nurse) at the Royal Marsden Hospital, leading a team in the field of breast cancer research. She is also a non-executive director of the local housing charity BHT (Brighton Housing Trust) Sussex.

A regional deputy chairman for the Conservatives in the south-east, she was a councillor for the Moulsecoomb & Bevendean ward on Brighton & Hove City Council between 2007 and 2011, and cabinet member for Housing. At the 2010 general election she stood in Caerphilly, coming second with 17% of the vote. She is a member of the Conservatives' Project Umubano, which visits Rwanda annually. In 2011 she was the Sussex No2AV coordinator for the referendum. She has lived in the area, close to the village of Falmer, for over ten years and is the author of *The Battle of Lewes 1264*. She is one of the original members of the Urban Shepherd scheme in Brighton & Hove, where sheep have been introduced to grazing in urban parks. ▪

Alex Chalk

CONSERVATIVE MP FOR CHELTENHAM

FORMER MP	Martin Horwood, Liberal Democrat, defeated
MAJORITY	6,516 (12.1%)
VOTE SHARE	46.1%
CHANGE	+5.0%
2ND PLACE	Lib Dem

www.alexchalk.com   @AlexChalkChelt

ALEX CHALK WAS brought up in Cheltenham, where his parents and other family members still live. He was educated at Winchester College before going to Oxford University in 1995, where he studied Modern History. He took a graduate diploma in Law at City University and was called to the Bar at Inns of Court School in 2001. As a barrister, working in the 6KBW College Hill Chambers, he has specialised in counter-terrorism, corporate crime (including phone hacking), homicide and serious fraud cases. He successfully prosecuted a Conservative council candidate who faked signatures and attempted to ballot-rig hundreds of postal votes. He was elected as a councillor in Hammersmith & Fulham in 2006, chairing the planning committee for four years. He was re-elected in 2010, but stood down. He is married to Sarah and the couple have two young daughters. ∎

Doug Chapman

SCOTTISH NATIONAL PARTY (SNP) MP FOR
DUNFERMLINE & WEST FIFE

FORMER MP	Thomas Docherty, Labour, defeated
MAJORITY	10,352 (18.5%)
VOTE SHARE	50.3%
CHANGE	+39.6%
2ND PLACE	Lab

@DougChapmanSNP

DOUG CHAPMAN SPENT eighteen years of his working life before politics with TSB Scotland in branch banking and, latterly, personnel management. Since then he has worked for Bruce Crawford MSP for six years, assisting with his shadow ministerial responsibilities of Transport, Energy and the Environment. He has worked as campaign manager at SNP headquarters and has been an active member of the party, holding convenor, organiser, membership secretary and political education officer roles. He was a Fife councillor representing the Rosyth ward between 2007 and 2012 and was a member of the executive committee and the Economic & Planning Advisory Group, and chair of the Education and Children's Services Committee.

Since 2012 he has been CoSLA's spokesperson for Education, Children and Young People and has served on a number of its taskforces and workforce groups. He is no stranger to elections, having stood as a candidate in Dunfermline West at the 1999 Scottish Parliament election, Dunfermline at the 2005 general election and a Westminster by-election in 2006, and for Kirkcaldy & Cowdenbeath in 2010. He has lived in Dunfermline for over twenty-three years and is married to a primary school teacher in Cowdenbeath. They have two children. ∎

Joanna Cherry QC

SCOTTISH NATIONAL PARTY (SNP) MP FOR
EDINBURGH SOUTH WEST

FORMER MP	Alistair Darling, Labour, stood down
MAJORITY	8,135 (15.8%)
VOTE SHARE	43.0%
CHANGE	+30.8%
2ND PLACE	Lab

@joannaccherry

BORN AND BRED in Edinburgh, Joanna Cherry gained a first-class Law degree from the University of Edinburgh in 1988. This was followed by a diploma in Legal Practice in 1990, Cherry having been a trainee solicitor at Brodies WS. She practised as an advocate for around twenty years, working on, among others areas, clinical and professional negligence, personal injury, fatal accident and public inquiries, mental health and human rights. She rose steadily through the legal ranks. She was a Standing Junior to the Scottish government in 2003. Between 2008 and 2011 she was an Advocate Depute and Senior Advocate Depute. In 2009 she became a Queen's Counsel. She returned to full-time practice with Hastie Stable in 2011. She has been a tutor at Edinburgh University, has written a legal textbook and has appeared before the UK Supreme Court.

Although a supporter of Scottish independence for over twenty years, she has only been a member of the SNP since 2008, with the public offices that she held precluding her from political activity for a number of years. She co-founded Lawyers for Yes during the referendum campaign. ■

Jo Churchill

CONSERVATIVE MP FOR BURY ST EDMUNDS

FORMER MP	David Ruffley, Conservative, stood down
MAJORITY	21,301 (35.9%)
VOTE SHARE	53.6%
CHANGE	+6.1%
2ND PLACE	Lab

@Jochurchill4

BORN IN MARCH 1964, Johanna Peta (Jo) Churchill is a businesswoman and county councillor from Mrs Thatcher's hometown, Grantham in Lincolnshire. Educated at Dame Alice Harpur School in Bedford, she has a first-class degree in Business and Occupational Psychology. She is the finance director of a scaffolding firm, South Lincolnshire Scaffolding (SLS). Her husband, Peter, is chairman of SLS Ltd. As a Lincolnshire county councillor representing Grantham and Barrowby, she has sat on the Adults Scrutiny Committee, the Children and Young People Scrutiny Committee, Lincolnshire Economic Action Partnership, Lincolnshire Forum for Agriculture and Horticulture and Lincolnshire Health and Wellbeing Board. She was a finalist in the South Cambridgeshire selection.

She is a former school governor and a director of Kesteven and Sleafor Academy Trust and actively campaigns for Breakthrough Breast Cancer, having been diagnosed with breast cancer in 2010 at the age of forty-six. She and her husband have four daughters. ∎

James Cleverly TD AM

CONSERVATIVE MP FOR BRAINTREE

FORMER MP	Brooks Newmark, Conservative, stood down
MAJORITY	17,610 (35.0%)
VOTE SHARE	53.8%
CHANGE	+1.2%
2ND PLACE	UKIP

https://jamescleverly.wordpress.com   @JamesCleverly

JAMES CLEVERLY WAS born in 1969 in Lewisham, London, to a Wiltshire-born father and a mother from Sierra Leone. He attended Riverston School and Colfe's School in south-east London. His intended career in the army was cut short by injury, so he returned to education, attaining a Business degree at Thames Valley University. Before entering politics he worked in the magazine and web publishing industry.

He has been the London Assembly member for Bexley & Bromley since his election in 2008. He has served on the Metropolitan Police Authority and the London Resilience Forum, has been the Mayor's youth ambassador and has sat on several Assembly committees including Counter-Terrorism, Environment and Regeneration. He is the chairman of the London Fire and Emergency Planning Authority and also the London Waste and Recycling Board, both mayoral appointments. He has stood in a number of elections including for the seat of Lewisham East in 2005 and the post of elected mayor of Lewisham in 2006. An officer in the Territorial Army for over twenty years, rising to the rank of major, until 2005 he was the officer commanding 266 (Para) Battery Royal Artillery (Volunteers). He was called up during the Iraq War in 2004, supporting mobilised TA soldiers and their employers. He is married to Susannah. ∎

Julie Cooper

LABOUR MP FOR BURNLEY

FORMER MP	Gordon Birtwistle, Liberal Democrat, defeated
MAJORITY	3,244 (8.2%)
VOTE SHARE	37.6%
CHANGE	+6.3%
2ND PLACE	Lib Dem

www.juliecooperforburnley.co.uk   @JulieForBurnley

A QUALIFIED ENGLISH teacher, Julie Cooper owned and ran Cooper's Chemist in Burnley with her husband Brian for twenty-three years. A Labour Party and union member for around thirty years, she has served on Burnley Borough Council, representing Bank Hall ward since 2005, and is the leader of the council. She has held a number of posts and positions including chair of East Lancashire Health and Wellbeing Partnership, Burnley's representative on Lancashire Health and Wellbeing Board, Lancashire Leaders' representative on Local Enterprise Partnership, a member of the Police and Crime Panel, a board member of East Lancashire Women's Refuge Association, a member of the executive committee of the Burnley Action Partnership and a member of the government special interest group to tackle far-right extremism. She stood as the Labour candidate in Burnley in 2010. She lives in the Briercliffe area of Burnley and has a son and a daughter. She was selected from an all-women shortlist. ▪

Alberto Costa

FORMER MP	Andrew Robathan, Conservative, stood down
MAJORITY	16,824 (31.2%)
VOTE SHARE	53.2%
CHANGE	+3.7%
2ND PLACE	Lab

www.albertocosta.org.uk

BORN IN 1972 to Italian parents who came to the UK in 1967, Alberto Costa was raised, educated and went to university in Glasgow, where he studied Law. While at Glasgow he was president of the Students' Representative Council. He was awarded a post-graduate diploma in Legal Practice at the University of Strathclyde Graduate Law School. He is a dual-qualified English and Scottish solicitor and Scottish notary public and has worked in London, Edinburgh and the USA. He worked in Whitehall for the Treasury Solicitor's Department and was a solicitor at Richards Butler international commercial law firm (now Reed Smith), representing large multinationals. More recently he founded Costa Carlisle Solicitors. He is an associate member of the Chartered Institute of Arbitrators and a member of the Institute of Directors.

He stood in Angus at the 2010 general election and in Southwark North & Bermondsey in 2005. He is married to Dr Maria Costa, a medical scientist, and the couple have two children. ▪

Ronnie Cowan

SCOTTISH NATIONAL PARTY (SNP) MP FOR INVERCLYDE

FORMER MP	Iain McKenzie, Labour, defeated
MAJORITY	11,063 (24.8%)
VOTE SHARE	55.1%
CHANGE	+37.6%
2ND PLACE	Lab

www.ronniecowan.com   @ronniecowan

BORN IN GREENOCK in 1959, Ronnie Cowan comes from a family of Clydeside joiners, mill-workers and weavers. His father was a goalkeeper for Morton and Scotland. He attended school in Inverclyde and has supported the SNP since the age of sixteen. He has worked in IT for thirty years, as a senior analyst for Playtex Products between 1978 and 1986, a consultant to Campbell Lee Computer Services between 1986 and 2001 and an IT manager for DuPont Powder Coatings until 2009. Since 2002 he has run his own IT company as a contract software developer, working with a number of companies including Robert Wiseman Dairies. He served briefly on the Argyll & Clyde Health Board in 1978.

During the referendum campaign he led Yes Inverclyde. ▪

Jo Cox

LABOUR MP FOR BATLEY & SPEN

FORMER MP	Mike Wood, Labour, stood down
MAJORITY	6,057 (12.0%)
VOTE SHARE	43.2%
CHANGE	+1.0%
2ND PLACE	Con

@Jo_Cox1

BATLEY-BORN JO COX (née Leadbeater) attended Heckmondwike Grammar School and Cambridge University, reading Social and Political Studies. Upon graduating in 1995, she worked for Joan Walley MP in the House of Commons, then joined Britain in Europe in 1998 as head of key campaigns. Her next move was to Brussels in 2000 to work for Glenys Kinnock MEP as a political adviser. She stayed in Brussels for her next job as head of the EU office for Oxfam between 2002 and 2005, then returned to the UK with Oxfam as head of policy and advocacy, before heading to New York to work as head of humanitarian campaigning in 2007. She then spent two years working with Sarah Brown as a director of her Maternal Mortality campaign, before becoming a strategy consultant advising Save the Children, the NSPCC, the White Ribbon Alliance for Safe Motherhood and the Freedom Fund on fighting modern slavery. She is the CEO and founder of a research company, UK Women, is on the board of the Burma Campaign and is national chair of Labour Women's Network. She is married and has two children. Before her selection, she used to live on a boat on the Thames. She was selected from an all-women shortlist. ∎

Neil Coyle

LABOUR MP FOR BERMONDSEY & OLD SOUTHWARK

FORMER MP	Simon Hughes, Liberal Democrat, defeated
MAJORITY	4,489 (8.7%)
VOTE SHARE	43.1%
CHANGE	+13.8%
2ND PLACE	Lib Dem

www.neilcoyle.org.uk   @coyleneil

BORN IN LUTON in December 1978 into a working-class family, Neil Coyle attended Wenlock, Ashcroft and Bedford schools before working in a variety of jobs to fund his studies at Hull University. He worked in China between 2001 and 2003 and, on returning to the UK, worked for the government's Equality Commission on campaigns and media, and as acting head of parliamentary affairs, latterly becoming policy manager for health and social care. He then had several senior policy roles with the National Centre for Independent Living, the Disability Alliance and Deafness Research UK.

A London Borough of Southwark councillor for the Newington ward since 2010, he was a deputy cabinet member, responsible for welfare, between 2011 and 2013. He helped found the Walworth Society, is a trustee for a mental health charity and the North Southwark Environment Trust and has worked with several other local community organisations. He lives in Newington with his wife Sarah, a landscape architect. ▪

Angela Crawley

SCOTTISH NATIONAL PARTY (SNP) MP FOR
LANARK & HAMILTON EAST

FORMER MP	Jim Hood, Labour, defeated
MAJORITY	10,100 (18.3%)
VOTE SHARE	48.8%
CHANGE	+27.8%
2ND PLACE	Lab

@CrawleyAngela

BORN AND RAISED in Hamilton, Angela Crawley attended John Ogilvie High School before studying Politics at Stirling University, graduating in 2009. During her studies she interned as a parliamentary assistant to Clare Adamson MSP. She spent the next two years working in Brighton as a tour co-ordinator for the Education Travel Group, before returning to Scotland to work for the Scottish government minister Bruce Crawford MSP between 2011 and 2013. She is currently completing her studying for an LLB degree in Law at the University of Glasgow, having interned briefly for Aamer Anwar & Co. in Glasgow.

Elected as a councillor for Hamilton South in South Lanarkshire Council in 2012, she has served on numerous council committees. She is the SNP spokesperson for Young People and Community Resources, is the national convenor of the SNP's youth wing, Young Scots for Independence, and sits on the party's ruling national executive committee. ■

Judith Cummins

LABOUR MP FOR BRADFORD SOUTH

FORMER MP	Gerry Sutcliffe, Labour, stood down
MAJORITY	6,450 (17.2%)
VOTE SHARE	43.4%
CHANGE	+2.2%
2ND PLACE	Con

www.judithcummins.org.uk   @JudithCummins

JUDITH CUMMINS, WHO is from a working-class background, began work early with the civil service and became active within the trade union movement. At the age of nineteen she was elected as branch secretary in the Civil and Public Service Association (CPSA). She was later awarded a scholarship by the union and put through Ruskin College, Oxford. She is also a member of GMB and Unison. She has worked in Westminster in Labour's parliamentary Whips' Office.

She was a full-time Leeds city councillor, representing Temple Newsam, and is a member of the executive committee, chair of the Audit Committee and a member of the executive of the West Yorkshire Fire Authority, with lead responsibility for auditing. She has also been a councillor for Bradford City Council, where she was whip for the Labour group. She states that one of her proudest achievements was as agent for Chris Leslie MP. Her husband, Mark, is employed by Bradford Metropolitan District Council. She was also shortlisted for Leeds East but was beaten by Richard Burgon. ▪

Byron Davies

CONSERVATIVE MP FOR GOWER

FORMER MP	Martin Caton, Labour, stood down
MAJORITY	27 (0.1%)
VOTE SHARE	37.1%
CHANGE	+5.1%
2ND PLACE	Lab

www.byrondavies.org.uk   @Byron_Davies

THE FIRST NON-LABOUR MP to represent the constituency since 2006, and only winning by twenty-seven votes, Byron Davies was born and raised in Gower. He was educated at Knelston County Primary School and Gowerton Boys' Grammar School, and has a degree in Law from the University of West London that he took as a mature student between 1994 and 1997. He was a police officer in London between 1971 and 2003, attaining senior rank as a detective in the Metropolitan Police. He was seconded to the UK National Crime Squad for several years and also to the European Union as an adviser on combating organised crime. He spent several years living and working in Eastern Europe, helping to prepare EU candidate countries for accession. Before his election to the Welsh Assembly he was an independent adviser, working with Axiom Consulting and B&S Europe, and is the owner of Blue Lines Solutions Europe Ltd. He is a Fellow of the Institute of Professional Investigators.

He was elected as a South Wales West regional Assembly member at the May 2011 election. He served on the Enterprise and Business Committee and was shadow Transport and Regeneration Minister and spokesperson on European Affairs. He is married to Gill and they have one son. ∎

Chris Davies

CONSERVATIVE MP FOR BRECON & RADNORSHIRE

FORMER MP	Roger Williams, Liberal Democrat, defeated
MAJORITY	5,102 (12.7%)
VOTE SHARE	41.1%
CHANGE	+4.5%
2ND PLACE	Lib Dem

www.chrisdavies.org.uk   @ChrisDavies4MP

CHRIS DAVIES WORKED as a rural auctioneer and estate agent for twenty years but more recently managed Hay Veterinary Group, one of Mid Wales's largest veterinary practices, based in Hay-on-Wye. Heavily engaged with countryside issues, he has been involved in the Royal Welsh Agricultural Society since his teens and is the main ring commentator at the Royal Welsh Show.

He was elected as a Powys county councillor in 2012 for the Glasbury ward. He stood unsuccessfully as the Conservative candidate in the 2011 Welsh Assembly election. He is a governor of local primary and secondary schools. He lives with his wife Liz and two young daughters in Glasbury-on-Wye. ▪

Dr James Davies

CONSERVATIVE MP FOR VALE OF CLWYD

FORMER MP	Chris Ruane, Labour, defeated
MAJORITY	237 (0.7%)
VOTE SHARE	39.0%
CHANGE	+3.8%
2ND PLACE	Lab

www.jamesdavies4mp.co.uk   @jamesdavies4mp

BORN IN ST Asaph, Dr James Davies is a local man, with his family hailing from Rhyl. Qualifying as a GP from Cambridge University in 2004, he trained at Glan Clwyd Hospital. He spent a year at the Bodelwyddan Hospital as a house officer and worked on the labour ward at the Countess of Chester Hospital. Before his election he worked as an NHS GP in a medical practice in Chester. He held a clinical champion role for dementia. He is a member of the British Medical Association and the Royal College of GPs.

He was elected to Denbighshire County Council in the ward of Prestatyn East in 2003 and has also served as a town councillor in Prestatyn. He has lived in Prestatyn since the early 1980s with his wife Nina, a district nurse. The couple have a baby son. ∎

Mims Davies

CONSERVATIVE MP FOR EASTLEIGH

FORMER MP	Mike Thornton, Liberal Democrat, defeated
MAJORITY	9,147 (16.5%)
VOTE SHARE	42.3%
CHANGE	+2.9%
2ND PLACE	Lib Dem

www.mimsdavies.org.uk   @mimsdavies

BORN IN JUNE 1975, Mims (Miriam) Davies has worked as a local radio presenter, reporter and producer. Most recently she worked as a road safety communications officer, working closely with the police, the AA and other organisations. She studied Politics at Swansea University. A mother of two, she lives in Haywards Heath and is married to an accountant and finance director of New River Retail plc, which owns land in Burgess Hill. Davies is a shareholder in New River Retail along with her husband.

She is councillor for Haywards Heath, Lucastes, is on Mid Sussex District Council, having been elected in May 2011, and also sits on Haywards Heath Town Council for the Lucastes & Bolnore ward. She is also a former local parish councillor in Hurstpierpoint and Sayers Common. She is southern regional chairman of the Conservative Women's Organisation. A keen runner, she has completed several marathons and other long-distance races. ▪

Martyn Day

SCOTTISH NATIONAL PARTY (SNP) MP FOR
LINLITHGOW & FALKIRK EAST

FORMER MP	Michael Connarty, Labour, defeated
MAJORITY	12,934 (21.0%)
VOTE SHARE	52.0%
CHANGE	+26.6%
2ND PLACE	Lab

http://martynday.scot @martynday4mp

BORN IN FALKIRK in 1971, Martyn Day was raised in Linlithgow and educated at the Linlithgow Academy. He was a personal banking manager with the Bank of Scotland until 1998. He has been a member of the Chartered Institute of Bankers in Scotland since 1994.

He joined his local branch of the SNP in 1989. A long-standing West Lothian councillor for sixteen years, representing Linlithgow since 1999, he held the Development and Transport portfolio on the council's executive between 2007 and 2012. Now in opposition, he acts as the spokesperson for Development and Transport and is the SNP group's whip. He also sits on the Licensing Committee and the Linlithgow Area Committee. He served as parliamentary election agent for Linlithgow in 1999, Linlithgow & East Falkirk in 2010 and Falkirk East in 2011. He is married to Debbie. ■

Thangam Debbonaire

LABOUR MP FOR BRISTOL WEST

FORMER MP	Stephen Williams, Liberal Democrat, defeated
MAJORITY	5,673 (8.8%)
VOTE SHARE	35.7%
CHANGE	+8.1%
2ND PLACE	Green

http://debbonaire.co.uk   @tdebbonaire

BORN IN 1966, Thangam Debbonaire is a keen musician, having attended the prestigious Chetham's School of Music in Manchester, playing the cello as well as participating in choral singing. From here she began her studies of Mathematics at the University of Oxford but failed to complete them. Instead, she finished her undergraduate education at St John's City College of Technology. She also has an MSc in Management, Development & Social Responsibility Studies from the School for Advanced Urban Studies (1995). Until her election she was research manager at Respect, a UK-based network of domestic violence perpetrator programmes. She has been a director of Domestic Violence Responses since 1997. She has also been national children's officer for Women's Aid National Office in England.

She is a trustee for a Bristol charity, WISH, supporting their work to help young people stop using violence, and a voluntary governor at Glenfrome Primary School. She stood for the local elections in Bristol in 2011 and was secretary of Ashley ward, women's officer for Bristol West CLP and a member of the executive committee. She also stood for the nomination in the constituency of Kingswood. ▪

Martin Docherty

SCOTTISH NATIONAL PARTY (SNP) MP
FOR DUNBARTONSHIRE WEST

FORMER MP	Gemma Doyle, Labour, defeated
MAJORITY	14,171 (27.7%)
VOTE SHARE	59.0%
CHANGE	+38.9%
2ND PLACE	Lab

www.martinjdocherty.com   @MartinJDocherty

BORN IN 1971 and raised in Clydebank, Martin Docherty left school at sixteen, but returned to higher education in his twenties, gaining an HNC and HND in Business Administration from colleges in Glasgow, a degree in Political Science and Government from the University of Essex and a Master's degree in Organisational Development from the Glasgow School of Art. He spent a decade working for West Dunbartonshire Community and Volunteering Services (WDCVS) as the policy and research lead. Since 2014 he has worked as a policy adviser to Volunteer Scotland.

He joined the SNP in 1991 and was elected as Scotland's youngest ever councillor, aged twenty-one, to the then Clydebank District Council in 1992. He was elected to Glasgow City Council in 2012, representing the Anderston/City ward and leads the SNP group on community planning. He has held a number of positions within the party including SNP Clydebank secretary, and chair and SNP liaison secretary for West Dunbartonshire. He is a member of Glasgow Community Planning Partnership Strategic Board and voluntary chair of Clydebank Restoration Trust. He is a former board member of Glasgow Housing Association and national secretary of the charity Cahonas Scotland. He lives in Whiteinch with his partner, John. ▪

Stuart Donaldson

SCOTTISH NATIONAL PARTY (SNP) MP FOR
ABERDEENSHIRE WEST & KINCARDINE

FORMER MP	Sir Robert Smith, Liberal Democrat, defeated
MAJORITY	7,033 (12.7%)
VOTE SHARE	41.6%
CHANGE	+25.9%
2ND PLACE	Con

@StuDonaldsonSNP

THE SON OF Scottish Public Health Minister Maureen Watt and the grandson of Hamish Watt, SNP MP for Banffshire and Moray between 1974 and 1979, Stuart Donaldson is one of several new young SNP MPs elected in 2015. Born in 1992, he grew up in Durris, was educated locally at Banchory Academy and then went on to Glasgow University. Upon graduating, he was going to go to China to work in the tourism industry but changed his plans when Christian Allard was made a north-east region MSP in 2013 following the death of Aberdeenshire Donside MSP Brian Adam. He worked as an assistant to Christian Allard until his selection. He was campaign co-ordinator for Yes Scotland in Aberdeenshire during the referendum campaign. ▪

Michelle Donelan

CONSERVATIVE MP FOR CHIPPENHAM

FORMER MP	Duncan Hames, Liberal Democrat, defeated
MAJORITY	10,076 (18.2%)
VOTE SHARE	47.6%
CHANGE	+6.5%
2ND PLACE	Lib Dem

http://michelledonelan.co.uk   @michelledonelan

COMING FROM THREE generations of small-business owners, Michelle Donelan was born and raised in a small village in Cheshire. She was educated locally at the County High School in Leftwich before studying History and Politics at York University. An international marketer, she worked in Sydney for one of Australia's leading publishing houses before returning to the UK to manage partnership marketing projects for The History Channel, a joint venture between BSkyB and AETN. Most recently, she managed international marketing campaigns for WWE (World Wrestling Entertainment) across 100 countries, working with broadcasters and charities. She was a member of the board of trustees of a volunteer centre in London before moving to Chippenham. Donelan made her first speech at a party conference aged fifteen, younger than William Hague at his famous appearance. She stood against former Labour minister John Healey in Wentworth & Dearne at the 2010 general election. ▪

Steve Double

CONSERVATIVE MP FOR ST AUSTELL & NEWQUAY

FORMER MP	Stephen Gilbert, Liberal Democrat, defeated
MAJORITY	8,173 (16.2%)
VOTE SHARE	40.2%
CHANGE	+0.2%
2ND PLACE	Lib Dem

www.stevedouble.org.uk   @stevedouble

STEVE DOUBLE WAS born and raised in St Austell and has always lived and worked in Cornwall. He has worked for a local church and is a director of two companies he founded: Bay Direct Media since 2001 and Phoenix Corporate since 2011. Before the election he was Deputy Mayor of St Austell Town Council and was previously a cabinet member on Cornwall Council. He is also a governor of his local primary school, an active member of the local church, a trustee of the St Austell Bay Community Trust and a member of Volunteer Cornwall. Married to his wife Anne for nearly thirty years, they have three children. ▪

Peter Dowd

LABOUR MP FOR BOOTLE

FORMER MP	Joe Benton, Labour, stood down
MAJORITY	28,704 (63.6%)
VOTE SHARE	74.5%
CHANGE	+8.0%
2ND PLACE	UKIP

@Peter_Dowd

BORN IN BOOTLE in 1957, Peter Dowd was educated at local primary and secondary schools and college, before gaining a degree at Liverpool University and a postgraduate degree and other qualifications at Lancaster University. He has been a social worker for much of his career and, before his election, was head of care delivery frameworks for 5 Boroughs Partnership NHS Trust. He was arguably the natural successor to former MP John Benton, having inherited his council seat for the Derby ward of Sefton Metropolitan Council in 1991 after Benton's election to Parliament. He would serve on the council for the next twenty-five years, as leader of the Labour group from 2008 and leader of the council from 2013. Since 2010 he has served the St Oswald ward. He also served on Merseyside County Council between 1981 and 1986 and was elected to Maghull Town Council in 2011.

He sat on the Liverpool City Region Cabinet, Liverpool City Region Combined Authority and Liverpool City Region Local Enterprise Partnership Board. He is a former member and chairman of Merseyside Fire and Rescue Service, and director of Merseyside Racial Equality Council, Netherton Feelgood Factory (social partnership), the Fire Support Network and Sefton Education Business Partnership. ▪

Oliver Dowden

CONSERVATIVE MP FOR HERTSMERE

FORMER MP	James Clappison, Conservative, stood down
MAJORITY	18,461 (36.9%)
VOTE SHARE	59.3%
CHANGE	+3.3%
2ND PLACE	Lab

www.oliverdowden.com

OLIVER DOWDEN WAS born and brought up in the constituency. He went to Parmiter's School near Watford and then read Law at Cambridge University. After working as teacher in Japan, he joined the Conservative Research Department in 2004, rising to deputy campaigns director. An account director at public affairs consultancy LLM, he worked for Hill & Knowlton for less than a year as managing consultant before returning to work for the Conservative Party with Andy Coulson. Working first as a political adviser, he was promoted to deputy chief of staff to the Prime Minister David Cameron in 2012, one of two (the other being Kate Fall). He was one of the unsuccessful shortlisted candidates for Croydon South in 2013 before his selection for Hertsmere in October 2014. He lives in the neighbouring constituency of St Albans with his wife Blythe and their two young children. ■

Flick Drummond

CONSERVATIVE MP FOR PORTSMOUTH SOUTH

FORMER MP	Mike Hancock, Liberal Democrat/Independent, de-selected
MAJORITY	5,241 (12.5%)
VOTE SHARE	34.8%
CHANGE	+1.6%
2ND PLACE	Lib Dem

www.flickdrummond.com   @FlickD

FLICK DRUMMOND WAS born in Aden in 1962, where her father was serving in the army. She was educated at Roedean and studied South-East Asian Studies at Hull University, and has since studied for a Master's in Global Politics at the University of Southampton. She has worked as an insurance broker and an OFSTED inspector. She was director of corporate affairs for the Conservative Middle East Council between 2010 and 2011.

She has been a Winchester city councillor and previously fought Southampton Itchen in 2005 and Portsmouth South in 2010. She is chair of governors of Milton Park Primary and is a trustee of Portsmouth Citizens Advice Bureau. She was previously a board member of Healthwatch and was on a community health council for nine years. The former Liberal Democrat MP, Mike Hancock, who was de-selected, could only manage sixth place standing as an Independent in 2015. Drummond lives with her family in Southsea. ∎

Tom Elliott MLA

ULSTER UNIONIST PARTY (UUP) MP FOR
FERMANAGH & SOUTH TYRONE

FORMER MP	Michelle Gildernew, Sinn Féin, defeated
MAJORITY	530 (1.0%)
VOTE SHARE	46.4%
CHANGE	+46.4%
2ND PLACE	Sinn Féin

@telliott_UUP

IN A SURPRISE result, Tom Elliott, leader of the Ulster Unionist Party between 2010 and 2012, defeated Sinn Féin's Michelle Gildernew to be elected. Born in 1963, he has been a member of the Northern Ireland Assembly for the constituency since 2003. He was educated at Ballinamallard Primary School and Duke of Westminster High School, Ballinamallard & Kesh. Afterwards, he earned a college certificate in Agriculture from the Enniskillen College of Agriculture. A farmer by background, he served part time in the Ulster Defence Regiment and the Royal Irish Regiment for eighteen years.

He was elected an Ulster Unionist councillor on Fermanagh District Council, representing Erne North, in 2001 and was re-elected in 2005 but resigned in 2010. In the Assembly he served as UUP spokesperson on Agriculture and Rural Affairs. He is currently vice-chair of the Agricultural Committee in Stormont and also sits as a member of the Committee for the Office of the First Minister and Deputy First Minister. He stood for election in the seat in 2005 and then in 2010, but stood down in favour of Independent Unionist Rodney Connor at the 2010 general election. He is married to Anne and has one daughter and one son. They live on the family farm near Ballinamallard. ▪

Marion Fellows

SCOTTISH NATIONAL PARTY (SNP) MP FOR
MOTHERWELL & WISHAW

FORMER MP	Frank Roy, Labour, defeated
MAJORITY	11,898 (24.7%)
VOTE SHARE	56.5%
CHANGE	+38.4%
2ND PLACE	Lab

http://marionfellows.org   @marion53f

BORN IN IRVINE, Marion Fellows was educated at Belmont High, Ayr, and Carrick Academy, Maybole, before graduating from Heriot-Watt University in Accountancy and Finance. She spent her early career in a variety of related roles in both the public and private sector, before spending nineteen years teaching business studies at West Lothian College. She is an active member of the EIS-CLA (College Lecturers Association), and has been a branch official and a member of the national Salary and Conditions Committee.

She stood for the Scottish Parliament in Motherwell & Wishaw against former First Minister Jack McConnell and achieved a 6.9% swing from Labour to the SNP. She has represented Wishaw on North Lanarkshire Council since 2012 and was a senior figure in the Yes Motherwell & Wishaw campaign. She is married, has raised three children and has lived in Wishaw and Bellshill for forty years. ∎

Suella Fernandes

CONSERVATIVE MP FOR FAREHAM

FORMER MP	Mark Hoban, Conservative, stood down
MAJORITY	22,262 (40.7%)
VOTE SHARE	56.1%
CHANGE	+0.8%
2ND PLACE	UKIP

www.suellafernandes.co.uk   @SuellaFernandes

SUELLA FERNANDES WAS born in Harrow in 1980 to parents who came to the UK from east Africa. Her father was an NHS nurse and a local councillor and candidate in Tottenham in the 2001 general election and in Brent East in the 2003 by-election. She attended a comprehensive, then an independent school, before reading Law at Queens' College, Cambridge, graduating in 2002. Having joined the Conservative Party at sixteen, she was chairman of the Cambridge University Conservative Association. Between 2002 and 2003 she studied Law at the Sorbonne, Université de Paris. Returning to the UK, she was the parliamentary researcher to shadow Attorney General Dominic Grieve MP between 2004 and 2005.

She was called to Middle Temple in 2005 on a Pegasus scholarship. She stood against Keith Vaz in Leicester East at the 2005 general election. She qualified as an attorney in New York in 2006. Since 2008 she has worked as a barrister at No. 5 Chambers, specialising in planning. She was on secondment to a law firm in Manhattan in 2010, which prevented her from standing at the 2010 election. She stood in the 2012 Greater London Assembly election. She is a co-founder, former chair and now trustee of the Africa Justice Foundation and a co-founder of the Michaela Community School, a free school in Brent. ▪

Margaret Ferrier

SCOTTISH NATIONAL PARTY (SNP) MP FOR
RUTHERGLEN & HAMILTON WEST

FORMER MP	Tom Greatrex, Labour, defeated
MAJORITY	9,975 (17.3%)
VOTE SHARE	52.6%
CHANGE	+36.5%
2ND PLACE	Lab

@MgtFerrierSNP

BORN AND BRED in Glasgow, Margaret Ferrier moved to Rutherglen in 1972, where she lived until 1990, and has lived in Cambuslang for fifteen years. She worked as a commercial sales supervisor for Terex Equipment Limited, a manufacturing construction company.

She joined the Rutherglen branch of the party in 2011 and stood in the Rutherglen South by-election for South Lanarkshire Council in 2013 but came third. She is an elected community councillor, chair of Halfway Community Council and has worked as a volunteer for the Citizens Advice Bureau. She is the mother of a grown-up daughter. ∎

Colleen Fletcher

LABOUR MP FOR COVENTRY NORTH EAST

FORMER MP	Bob Ainsworth, Labour, stood down
MAJORITY	12,274 (29.1%)
VOTE SHARE	52.2%
CHANGE	+2.9%
2ND PLACE	Con

COLLEEN FLETCHER WAS born and bred in Coventry into a political family. Her mother was a local councillor. She went to school locally at Lyng Hall Comprehensive. Later she attended Henley College. She began her career at General Electric Company (GEC) in Coventry and her last employment before her election was as a customer services officer with Orbit Housing Group. She has been a councillor on Coventry City Council for thirteen years over three different terms of office, representing Upper Stoke ward in the parliamentary constituency. She has been a cabinet member for Community Safety and head of Scrutiny Co-Ordination, and chaired the Labour group. She currently sits on the cabinet advisory panel on School Organisation, the Health and Social Care scrutiny board and the Public Services, Energy and Environment scrutiny board. She was also appointed by the council to the Annie Bettmann Foundation, Coventry Ambassadors Social Enterprise Board and the Lyng Hall Trust Limited.

A member of the Labour Party for over forty years, she is a member of the National Policy Forum and an officer of the West Midlands Regional Board. She was selected from an all-women shortlist and is Coventry's first female MP since 1979. She is married with two adult sons. ∎

Kevin Foster

CONSERVATIVE MP FOR TORBAY

FORMER MP	Adrian Sanders, Liberal Democrat, defeated
MAJORITY	3,286 (6.8%
VOTE SHARE	40.7%
CHANGE	+2.0%
2ND PLACE	Lib Dem

www.kevinjfoster.com   @kevin_j_foster

BORN IN PLYMOUTH in 1978, Kevin Foster spent his childhood in Devon, the son of a labourer and painter at Devonport Dockyard and a primary school teaching assistant. He was educated at Hele's School, a comprehensive in Plympton, and studied a Law degree and Master's (LLM) in International Economic Law at the University of Warwick. In 2002 he was called to the Bar by Inner Temple. He first worked for an MEP in the West Midlands before becoming a criminal defence paralegal for Howell & Co. in 2003. Having been elected as a councillor on Coventry City Council in 2002 for Cheylesmore, he gave up his paralegal job in 2004 and was made cabinet member for City Services. Between 2005 and 2011 he was company secretary of AW Computech Ltd.

He was made deputy leader of the council in 2008 and became leader of the Conservative group in 2011. He stepped down from this role in 2013 upon his selection and resigned from the council in 2014 to focus on his campaign. He first joined the Conservative Party in 1995 and stood for Coventry South at the 2010 general election. He is a practising Christian and a prolific tweeter. ∎

Vicky Foxcroft

LABOUR MP FOR LEWISHAM DEPTFORD

FORMER MP	Dame Joan Ruddock, Labour, stood down
MAJORITY	21,516 (45.4%)
VOTE SHARE	60.2%
CHANGE	+6.6%
2ND PLACE	Con

@vickyfoxcroft

VICKY FOXCROFT WAS born in Chorley and grew up in the north-west in a single-parent household. Her father worked for Leyland Motors for thirty-eight years. She was the first person in her family to go to university and gained a BA from De Montfort University in 2000. In 2002 she joined the Amalgamated Engineering and Electrical Union (AEEU) as a research officer. She was political officer at the union Amicus between 2005 and 2009, and since 2009 has been the finance sector officer, representing high-street bank workers, particularly at HSBC, for Unite the Union.

A Labour Party member for more than seventeen years, she moved to Lewisham Deptford more than a decade ago and has lived in the constituency for most of her adult life. She has held many positions in the party, including chair of Labour Students, women's officer of the constituency, trades union officer and campaigns officer, and has sat on the National Policy Forum. She is a Lewisham borough councillor, representing Brockley ward, and is the chair of Lewisham Labour group of councillors. She is married. ▪

Lucy Frazer QC

CONSERVATIVE MP FOR CAMBRIDGESHIRE SOUTH EAST

FORMER MP	Sir James Paice, Conservative, stood down
MAJORITY	16,837 (28.3%)
VOTE SHARE	48.5%
CHANGE	+0.5%
2ND PLACE	Lib Dem

www.lucyfrazer.org.uk

LUCY FRAZER IS one of the youngest women QCs in the country. Growing up in Yorkshire, she studied Law at Newnham College, Cambridge. Both her sisters left school at sixteen and she was the only child in her family to go to university. In 1993 she became one of the few women presidents of the Cambridge Union Society, the previous woman having been Clare Balding. She was called to the Bar at Middle Temple in 1996 and was made a Queen's Counsel in 2013. Since 1998 she has worked as a barrister at South Square chambers in Gray's Inn, specialising in restructuring and insolvency, commercial banking, financial services, and company and civil fraud. She has regularly acted for HMRC and the Serious Organised Crime Agency in claims involving tax fraud.

She is a governor of a state school and deputy chair of Hampstead & Kilburn Conservative Association. Her selection at an open primary was controversial, following claims that mistakes were made in counting the votes. She is married to David and they have two children. ∎

Marcus Fysh

CONSERVATIVE MP FOR YEOVIL

FORMER MP	David Laws, Liberal Democrat, defeated
MAJORITY	5,313 (9.3%)
VOTE SHARE	42.5%
CHANGE	+9.6%
2ND PLACE	Lib Dem

www.marcusfysh.org.uk   @MarcusFysh

BORN IN 1970, Marcus Fysh moved to England from Australia at the age of three. He went to school in Bristol, London and Hampshire, before going to Oxford University to study Literature. He joined fund management firm Mercury Asset Management in London in 1993, and in 2003 he set up his own investment business with a focus on the Asia Pacific region, Europe and the UK, specialising in farming, housing development and medical research.

He is a Somerset county councillor for the Coker division and a South Somerset district councillor since 2001, representing the Yeovil South ward. He was the deputy leader of the Conservative group on the council. He was selected in an open primary. He lives just outside Yeovil, in East Coker, with his wife and baby daughter. ∎

Stephen Gethins

SCOTTISH NATIONAL PARTY (SNP) MP FOR
FIFE NORTH EAST

FORMER MP	Sir Menzies Campbell, Liberal Democrat, stood down
MAJORITY	4,344 (9.6%)
VOTE SHARE	40.9%
CHANGE	+26.7%
2ND PLACE	Lib Dem

@StephenGethins

STEPHEN GETHINS IS a former special adviser to Alex Salmond as First Minister and has worked in the European Parliament and the Westminster Parliament. Originally from Perthshire, he studied Scots and International Law at the University of Dundee, including a year at Universiteit Antwerpen in Belgium. In 2001 he became a project co-ordinator for Saferworld on a small arms and light weapons control project across the South Caucasus and the Balkans. In 2003 he became the head of press and communications, and subsequently chief of staff, to the SNP group of MPs in Westminster. While in Westminster, he studied for a research Master's in Politics and International Affairs at the University of Kent.

In 2005 he became a policy adviser to the Committee of the Regions in the European Parliament. Staying in Brussels, he worked for Scotland Europa as a senior executive. He also briefly worked for Pagoda Public Relations. In 2009 he was appointed as a special adviser to Alex Salmond with responsibility for finance, energy and climate change, rural affairs, and Europe and international affairs. Since 2013 he has worked as an independent communications consultant and political commentator in Edinburgh. He was the fourth candidate on the SNP list for the European elections in 2014. He is married with a baby daughter. ∎

Nusrat Ghani

CONSERVATIVE MP FOR WEALDEN

FORMER MP	Charles Hendry, Conservative, stood down
MAJORITY	22,967 (40.3%)
VOTE SHARE	57.0%
CHANGE	+0.5%
2ND PLACE	UKIP

@Nusrat_Ghani

BORN IN KASHMIR, Nusrat Ghani moved to Britain as a child and was educated in state schools in Birmingham, at Cadbury Sixth Form College and at the University of Central England, the first woman in her family to go to university. She later gained a Master's in International Relations from Leeds University. She has had a very varied career, beginning in the City working for Goldman Sachs as an emerging markets team assistant in 1996. A year later she moved into public affairs and has been head of public affairs for Age Concern, for Breakthrough Breast Cancer between 2000 and 2001, and for the BBC World Service between 2002 and 2007. Since then she has been a director of an international media development agency.

She joined the Conservative Party in 2009, in response to David Cameron's call for a wider range of people to offer themselves as candidates. At the 2010 general election she stood as a late replacement candidate in Birmingham Ladywood. She was a team leader in west London for Boris Johnson's mayoral campaign between 2011 and 2012. She was selected for Wealden in December 2013 in an open primary. She is married. ▪

Patricia Gibson

SCOTTISH NATIONAL PARTY (SNP) MP FOR
AYRSHIRE NORTH & ARRAN

FORMER MP	Katy Clark, Labour, defeated
MAJORITY	13,573 (25.2%)
VOTE SHARE	53.2%
CHANGE	+27.2%
2ND PLACE	Lab

@PGibsonSNP

PATRICIA GIBSON (NÉE Duffy) was born and brought up in Govan. She attended Glasgow University, where she gained an MA (Hons) in Politics and a post-graduate diploma in Education. She was an English teacher for sixteen years at Airdrie Academy and then for eight years at St Ninian's High, just outside Greater Pollok.

She joined the SNP in 1997 and is a former Glasgow city councillor for Greater Pollok. She is the SNP spokesperson for Education in the city and has been Pollok constituency secretary. She fought the seat at the 2010 general election. She is married to local SNP MSP Kenneth Gibson, who represents Cunningham North, and has been a policy adviser to her husband since 2007. The couple live in Kilbirnie and have a young child. ∎

Patrick Grady

SCOTTISH NATIONAL PARTY (SNP) MP FOR
GLASGOW NORTH

FORMER MP	Ann McKechin, Labour, defeated
MAJORITY	9,295 (25.2%)
VOTE SHARE	53.1%
CHANGE	+41.2%
2ND PLACE	Lab

www.patrickgrady.org   @grady_patrick   @GradySNP

BORN IN 1980, Patrick Grady moved to Glasgow from Inverness in 1997 to study History at the University of Strathclyde. After spending a few years living and working in Malawi and London as an advocacy manager for SCIAF, the official aid agency of the Catholic Church in Scotland, he returned to Glasgow in 2007 and currently works as a policy officer in the Scottish Parliament. He is a vice-chair of the board of trustees of NIDOS (Network of International Development Organisations in Scotland).

Since joining the SNP at the age of seventeen, Patrick has held a variety of posts, including national secretary of the Federation of Student Nationalists, and was recently elected convenor of Glasgow Kelvin SNP Constituency Association. He was appointed the national secretary of the party in 2012. He stood for Glasgow North at the 2010 general election. ∎

Peter Grant

SCOTTISH NATIONAL PARTY (SNP) MP FOR GLENROTHES

FORMER MP	Lindsay Roy, Labour, stood down
MAJORITY	13,897 (29.2%)
VOTE SHARE	59.8%
CHANGE	+38.1%
2ND PLACE	Lab

@GlenCentFifeSNP

PETER GRANT WAS brought up in Lanarkshire in a working-class family. He graduated from Glasgow University and worked as a physics teacher in Ayrshire and Fife before retraining as an accountant. He has a professional qualification in public sector finance and has worked in a number of local government and NHS finance roles. In August 2013 he gave up a part-time job as a finance manager to spend more time working for the Yes campaign.

He has been a Fife councillor since 1992, representing Glenrothes West and Kinglassie. He has served for five years as leader of Fife Council, the first ever non-Labour leader of the council, and is still leader of the SNP group. He is a member of the executive committee of Fife Partnership Board. He previously stood as a Westminster parliamentary candidate in the Glenrothes by-election in 2008, when he lost, confounding all expectations. He has been married for thirty years to Fiona, a local GP and fellow Fife councillor, and has lived in the constituency since 1983. ▪

Neil Gray

SCOTTISH NATIONAL PARTY (SNP) MP FOR
AIRDRIE & SHOTTS

FORMER MP	Pamela Nash, Labour, defeated
MAJORITY	8,779 (19.8%)
VOTE SHARE	53.9%
CHANGE	+30.4%
2ND PLACE	Lab

@NeilGray3

BORN AND BROUGHT up in the Orkney Isles, Neil Gray attended Kirkwall Grammar School before studying at Stirling University, graduating with a first-class degree in Politics and Journalism in 2008. He worked as a contract producer and reporter for BBC Radio Orkney between 2003 and 2008, and for local newspaper titles. He moved to the SNP's press and research office in Holyrood as an intern for four months and was subsequently employed full time by Alex Neil MSP in his constituency office in August 2008. He became Neil's office manager in 2011. A keen athlete who won many sporting awards at school and university, he represented Scotland at the 400 metres until injury ended his career. He is married with a baby daughter. ▪

Christopher Green

CONSERVATIVE MP FOR BOLTON WEST

FORMER MP	Julie Hilling, Labour, defeated
MAJORITY	801 (1.6%)
VOTE SHARE	40.6%
CHANGE	2.3%
2ND PLACE	Lab

www.chris-green.org.uk   @Chris11Green

CHRISTOPHER GREEN IS a scientific instrumentation engineer by training and had a successful career in the pharmaceutical and manufacturing industry in the north-west. He has also promoted science and engineering in primary schools and taught English in Rwanda, and was a member of the Territorial Army for several years prior to entering politics.

He has twice stood for election to Manchester City Council, in Chorlton Park in 2008 and Didsbury in 2011. He was the Conservative parliamentary candidate in Manchester Withington at the 2010 general election, increasing the Conservative share of the vote. He was deputy chairman of the Manchester Federation from 2009 to 2012 and remains a member of the Greater Manchester Area Committee. ∎

Margaret Greenwood

LABOUR MP FOR WIRRAL WEST

FORMER MP	Esther McVey, Conservative, defeated
MAJORITY	417 (1.0%)
VOTE SHARE	45.1%
CHANGE	+8.9%
2ND PLACE	Con

www.margaretgreenwood.org.uk   @MGreenwoodWW

MARGARET GREENWOOD IS a former
web consultant and English teacher, working in various schools, colleges and adult
education centres in the Wirral and Liverpool. She also taught literacy to adult
learners and worked with adults with special needs. Additionally she has worked
as a travel writer. She has lived in Liverpool for over twenty years and is a founder
member of Defend our NHS.

In a hard-fought and sometimes bitter contest, she narrowly defeated former
Employment Minister Esther McVey, the
most senior Conservative to lose their seat
in 2015. ∎

Louise Haigh

LABOUR MP FOR SHEFFIELD HEELEY

FORMER MP	Megg Munn, Labour, stood down
MAJORITY	12,954 (30.8%)
VOTE SHARE	48.2%
CHANGE	+5.6%
2ND PLACE	UKIP

www.louisehaigh.org.uk   @LouHaigh

LOUISE HAIGH WAS born and grew up in Sheffield in a single-parent family. Her grandfather was an FBU (Fire Brigades Union) official in Chesterfield and her uncle was an NUM (National Union of Mineworkers) member who went on strike in 1984. She started work as a local call centre worker at Ant Marketing but then was able to attend university. She trained youth workers in the Midlands on how to deal with issues such as teen pregnancy, drug and alcohol misuse, and child protection. She became a parliamentary researcher to a shadow minister focusing on children and young people. She was also a co-ordinator of the All-Party Parliamentary Group on International Corporate Responsibility. During her time in Westminster she was secretary of the parliamentary staff branch of Unite. Most recently, she has been working at insurance company Aviva. ∎

Luke Hall

CONSERVATIVE MP FOR THORNBURY & YATE

FORMER MP	Steve Webb, Liberal Democrat, defeated
MAJORITY	1,495 (3.1%)
VOTE SHARE	41.0%
CHANGE	+3.9%
2ND PLACE	Lib Dem

www.lukehall.org.uk

28-YEAR-OLD LUKE HALL succeeded in defeating former Pensions Minister Steve Webb. He was born and grew up locally in South Gloucestershire and now lives in Westerleigh. He attended local state schools and has worked in retail since the age of sixteen. He started on the shop floor and progressed to become the store manager of Lidl in Yate at the age of twenty. He was later promoted to district manager and was an area manager for the southwest for the Farmfoods supermarket chain before his election.

An active member of the local Conservative Party since 2009, he has been a constituency chairman in South Gloucestershire and has served as the deputy chairman of the Bristol & South Gloucestershire Conservatives. He was nominated for the 2013 National Conservative Excellence Awards for his campaigning in South Gloucestershire. ▪

Harry Harpham

LABOUR MP FOR SHEFFIELD BRIGHTSIDE
& HILLSBOROUGH

FORMER MP	David Blunkett, Labour, stood down
MAJORITY	13,807 (34.5%)
VOTE SHARE	56.6%
CHANGE	+1.6%
2ND PLACE	UKIP

www.harryharpham.com   @sheffharry

BORN IN 1954 in Nottingham, Harry Harpham left school at sixteen and went down the pits. He spent a full year on strike in 1984/85 as an NUM member at Clipstone Colliery. He is the only member of the new intake of Labour MPs to come from a mining background. In 1985 he moved to Sheffield and, after studying at Northern College, he progressed to Sheffield University, graduating with an honours degree. He worked as a researcher for the retiring MP David Blunkett.

A member of the Labour Party for over twenty years, after two previous attempts he was elected to Sheffield City Council in 2000 to represent the Manor ward and then Darnall ward in 2004. He held several portfolios as a cabinet member and was deputy leader and cabinet member for Homes and Neighbourhoods. He stood down as a deputy leader in March 2015 but continued his role as cabinet member until the election. As chairman of South Yorkshire's Police and Crime Panel, he called for Shaun Wright, the former Police and Crime Commissioner for South Yorkshire, to resign in 2014. He is a school governor and Unite sponsored. He lives in Burngreave with his partner, who works for Sheffield Teaching Hospitals NHS Trust. He has adult children. ∎

Carolyn Harris

LABOUR MP FOR SWANSEA EAST

FORMER MP	Siân James, Labour, stood down
MAJORITY	12,028 (35.8%)
VOTE SHARE	53.0%
CHANGE	+1.5%
2ND PLACE	UKIP

www.carolynharris4labour.co.uk   @carolynharris24

CAROLYN HARRIS HAS lived and worked in the constituency all her life and worked for the previous MP. She was educated locally and returned to education in her thirties, getting a degree in Social History and Social Policy in 1998. She formerly worked with several charitable and community action groups. She was project manager for the Guiding Hands Charity between 1998 and 2000. She was then appointed Wales regional director for Community Logistics, and Wales regional manager for a children's cancer charity in 2003. Since 2005 she has worked as the parliamentary assistant and constituency manager for Siân James MP, managing her constituency team and office.

She has been a member of the Labour Party for eighteen years. She is a member of Unison and has held a number of branch and constituency offices. She is a governor of two local schools. She belongs to several church and community groups. She is married to David and they have two sons. ∎

Helen Hayes

LABOUR MP FOR DULWICH & WEST NORWOOD

FORMER MP	Dame Tessa Jowell, Labour, stood down
MAJORITY	16,122 (31.4%)
VOTE SHARE	54.1%
CHANGE	+7.5%
2ND PLACE	Con

www.helenhayes.org.uk   @helenhayes

HELEN HAYES GREW up in the north-west, where her parents were both public sector workers. She attended a local comprehensive school and then studied Politics, Philosophy and Economics at the University of Oxford, and Social Policy at the London School of Economics. She is a chartered town planner, and set up and ran a consultancy practice specialising in planning and urban design, Urban Practitioners, for fourteen years. In 2011 she joined Allies and Morrison, a large architecture practice based in Southwark, as a partner, helping to establish Allies and Morrison Urban Practitioners. She is a chartered member of the Royal Town Planning Institute and member of the Academy of Urbanism.

She has lived in Brixton and Dulwich for the last seventeen or so years. A member of the Labour Party for all her adult life, she was elected to Southwark Council in the College ward in 2010. She is chair of Dulwich Community Council, a trustee of the Turner Contemporary Gallery in Margate and a member of King's College Hospital NHS Foundation Trust. She lives in Sydenham Hill with her husband, Ben Jupp, and two daughters. He is a director at Social Finance and formerly worked in the Cabinet Office and Demos. ∎

Sue Hayman

LABOUR MP FOR WORKINGTON

FORMER MP	Sir Tony Cunningham, Labour, stood down
MAJORITY	4,686 (12.2%)
VOTE SHARE	42.3%
CHANGE	-3.2%
2ND PLACE	Con

@SueHayman1

BORN IN 1962, Sue Hayman has a degree in English Literature from Anglia Ruskin University. She was the constituency office manager for Tess Kingham, former MP for Gloucester, from 1997 until 2001. She is a qualified copywriter and has worked as account director and then head of public affairs for Cumbria-based Copper Consultancy. She was a self-employed communications consultant until her election.

An active member of the Labour Party for twenty years, she was elected to Cumbria County Council, representing Howgate, in 2013. She was vice-chair of the council's Children Scrutiny Committee. Between 2008 and 2011 she was a steering committee member of the Labour Finance and Industry Group. She stood as the Labour candidate in Preseli Pembrokeshire in 2005 and in Halesowen and Rowley Regis at the 2010 general election. She also stood in the European Parliament election in 2004. She is a former trustee of Asha Women's Centre. She lives with her husband, Ross, in Ullock, in between Workington and Cockermouth. He works for Copper Consultancy as regional director (north) and is a former head of UK media relations for National Grid. They have grown-up children. ∎

James Heappey

CONSERVATIVE MP FOR WELLS

FORMER MP	Tessa Munt, Liberal Democrat, defeated
MAJORITY	7,585 (13.3%)
VOTE SHARE	46.1%
CHANGE	+3.6%
2ND PLACE	Lib Dem

www.jamesheappey.org.uk   @JSHeappey

JAMES HEAPPEY WAS an army major until 2012 and has since worked in the House of Commons. He attended Queen Elizabeth's Hospital School in Bristol and graduated from the University of Birmingham in 2003, having studied Political Science. He joined the army and attended the Royal Military Academy, Sandhurst. He served as an officer in the Royal Gloucestershire, Berkshire and Wiltshire regiment and then The Rifles, the county regiment for Somerset, in Kabul in 2005, Northern Ireland in 2006, Basra in 2007 and Sangin in Helmand Province in 2009. He also served in Kenya, and in 2011 he was posted to the Ministry of Defence in London, where he worked as executive officer on the General Staff and was promoted to major in 2012. Leaving the army, he worked for ten months as a parliamentary assistant to North Somerset MP Dr Liam Fox. Since his selection in 2013, he worked as a self-employed consultant developing strategy and change management. He is chairman of the Highbridge Community Development Fund Grants Panel. He lives in Axbridge with his wife Kate and son. ▪

Peter Heaton-Jones

CONSERVATIVE MP FOR DEVON NORTH

FORMER MP	Sir Nick Harvey, Liberal Democrat, defeated
MAJORITY	6,936 (13.3%)
VOTE SHARE	42.7%
CHANGE	+6.7%
2ND PLACE	Lib Dem

www.peterheatonjones.org.uk   @PeterNorthDevon

BORN IN 1963, Peter Heaton-Jones began a broadcasting career after graduating from the University of London. Working first for commercial radio, he joined the BBC in 1986 and worked as a reporter, producer and news presenter for BBC Essex. He joined BBC Radio 5 Live when it opened in 1994 and was a presenter and editor. In 1997, he moved to Australia to join the Australian Broadcasting Corporation in Sydney, becoming head of marketing for several radio stations, but left after three years. He returned to the UK in 2000 and joined BBC Radio Swindon. He left full-time broadcasting in August 2006.

Joining the Conservative Party after leaving the BBC, he returned to Australia for a year and worked on a successful election campaign in New South Wales. He acted as agent and campaign director for the Conservative candidates in Swindon at the 2010 election. After the election he was appointed senior parliamentary assistant to the Swindon MPs Robert Buckland and Justin Tomlinson. He served as a councillor on Swindon Borough Council for the Abbey Meads ward between 2010 and 2014, appointed as chair of the Economic Scrutiny Committee. He has been a parish councillor and is a school governor. ∎

Drew Hendry

SCOTTISH NATIONAL PARTY (SNP) MP FOR INVERNESS,
NAIRN, BADENOCH & STRATHSPEY

FORMER MP	Danny Alexander, Liberal Democrat, defeated
MAJORITY	10,809 (18.8%)
VOTE SHARE	50.1%
CHANGE	+31.4%
2ND PLACE	Lib Dem

@drewhendrySNP

DREW (ANDREW) HENDRY was born in 1964 and lived and worked in Edinburgh as a retail manager and director with Swedish electrical firm Electrolux for twenty years. In 1999 he and his wife moved to Tore in the Black Isle. He founded a company, Teclan, in Inverness, which offers services for company websites.

He was first elected at the 2007 election for the Aird & Loch Ness ward on Highland Council. He was appointed leader of the SNP Highland Council group in 2011, replacing John Finnie, who had become a list MSP for the Highlands and Islands. In 2012 he took the second seat in the ward and, in the resulting coalition formed to run the council, he was appointed leader. He is a former board member of Cairngorm National Park Authority and Highland Opportunities Limited, and was a director of Inverness City Heritage Trust. He stood as a candidate in the 2009 European election. He is married to Jackie and they have four children. ∎

Simon Hoare

CONSERVATIVE MP FOR DORSET NORTH

FORMER MP	Bob Walter, Conservative, stood down
MAJORITY	21,118 (39.6%)
VOTE SHARE	56.6%
CHANGE	+5.6%
2ND PLACE	UKIP

BORN IN 1969, Simon Hoare studied Modern History at Oxford University. On graduating, he worked at Conservative HQ before becoming personal assistant to the leader of Kingston upon Thames Council. He then began a career in public relations, starting with Charles Barker in the 1990s. He was head of property and planning at Ketchum, an account director at PPS, and external affairs director at the Environmental Services Association. He set up his own agency, Community Connect, before integrating with Four Politics, the public affairs arm of Four Communications.

He stood in Cardiff South & Penarth at the 2010 general election and Cardiff West in 1997. He is an Oxfordshire county councillor for Witney West & Bampton, serving as cabinet member for Resources, and a West Oxfordshire district councillor for Hailey, Minster Lovell & Leafield since 2004. He is a former political officer of the Tory think tank the Bow Group, and is a member of the Tory Reform Group. He is a governor of South Central Ambulance Trust. He is married to Kate and has three young daughters. ∎

Kate Hollern

LABOUR MP FOR BLACKBURN

FORMER MP	Jack Straw, Labour, stood down
MAJORITY	12,760 (29.0%)
VOTE SHARE	56.3%
CHANGE	+8.5%
2ND PLACE	Con

http://kateforblackburn.org.uk @CllrKate

BORN IN DUMBARTON, Scotland, in 1955, Kate Hollern moved to Blackburn with her family in 1977. Having not attended university, she was employed as a manager at Newman's shoe factory before becoming contracts manager at Blackburn College.

She was first elected to Blackburn with Darwen Council in 1995. In a local government career spanning eighteen years, she led the Labour group from 2004 and was leader of the council from 2004 until 2007, regaining control in 2010. She was chair of the North West Assembly from 2007 to 2008 and is presently chair of the Lancashire Police and Crime Panel. She is a member of the LGA Innovation Board and the CLG's Special Integration Group. She has served on numerous local bodies and associations. She was selected from an all-women shortlist. She is divorced, lives in Darwen with her partner and has two daughters. ∎

Kevin Hollinrake

CONSERVATIVE MP FOR THIRSK & MALTON

FORMER MP	Anne McIntosh, Conservative, de-selected
MAJORITY	19,456 (37.2%)
VOTE SHARE	52.6%
CHANGE	-0.3%
2ND PLACE	Lab

@kevinhollinrake

BORN IN 1963, Kevin Hollinrake attended a local comprehensive, Easingwold School, in North Yorkshire before embarking upon a Physics degree at Sheffield Polytechnic in 1981. He abandoned the degree halfway through and instead began selling army surplus clothes on street markets. He says that he started several businesses in his early twenties before applying for a job as a trainee valuer for an estate agent in York. He was an area manager for Prudential Property Services, first for Haxby, then Burnley, Todmorden and Hebden Bridge between 1987 and 1991, when he was made redundant. In 1992 he co-founded Hunters Estate Agents, which has gone on to become one of the most successful estate agents in the north of England, with over 100 branches across the UK. He is also chairman of Shoptility.com, a shopping search engine, and a co-founder of Vizzi-home, providing market intelligence for the property sector. He held his first directorship at the age of twenty-nine at Movie World (York) Limited and has held at least fourteen directorships subsequently. He is married to Nikky and the couple have four children. ∎

Ben Howlett

CONSERVATIVE MP FOR BATH

FORMER MP	David Wright, Labour, defeated
MAJORITY	3,833 (8.1%)
VOTE SHARE	37.8%
CHANGE	+6.4%
2ND PLACE	Lib Dem

www.ben4bath.co.uk   @ben4bath

BEN HOWLETT ATTENDED Manningtree High School and studied History and Politics at Durham University, where he was president of the student union, before completing a Master's in Economic History at Sidney Sussex College, Cambridge, in 2008. He joined Venn Group as a recruitment consultant but left less than two years later, and in November 2010 he set up Finegreen Associates, a recruitment consultancy with a particular focus on health sector executive appointments. The firm is owned by Accountants in Demand Limited. Between 2007 and 2010 he also worked part time as stakeholder manager for Syed Kamall MEP.

While still studying, he served as a local councillor in north-east Essex on Tendring District Council between 2005 and 2007. He was the elected national chairman of Conservative Future from 2010 to 2013. He is a member of LGBTory, the group for lesbian, gay, bisexual and trans Conservatives. ■

Nigel Huddleston

CONSERVATIVE MP FOR WORCESTERSHIRE MID

FORMER MP	Sir Peter Luff, Conservative, stood down
MAJORITY	20,532 (39.3%)
VOTE SHARE	57.0%
CHANGE	+2.5%
2ND PLACE	UKIP

www.nigelhuddleston.com   @HuddlestonNigel

NIGEL HUDDLESTON WAS born and raised in Lincolnshire and attended the Robert Pattinson Comprehensive School in North Hykeham before going on to study Philosophy, Politics and Economics at Oxford University, graduating in 1992. With both parents from a solidly working-class background, he was the first person in his family to go to university and the first person from his school to go to Oxford. After Oxford, he joined Arthur Andersen as a management consultant before studying for a Master's in Entertainment Management at the Anderson School of Management at the University of California, Los Angeles (UCLA). He joined Deloitte in 2002 and rose to become a director, working primarily with the entertainment and travel and tourism industries both in the US and the UK. In 2011 he joined Google as industry head of travel.

He stood as the Conservative candidate in Luton South at the 2010 general election. He is a board member of the Tory Reform Group. He is currently the councillor for Wheathampstead on St Albans City and District Council. He now lives in Worcestershire with his American wife Melissa, a Bedfordshire University exam marker, whom he met at UCLA. They have two young children. ▪

Dr Rupa Huq

LABOUR MP FOR EALING CENTRAL & ACTON

FORMER MP	Angie Bray, Conservative, defeated
MAJORITY	274 (0.5%)
VOTE SHARE	43.2%
CHANGE	+13.1%
2ND PLACE	Con

http://rupa4ealingactonlabour.wordpress.com   @RupaHuq

RUPA HUQ WAS born in 1972 and grew up in Ealing, attending Notting Hill & Ealing High School. Her Bangladeshi parents came to Britain in the 1960s and ran an Indian restaurant in Soho. She graduated from Cambridge University in Political and Social Sciences and Law. In 1999, she completed a PhD in Cultural Studies at the University of East London, which included study at Strasbourg II University. During this time she also worked at the European Parliament for a Labour MEP. From 1998 to 2004 she lectured at the University of Manchester, and since 2004 has been a senior lecturer in Sociology and Criminology at Kingston University, specialising in youth culture and pop music.

She published her first book, *Beyond Subculture*, in 2006.

She has worked as a researcher for Tony Banks and Patricia Hewitt. In 2004 she stood as a Labour candidate in the North West at the European Parliament election. At the 2005 general election she stood in the safe Conservative seat of Chesham & Amersham. She was the Deputy Mayoress of Ealing between 2010 and 2011. Her younger sister is the former *Blue Peter* presenter Konnie Huq. She is also a DJ under the stage name Dr Huq. She has a young son. ▪

Imran Hussain

LABOUR MP FOR BRADFORD EAST

FORMER MP	David Ward, Liberal Democrat, defeated
MAJORITY	7,084 (17.1%)
VOTE SHARE	46.6%
CHANGE	+13.8%
2ND PLACE	Lib Dem

IMRAN HUSSAIN WAS born in Bradford and went to school locally. His family is from Mirpur in Pakistan. He qualified as a barrister at Lincoln's Inn, London, and from 2003 worked mainly as a criminal defence lawyer, for Altaf Solicitors.

He joined the Labour Party at seventeen and has been a Bradford city councillor, representing the Toller ward, since 2002. He is deputy leader of the council and holds the Safer and Stronger Communities portfolio. He is a member of West Yorkshire Police and Crime Panel and West Yorkshire Combined Authority. He is a former primary school governor. Chair of the Bradford West constituency party for the last ten years, he unsuccessfully fought George Galloway at the by-election in 2012. He is a member of Unite, Unison, GMB and the Co-operative Party. ∎

Ranil Jayawardena

CONSERVATIVE MP FOR HAMPSHIRE NORTH EAST

FORMER MP	James Arbuthnot, Conservative, stood down
MAJORITY	29,916 (55.4%)
VOTE SHARE	65.9%
CHANGE	+5.3%
2ND PLACE	Lib Dem

www.tellranil.com   @TellRanil

RANIL JAYAWARDENA IS the son of a Sri Lankan father who migrated to Britain in the 1970s. He was educated at Robert May's School in Odiham and then Alton College, before studying Government at the London School of Economics and Political Science. His career has been in financial services, and since 2010 he worked for Lloyds Banking Group, latterly as a senior manager. His role included advocacy with MPs and MEPs on banking regulation.

He has served as a councillor on Basingstoke & Deane Borough Council since 2008, representing Bramley & Sherfield. He was the deputy leader of the council from 2012 and served as the cabinet member for Finance and Property from 2011 until 2012. He was selected in an open primary contest. He is married and had a child just before the general election. ∎

Andrea Jenkyns

CONSERVATIVE MP FOR MORLEY & OUTWOOD

FORMER MP	Ed Balls, Labour, defeated
MAJORITY	422 (0.9%)
VOTE SHARE	38.9%
CHANGE	+3.6%
2ND PLACE	Lab

www.andreajenkyns.co.uk @andreajenkyns

ANDREA JENKYNS WAS born and bred in Yorkshire, the daughter of a former Hull lorry driver turned transport businessman. Educated in Holderness, she left school with a BTEC in business finance and went straight into the retail sector, working her way up from retail assistant to area manager of forty branches. She was also international business development manager for an executive management training company with clients in Europe and Asia. She is a semi-professional singer (soprano) and has owned her own record label and recording studio, and been a music tutor teaching in three secondary schools, and a musical director at two performing arts academies. In her mid-thirties she decided to re-train, and studied for a diploma in Economics through the Open University and a degree in International Relations and Politics from the University of Lincoln at the age of forty.

She was elected in 2009, by sixteen votes, to Lincolnshire County Council, having been called in as a last-minute replacement two weeks before the nominations closed. She held the seat until 2013, serving as the executive support councillor for Community Safety. She has been a trustee and East Midlands representative for MRSA Action UK since 2012. The charity's goals are particularly personal to her, as her father died from the hospital superbug MRSA in 2011. ∎

Boris Johnson

CONSERVATIVE MP FOR UXBRIDGE & RUISLIP SOUTH

FORMER MP	Sir John Randall, Conservative, stood down
MAJORITY	10,695 (23.9%)
VOTE SHARE	50.2%
CHANGE	+2.0%
2ND PLACE	Lab

www.boris-johnson.com @MayorofLondon

ALEXANDER BORIS DE Pfeffel Johnson, or simply 'Boris', was born in New York City in 1964, a distant relative of King George II and David Cameron, and the son of a former Conservative MEP. He was educated at the European School of Brussels, Ashdown House School, Eton College and Balliol College, Oxford, where he read Classics. He was elected president of the Oxford Union on his second attempt. As a trainee journalist, he worked for *The Times* until being sacked and then the *Daily Telegraph*, becoming assistant editor in 1994. He was the editor of *The Spectator* between 1999 and 2005. He was selected as the Conservative candidate for Clwyd South in 1997 and was elected as the Conservative MP for Henley in 2001, succeeding Michael Heseltine. He served as a shadow Culture Minister and then in Higher Education. He was elected as the Mayor of London in 2008, having defeated incumbent Ken Livingstone, and resigned his seat in Parliament. Mayor during the hosting of the highly successful 2012 London Olympics, he was re-elected in 2012, again defeating Livingstone. In August 2014 he announced his intention to stand again as an MP. He is an author and historian. He is married to his second wife, Marina Wheeler, a barrister, and they have two daughters and two sons. ∎

Gerald Jones

LABOUR MP FOR MERTHYR TYDFIL & RHYMNEY

FORMER MP	Dai Havard, Labour, stood down
MAJORITY	11,513 (35.2%)
VOTE SHARE	53.9%
CHANGE	+10.2%
2ND PLACE	UKIP

@gerald_jones3

BORN IN 1970, Gerald Jones was the deputy leader of Caerphilly County Borough Council from 2012 and cabinet member for Housing. Elected to represent the ward of New Tredegar in 2003, he worked as the chief development officer for the Gwent Association of Voluntary Organisations (GAVO). He was a volunteer director of the charity White Rose Resource Centre, a trustee of Phillipstown Residents & Community Association and secretary of New Tredegar Communities Partnership. He is a member of the Association of Public Services Excellence, the Consortium of Local Authorities Wales (CLAW), the Joint Council for Wales, the Local Government Association and the Welsh Local Government Association. Politically, he is a member of the GMB union and the Co-operative Party. ∎

Seema Kennedy

CONSERVATIVE MP FOR SOUTH RIBBLE

FORMER MP	Lorraine Fullbrook, Conservative, stood down
MAJORITY	5,945 (11.4%)
VOTE SHARE	46.4%
CHANGE	+1.0%
2ND PLACE	Lab

www.seemakennedy.co.uk   @SeemaKennedy

SEEMA KENNEDY WAS born in Blackburn in 1974, the daughter of an Iranian father who came to the UK in the 1960s and an Irish Catholic mother from Lancashire. At six weeks old, she went to live in Iran, but the family was forced to flee because of the Islamic Revolution. Returning to the UK, she spent her childhood in the Ribble Valley, attending Westholme School in Blackburn. At Cambridge University she gained a First in Oriental Studies, French and Persian and then attended the College of Law in London. She joined City law firm Slaughter and May as a trainee solicitor in 2000 and moved to Bevan Brittan in 2003, specialising in commercial property at both. She joined the family business, Tustin Developments, as a director in 2006, advising on the company's property portfolio in the north-west.

She stood in Ashton-under-Lyne in 2010 and was elected in 2014 as a St Albans district councillor for the ward of Marshalswick South. She is a trustee of St Giles Trust for Children, a founder of the Hertfordshire End Loneliness Project and a member of Conservative Women's Organisation's Forums Steering Group. She is married to Paul and they have three young boys. ▪

George Kerevan

SCOTTISH NATIONAL PARTY (SNP) MP FOR EAST LOTHIAN

FORMER MP	Fiona O'Donnell, Labour, defeated
MAJORITY	6,803 (11.5%)
VOTE SHARE	42.5%
CHANGE	+26.5%
2ND PLACE	Lab

@GeorgeKerevan

GEORGE KEREVAN WAS born in Glasgow in 1949. He was educated at Kingsridge Secondary School in Drumchapel and the University of Glasgow, graduating with a First in Political Economy. From 1975 until 2000 he was an economics lecturer at Napier College (Napier University from 1992), specialising in energy economics. He was associate editor of *The Scotsman* from 2000 to 2009 and was chief executive and producer at What If Productions (Television) Ltd, producing documentaries. He continues to write a weekly column for *The Scotsman*.

In his youth he was in the International Marxist Group, before serving three terms as a Labour councillor on Edinburgh City Council between 1984 and 1996. He is a former chair of the Edinburgh Tourist Board and served on the Scottish Enterprise local board for Edinburgh and the Edinburgh Festival council. He founded the Edinburgh Science Festival and is a co-organiser of the Prestwick World Festival of Flight. He joined the Scottish National Party in 1996 and stood for election in Edinburgh East at the 2010 general election. He is married to Angela Wrapson, an international arts consultant. ▪

Calum Kerr

SCOTTISH NATIONAL PARTY (SNP) MP FOR
BERWICKSHIRE, ROXBURGH & SELKIRK

FORMER MP	Michael Moore, Liberal Democrat, defeated
MAJORITY	328 (0.6%)
VOTE SHARE	36.6%
CHANGE	+2.2%
2ND PLACE	Con

www.calumkerr.scot @calumrkerr

BORN AND RAISED in Gala and the Scottish borders, Calum Kerr was educated at Peebles High School, where his father was head teacher. He graduated from St Andrews University in 1994 with a History degree. He has spent his career working in telecommunications for several companies. He began work as an account manager for Philips Business Communications in 1995, moving to Nortel Networks in 1998. In 2009 he joined telecoms company Avaya, becoming a practice consultant in 2012 and practice leader in 2014. He is also a director of Advice Direct Scotland, a charity that provides debt, employment and consumer advice.

He is secretary of the Midlothian South, Tweeddale & Lauderdale SNP constituency association and was chair of Yes Scottish Borders and Yes Tweeddale. He lives in Cardrona with his wife, who works for the NHS, and their three children. ∎

Danny Kinahan MLA

ULSTER UNIONIST PARTY (UUP) MP FOR ANTRIM SOUTH

FORMER MP	Dr William McCrea, Democratic Unionist Party (DUP), defeated
MAJORITY	949 (2.6%)
VOTE SHARE	32.7%
CHANGE	+2.3%
2ND PLACE	DUP

@DdeBK

IN ONE OF the big surprises of the election, Danny Kinahan defeated the veteran Dr William McCrea. Kinahan was born in Belfast in 1958 and educated at Stowe School and the University of Edinburgh, studying Commerce and Finance. Having joined the British Army in 1977 while studying, he served for nearly eight years as a captain in the Blues and Royals (Royal Horse Guards), seeing service in Cyprus, the Falklands and Northern Ireland. He then was a PR manager for Short Brothers and spent fifteen years as Christie's Northern Ireland representative. Since 2003 he has been a partner in Castle Upton Gallery and worked as an art dealer. He remains an honorary colonel in the North Irish Horse.

A member of the Ulster Unionist Party since 1998, he was a member of Antrim Borough Council from 2005 until 2010. He stood unsuccessfully for the UUP in South Antrim in the Assembly election of 2007, but replaced David Burnside as the MLA in 2009 when Burnside stepped down from the Assembly. He was re-elected in 2011 and was appointed chair of the Audit Committee and deputy chair of the Education Committee. He also sits on the Enterprise, Trade and Investment Committee. ∎

Stephen Kinnock

LABOUR MP FOR ABERAVON

FORMER MP	Hywel Francis, Labour, stood down
MAJORITY	10,445 (33.1%)
VOTE SHARE	48.9%
CHANGE	-3.0%
2ND PLACE	UKIP

www.stephenkinnock.co.uk   @Skinnock

STEPHEN KINNOCK WAS born in Tredegar in 1970, the son of Neil Kinnock, former leader of the Labour Party, and Glenys Kinnock, former Labour MEP and Europe Minister. After attending Drayton Manor High School, he won a degree in Modern Languages from Queens' College, Cambridge, and an MA from the College of Europe in Bruges in 1993, having won a scholarship. He speaks five languages fluently. He worked as a research assistant at the European Parliament in Brussels before becoming a British Council Development and Training Services executive, based in Brussels, in 1997. He was promoted to become British Council's Brussels director in 2002

and subsequently worked in St Petersburg and Sierra Leone with the organisation. He joined the World Economic Forum in 2009 as director, head of Europe and Central Asia, based in Geneva. In 2012 he was appointed managing director of advisory firm Xynteo.

Since 1996, he has been married to Danish Prime Minister Helle Thorning-Schmidt, whom he met when they were both studying at the College of Europe in Bruges. They have two daughters. He is the leading member of the group of aspiring Labour political offspring that the press has dubbed the 'Red Princes'. ■

Julian Knight

CONSERVATIVE MP FOR SOLIHULL

FORMER MP	Lorely Burt, Liberal Democrat, defeated
MAJORITY	12,902 (23.6%)
VOTE SHARE	49.2%
CHANGE	+6.7%
2ND PLACE	Lib Dem

www.julianknight.org.uk @ukmoneyguru (work) @julianknight15 (political)

BORN IN 1972 on a council estate near Chester, Julian Knight had a tough upbringing, with his father leaving the family home when he was ten. He attended Chester Catholic High School and became the first member of his family to go to university, studying History at the University of Hull. He succeeded in entering journalism, worked for *Moneywise* at Reader's Digest and joined the BBC in 2002, becoming personal finance and consumer affairs correspondent. He has been the money and property editor at *The Independent* since 2007. He has published seven books in the 'Dummies' series, including *British Politics for Dummies*, *Cricket for Dummies* and *The Euro Crisis for Dummies*.

He is a cricket enthusiast, a former youth coach and captain, and has been a club cricketer for over twenty years. He lives in Olton, Solihull, and is recently married to Philippa, a former nurse who works for a children's charity. ▪

Dr Peter Kyle

LABOUR MP FOR HOVE

FORMER MP	Mike Weatherley, Conservative, stood down
MAJORITY	1,236 (2.4%)
VOTE SHARE	42.3%
CHANGE	+9.3%
2ND PLACE	Con

www.facebook.com/hoveandportslade   @peterkyle

BORN IN 1970 in West Sussex, Peter Kyle grew up in Bognor Regis, attending the local comprehensive school. He spent five years working for Children on the Edge, a charity set up by Body Shop founder Anita Roddick, becoming an aid worker in Eastern Europe and the Balkans during the Bosnian conflict. He later became a trustee of the charity. Moving to Brighton in 1996, he became the first member of his family to go to university, studying a degree in Geography with Development and Environmental Studies at Sussex University. His doctorate on Community Economic Development followed, conducting his research in South Africa.

While doing his PhD he co-founded a video production company called Fat Sand Productions and remains a non-executive director. In 2006 he worked as a special adviser to Hilary Armstrong as Minister for the Cabinet Office, primarily working on social exclusion policy. He joined ACEVO, the membership body for charities and social enterprises, as deputy CEO in 2007, and in 2013 became CEO of Working for Youth. He is an unpaid non-executive director of Charities Aid Foundation (CAF) Bank, is a governor for two community colleges and was a trustee of Pride for three years. He stood unsuccessfully in Brighton Kemptown in 2010. ∎

Chris Law

SCOTTISH NATIONAL PARTY (SNP) MP FOR DUNDEE WEST

FORMER MP	Jim McGovern, Labour, defeated
MAJORITY	17,092 (38.2%)
VOTE SHARE	61.9%
CHANGE	+33.0%
2ND PLACE	Lab

http://chrislaw.scot   @ChrisLawSNP

BORN IN DUNDEE in 1969, Chris Law trained as a French chef in his youth before going to college and then to St Andrews University, graduating with a first-class degree in Cultural and Social Anthropology. He spent part of his degree studying in India at Madras College, when he started his first business, running expeditions to the world's highest roads in the Himalayas on 1950s motorcycles. For the past eleven years he has been running his own business, CMAL Limited, as a financial adviser. He is also an occasional social documentary filmmaker. He is an SNP political engagement officer and treasurer. During the 2014 referendum campaign he was the founder of the 'Spirit of Independence' road tour of communities in a refurbished 1950s Green Goddess fire engine. He has lived in Glasgow's West End for thirty years. ∎

Clive Lewis

LABOUR MP FOR NORWICH SOUTH

FORMER MP	Simon Wright, Liberal Democrat, defeated
MAJORITY	20,493 (35.9%)
VOTE SHARE	54.3%
CHANGE	+4.9%
2ND PLACE	Con

www.facebook.com/labourclivelewis   @labourlewis

BORN IN LONDON, Clive Lewis is the son of a Grenadian father and an English mother. Brought up in Northampton from the age of three, he attended local comprehensives and read Economics at the University of Bradford, the first graduate of his family. Having been elected president of his student union at Bradford, he became vice-president for education for the National Union of Students. He studied a post-graduate diploma in Newspaper Journalism and worked on local newspapers for eighteen months. He won a place on the BBC News trainee scheme and has worked for the past twelve years as a regional BBC reporter, first as a reporter for BBC *Look East* news, and in 2007 as

the eastern region's chief political reporter. Following his selection as a candidate in 2011, he continued working for the BBC in a non-editorial role.

He joined the Army Reserves in 2003, attended the Military Academy at Sandhurst in 2006, becoming a lieutenant in the 7 Rifles, and completed a combat tour of Afghanistan in 2009. He has been actively involved with the Future Trust charity and is a local secondary school associate governor. He is a Unite-sponsored candidate. He has lived in Norwich since 2001. ∎

Rebecca Long-Bailey

LABOUR MP FOR SALFORD & ECCLES

FORMER MP	Hazel Blears, Labour, stood down
MAJORITY	12,541 (29.0%)
VOTE SHARE	49.4%
CHANGE	+9.3%
2ND PLACE	Con

www.rebeccalongbailey.com @RLong_Bailey

REBECCA LONG-BAILEY WAS born in Old Trafford to Irish parents, her father working as a Salford docker for Shell and acting as a trade union representative. She attended Catholic High School in Chester and started working at sixteen. As well as shops, call centres and a furniture factory, she worked in a pawnshop for many years in the 1990s. While working, she studied Politics and Sociology at Manchester Metropolitan University as a mature student. She then worked full time in an administrative role while studying for her Law degree. Having qualified, she joined Halliwells solicitors in 2003. From 2006 she was a solicitor with Hill Dickinson, specialising in health care, NHS contracts and commercial property.

Sponsored by Unite, she came through an acrimonious selection process for the Salford & Eccles candidacy that saw resignations and threats of legal action. She previously sought the Labour candidacy in Weaver Vale. She is married to Stephen and they have one son. ▪

Holly Lynch

LABOUR MP FOR HALIFAX

FORMER MP	Linda Riordan, Labour, stood down
MAJORITY	428 (1.0%)
VOTE SHARE	40.0%
CHANGE	+2.6%
2ND PLACE	Con

@HollyLynch5

HOLLY LYNCH, AGED twenty-eight, was born and raised in Northowram, the daughter of a police officer and a nurse. She went to school at Northowram Primary and Brighouse High, and gained a degree from Lancaster University in History and Politics. She worked in export sales and marketing for Matrix Technology Solutions, an SME technology company headquartered in Halifax. She has taken CIM Professional Certificate in Marketing at Leeds Metropolitan University. She works as a communications officer for Linda McAvan MEP, who represents Yorkshire and the Humber. She was one of the last Labour candidates to be selected. She married in December 2014. ∎

Craig Mackinlay

CONSERVATIVE MP FOR SOUTH THANET

FORMER MP	Laura Sandys, Conservative, stood down
MAJORITY	2,812 (5.7%)
VOTE SHARE	38.1%
CHANGE	-9.9%
2ND PLACE	UKIP

www.craigmackinlay.com   @cmackinlay

CRAIG MACKINLAY SUCCESSFULLY fought off the strong challenge from his former UKIP colleague Nigel Farage. He was born in Chatham and raised in Kent. He went to school at Rainham Mark Grammar School and studied Zoology and Comparative Physiology at the University of Birmingham. He trained as a chartered accountant and tax adviser and is a partner in a Chatham firm, Beak Kemmenoe Chartered Accountants. He has also been involved in the family's wholesale food business.

His political life began in the Anti-Federalist League, before joining UKIP and then the Conservatives. He stood for Gillingham in 1992 for the Anti-Federalist League, and then for Gillingham in 1997 and 2005 and for Totnes in 2001 for UKIP. He also stood as a UKIP candidate at the 1994, 1999 and 2004 European elections. He was temporary leader of UKIP in 1997 and has been deputy leader, vice-chairman and treasurer. He resigned from UKIP in 2005, joined the Conservatives and was elected as a councillor on Medway Council, and re-elected in 2011, representing the River ward. He stood as the Conservative candidate for the Kent Police and Crime Commissioner elections in 2012. He has served as a magistrate and is a trustee of four local charities. His wife, Kati, works as a locum pharmacist. ∎

David Mackintosh

CONSERVATIVE MP FOR NORTHAMPTON SOUTH

FORMER MP	Brian Binley, Conservative, stood down
MAJORITY	3,793 (9.8%)
VOTE SHARE	41.6%
CHANGE	+0.7%
2ND PLACE	Lab

www.davidmackintosh.org.uk   @davidmackintosh

DAVID MACKINTOSH WAS born in Northampton and grew up in the country, attending Roade School before studying at Durham University between 1997 and 2001. He worked as a political counsellor in the European Parliament until 2004 and has continued to work as a consultant to the Conservative Party. He was elected to Northamptonshire County Council for Billing & Rectory Farm in 2009 and Northampton Borough Council for Rectory Farm in 2011. He was the leader of Northampton Borough Council until his election and also served as cabinet member for Community Services. He represents the council on the board of the Royal and Derngate Theatres, Northamptonshire Enterprise Partnership and the South East Midlands Local Enterprise Partnership. He is a patron of the Hope Centre homeless charity in Northampton and of the Caring and Sharing Trust, a school governor at a local primary school and the chairman of the KidsAid Foundation. He was selected at an open primary in December 2013. ∎

Justin Madders

LABOUR MP FOR ELLESMERE PORT & NESTON

FORMER MP	Andrew Miller, Labour, stood down
MAJORITY	6,275 (13.4%)
VOTE SHARE	47.8%
CHANGE	+3.1%
2ND PLACE	Con

www.justinmadders.com   @justinmadders

BORN IN 1972, Justin Madders grew up in the constituency and was the first member of his family to go to university. He gained a Law degree from the University of Sheffield in 1994. He was a trainee with Mace & Jones in Knutsford, qualifying in 1998, and has since worked with the Paul Rooney Partnership in Liverpool, Whittles Solicitors in Manchester, Thompsons Solicitors and Walker Smith Way in Chester since 2011. He works primarily in employment law, representing only employees and trade union members, and has represented a number of sportsmen.

He was elected to Ellesmere Port & Neston Council in 1998 and served until 2009, including as leader for the past two years. He was elected to Cheshire West & Chester Council in 2008 and was the leader of the Labour group from 2011 until 2014. As a councillor, he was appointed to Ellesmere Port Development Board, Ince Marshes Recovery Park Forum and the West Cheshire Strategy Board. He also sat on the management board of Merseyside Employment Law. He stood against George Osborne in Tatton at the 2005 general election. He lives in Little Sutton with his wife, Nicole Meardon, a fellow Cheshire West & Chester councillor and teacher. The couple have three children. ▪

Alan Mak

CONSERVATIVE MP FOR HAVANT

FORMER MP	David Willetts, Conservative, stood down
MAJORITY	13,920 (31.1%)
VOTE SHARE	51.7%
CHANGE	+0.6%
2ND PLACE	UKIP

www.alanmak.org.uk   @AlanMak4MP @AlanMakUK

ALAN MAK IS the first Chinese member of the House of Commons. He was born in 1983 just outside York. Both his parents came to the UK in the 1960s from Guangdong in southern China. When his state secondary school was closed down, he applied successfully for a scholarship to the independent St Peter's School in York. He read Law at Peterhouse, Cambridge, and completed a post-graduate Law and Business diploma at the Oxford Institute of Legal Practice. He spent a year as a researcher and speech-writer to Ed Vaizey MP, before joining City law firm Clifford Chance as a trainee solicitor, qualifying in 2009. He has also worked as a research associate at the Adam Smith Institute. He has been a non-executive director of the Havas UK Group, an advertising and communications company, since 2012.

A Conservative member since seventeen, he has served on the Globalisation and Global Poverty Policy Group and has been executive officer of the Conservative Rural Affairs Group. He has been a member of the TheCityUK China–Britain Business Council's China Advisory Committee, a Young Global Shaper at the World Economic Forum and a co-founder of the 48 Group Young Icebreakers. He is also a trustee of school charity Magic Breakfast and a primary school governor. ∎

Kit Malthouse AM

CONSERVATIVE MP FOR HAMPSHIRE NORTH WEST

FORMER MP	Sir George Young, Conservative, stood down
MAJORITY	23,943 (43.4%)
VOTE SHARE	58.1%
CHANGE	-0.2%
2ND PLACE	UKIP

http://kitmalthouse.com   @kitmalthouse

CHRISTOPHER 'KIT' MALTHOUSE was born in 1966 in Liverpool. Educated at Liverpool College, he studied Politics and Economics at the University of Newcastle. He trained as a chartered accountant at Touche Ross & Company (now Deloitte), qualifying in 2004. He worked as finance director of the Cannock Group, led the management buyout of the Country Finance part of the group, and remains chairman. In 2006 he was a founder director of Alpha Strategies PLC, where he remains a director.

He was elected to Westminster City Council in 1998 and served as Conservative chief whip, deputy leader and cabinet member for Finance before he stood down from the council in May 2006. In 2008 he was elected as the Conservative member for the London Assembly seat of West Central. Two days later he was appointed Deputy Mayor for Policing by Boris Johnson. Re-elected in 2012, he was appointed London's first Deputy Mayor for Business and Enterprise. Following his selection in 2014, he stepped down as Deputy Mayor to focus on his constituency. He was formerly married to Tracy-Jane Newall, a barrister now married to Adam Afriyie, Conservative MP for Windsor. He is married to Juliana Farha, a Canadian-born journalist and businesswoman, and they have three children. ▪

Scott Mann

CONSERVATIVE MP FOR CORNWALL NORTH

FORMER MP	Dan Rogerson, Liberal Democrat, defeated
MAJORITY	6,621 (13.7%)
VOTE SHARE	45.0%
CHANGE	+3.3%
2ND PLACE	Lib Dem

@CllrScottMann

SCOTT MANN WAS born in Wadebridge in the constituency and spent all his childhood there, going to Wadebridge School, the local comprehensive. He has spent his whole working life in Cornwall, working as a postman since 1996, most recently only part time, combining work with his local government duties. He first represented Wadebridge on North Cornwall District Council, and since 2009 has been a Cornwall county councillor. He resigned as deputy leader of the Conservative group on the council in 2012 in protest over funding for a proposed sports stadium. A Conservative branch chairman, he was selected as the Conservative candidate for Cornwall North in January 2013.

He is married to Alice and they have one daughter. ■

Rob Marris

LABOUR MP FOR WOLVERHAMPTON SOUTH WEST

FORMER MP	Paul Uppal, Conservative, defeated
MAJORITY	801 (2.0%)
VOTE SHARE	43.2%
CHANGE	+4.2%
2ND PLACE	Con

www.robmarris.net

ANOTHER FORMER LABOUR MP returning to Parliament, Rob Marris lost the seat in 2010. Born in Wolverhampton in 1995, he is the son of a radiologist and a local magistrate. He attended Birchfield Preparatory and St Edward's School in Oxford. Moving to Canada, he worked briefly as a lumberjack before studying History and Sociology at the University of British Columbia in Vancouver, gaining a Double First. He returned to the UK after nine years and qualified as a solicitor, having trained with Thompsons, a legal practice specialising in union law and representation. He was elected in Wolverhampton South West in 2001. He served on the Work and Pensions and Trade and Industry Select Committees and served as a parliamentary private secretary to Shaun Woodward in the Northern Ireland Office from 2007 until 2010. He won the Backbencher of the Year award in 2008. After losing his seat, he announced plans to run a free legal advice surgery.

A committed environmentalist, it is claimed that he was the 204th member worldwide to join Greenpeace. He is honorary president of the Wolves on Wheels cycle campaign. ∎

Rachael Maskell

LABOUR MP FOR YORK CENTRAL

FORMER MP	Hugh Bayley, Labour, stood down
MAJORITY	6,716 (14.1%)
VOTE SHARE	42.4%
CHANGE	+2.4%
2ND PLACE	Con

www.rachaelmaskell.com   @RachaelMaskell

RACHAEL MASKELL WAS a senior physiotherapist in acute medicine in Norfolk and Norwich NHS Trust before becoming a full-time trade unionist. Having studied at the University of East Anglia, she became a trade union representative shortly after joining the NHS. In 1998 she became an organiser for the TUC, and joined Unite the following year as a regional officer. In 2003 she was made Unite's national officer for equalities, and a year later national officer for community, youth workers and the not-for-profit sector. She is currently head of health at Unite.

A Labour Party member for twenty-four years, she sits on the party's national executive committee. She was unable to secure a candidacy for a seat in 2010 but was shortlisted for Leicester West and Erith & Thamesmead. She is a former vice-chair of the Christian Socialist Movement. She lives in the Guildhall area of York. ▪

Chris Matheson

LABOUR MP FOR CITY OF CHESTER

FORMER MP	Stephen Mosley, Conservative, defeated
MAJORITY	93 (0.2%)
VOTE SHARE	43.2%
CHANGE	+8.2%
2ND PLACE	Con

http://chesterlabour.com/chris-matheson-for-mp   @Chris_Matheson

CHRISTIAN (CHRIS) MATHESON was born at Warrington General Hospital but grew up in rural Cheshire, before later studying Economics and Politics at the London School of Economics and Political Science. He previously worked as a manager in the electricity industry before joining the trade union movement full time. He used to work for Sir Ken Jackson, leader of the Amalgamated Engineering and Electrical Union (AEEU) before it merged with the TGWU to form Unite. He has held a number of posts including PA to the joint general secretaries in 2008, and head of executive administration and support. He is currently national (industrial) officer at Unite. He is a member of Labour's North West Regional Party Board. He lives in Hoole with his family, wife Katherine and their two daughters. He rents a flat to Middlesbrough's Labour MP Tom Blenkinsop, a former union official. ∎

Dr Tania Mathias

CONSERVATIVE MP FOR TWICKENHAM

FORMER MP	Dr Vince Cable, Liberal Democrat, defeated
MAJORITY	2,017 (3.3%)
VOTE SHARE	41.3%
CHANGE	+7.2%
2ND PLACE	Lib Dem

www.tania4twickenham.co.uk   @tania_mathias

DR TANIA MATHIAS provided another of the main shocks of the election, defeating her veteran Liberal Democrat opponent Dr Vince Cable, who had held the seat since 1997. She attended St Paul's Girls' School and studied Medicine at Oxford University. Soon after graduating, she worked as a refugee health officer for the United Nations Relief and Works Agency (UNRWA) in the Gaza Strip and Africa between 1991 and 1993. She has also worked in North Bihar, India and south China. She is an NHS medical doctor and independent psychotherapeutic practitioner. She is a member of the British Medical Association and British Association of Counselling and Psychotherapy.

She has been a Richmond Borough Councillor since 2010, representing Hampton Wick, and sits on the planning committee. She is a member of the Conservative Councillors' Association. She is a school governor for St John the Baptist Junior School. She was selected by constituents at an open primary. She lives on a residential island in the Thames, just upstream from Teddington Lock, and has lived in the constituency for fifteen years. ■

Callum McCaig

SCOTTISH NATIONAL PARTY (SNP) MP FOR
ABERDEEN SOUTH

FORMER MP	Anne Begg, Labour, defeated
MAJORITY	7,230 (14.9%)
VOTE SHARE	41.6%
CHANGE	+29.8%
2ND PLACE	Lab

@callum_mccaig

CALLUM MCCAIG WAS born in Edinburgh in 1985, but grew up in Aberdeen. He was educated at Cults Academy, graduated with a degree in Politics from Edinburgh University and then worked for SNP MSPs Maureen Watt and then Kevin Stewart as a parliamentary assistant.

He was first elected in 2007 to Aberdeen City Council in the ward of Kincorth, Nigg & Cove. In 2011 he took over as leader of the SNP group on the council. After two by-elections in that year, the SNP became the largest party on the council and this resulted in him becoming leader of the council. At the age of twenty-six, he was one of the youngest council leaders in the UK. He was re-elected in 2012 and remains the SNP group leader but is no longer council leader, the Scottish Labour Party having formed an administration with the support of the Conservatives and Independents. He was appointed to North East Scotland Transportation Partnership and Social Investment North East. He is a former director of Aberdeen Renewable Energy Group and Aberdeen Bid Company Limited. ∎

Stewart McDonald

SCOTTISH NATIONAL PARTY (SNP) MP FOR
GLASGOW SOUTH

FORMER MP	Tom Harris, Labour, defeated
MAJORITY	12,269 (25.2%)
VOTE SHARE	54.9%
CHANGE	+34.7%
2ND PLACE	Lab

@StewartMcDonald

STEWART MCDONALD WAS born in the constituency and has lived in the Southside all his life, apart from a spell as a tour guide in the Canary Islands. His political career started in 2009, when he began working for Anne McLauglin MSP on campaigns and research as a parliamentary researcher. Before his election he worked for Cathcart MSP James Dornan as a caseworker.

He joined the Scottish National Party in 2006 and was campaign manager for the Cathcart constituency in the 2011 Holyrood election. He stood unsuccessfully for the Linn ward in the 2012 elections to Glasgow City Council. He is the convenor of Out for Independence, the organisation of LGBT members of the SNP. ■

Stuart McDonald

SCOTTISH NATIONAL PARTY (SNP) MP FOR CUMBERNAULD,
KILSYTH & KIRKINTILLOCH EAST

FORMER MP	Gregg McClymont, Labour, defeated
MAJORITY	14,752 (29.9%)
VOTE SHARE	59.9%
CHANGE	+36.1%
2ND PLACE	Lab

@StuartMcD_SNP

STUART MCDONALD GREW up in Milton of Campsie in the constituency and still lives there. He attended Kilsyth Academy before studying Scots Law at Edinburgh University between 1996 and 2000, including an exchange year at Katholieke Universiteit Leuven in Antwerp. He undertook a diploma in Legal Practice at Edinburgh University. He was a trainee solicitor with Simpson & Marwick before working as a solicitor with NHS Scotland for two years and the Immigration Advisory Service for over four years. In 2009 he became a parliamentary researcher to Shirley-Anne Somerville MSP and Jim Eadie MSP in the Scottish Parliament. He was a senior researcher for Yes Scotland during the referendum campaign. Until his election he worked for a Glasgow-based anti-racism charity.

He joined the SNP at sixteen and has been active in the Cumbernauld & Kilsyth SNP Constituency Association for twenty years. He served the SNP as a campaign manager for the 2010 Westminster elections. He is a member of Unite the Union. ▪

Natalie McGarry

SCOTTISH NATIONAL PARTY (SNP) MP FOR GLASGOW EAST

FORMER MP	Margaret Curran, Labour, defeated
MAJORITY	10,387 (24.5%)
VOTE SHARE	56.9%
CHANGE	+32.1%
2ND PLACE	Lab

www.nataliemcgarry.com   @nataliemcgarry

NATALIE MCGARRY WAS born and raised in Inverkeithing, studied Law at Aberdeen University and works as a policy adviser for a voluntary sector organisation. She has previously worked in HR and as a community officer for unemployed parents. Her mother has been an SNP councillor in Fife since 1986 and her aunt is Tricia Marwick, the Presiding Officer (Speaker) of the Scottish Parliament.

She was one of the activists to set up Women for Independence in 2012. She fought in the 2014 European Parliament elections and was the SNP's candidate for the 2014 Cowdenbeath by-election, but lost to Labour's Alex Rowley. She has been convenor of the party's Glasgow region for several years. She is the partner of Glasgow Conservative councillor David Meikle. ▪

Conor McGinn

LABOUR MP FOR ST HELENS NORTH

FORMER MP	Dave Watts, Labour, stood down
MAJORITY	17,291 (37.4%)
VOTE SHARE	57.0%
CHANGE	+5.3%
2ND PLACE	Con

@ConorM

CONOR MCGINN WAS born in Bessbrook, County Armagh, in 1984, the son of a former Newry Sinn Féin councillor, Pat McGinn. He was educated at St Paul's High School in Bessbrook, before travelling to London at the age of eighteen to study History, Politics and Irish Studies at London Metropolitan University between 2003 and 2007. He has worked for a mental health charity and the Irish Council for Prisoners Overseas. He has also been a public relations and government affairs consultant. He worked as the political adviser to the shadow Secretary of State for Defence, Vernon Coaker MP, from 2013.

He was the chair of the Young Fabians between 2006 and 2007 and was vice-chair of Young Labour, a post he resigned from in protest at the party's campaign over the Human Fertilisation and Embryology Bill. He stood unsuccessfully as a council candidate in Islington in 2006 and 2010. He was the chair of the Labour Party Irish Society until 2012. He has represented the twenty-one affiliated socialist societies on the Labour Party national executive committee since 2011. He is married to Katie Groucutt, a former political adviser to Owen Smith MP, shadow Secretary of State for Wales, and Islington councillor. They have one son. ▪

Anne McLaughlin

SCOTTISH NATIONAL PARTY (SNP) MP FOR
GLASGOW NORTH EAST

FORMER MP	Willie Bain, Labour, defeated
MAJORITY	9,222 (24.4%)
VOTE SHARE	58.1%
CHANGE	+43.9%
2ND PLACE	Lab

www.indygalinspired.blogspot.co.uk   @AnneMcLaughlin

ANNE MCLAUGHLIN LIVED in Aldershot, Hampshire, as a child until 1975, when her parents moved to Greenock in Scotland. She attended Port Glasgow High School and gained a degree in Dramatic Studies at the Royal Scottish Academy of Music and Drama at the University of Glasgow. She has been a member of the SNP for over twenty years, first working as a researcher to MSP Bob Doris. She contested Glasgow Rutherglen in 2001 (Westminster), Glasgow Rutherglen in 2003 (Holyrood) and Glasgow Springburn in 2007 (Holyrood). She was the campaign co-ordinator for the successful Glasgow East by-election in 2008.

She automatically became a regional member for Glasgow in the Scottish Parliament in 2009, following the death of Bashir Ahmad, as the next person on the SNP's regional list. She was defeated in the Glasgow Provan constituency in 2011 and was unsuccessful later the same year in the Inverclyde UK Parliament by-election. Since 2012 she has run her own consultancy firm. She is a member of the SNP's NEC, is national political education convenor for the SNP and was the campaign co-ordinator for Yes Scotland in the Provan area. With her fiancé, who is Jamaican by birth, she has been the business development and events manager for the African Caribbean Network Glasgow. ▪

John McNally

SCOTTISH NATIONAL PARTY (SNP) MP FOR FALKIRK

FORMER MP	Eric Joyce, Labour/Independent, stood down
MAJORITY	19,701 (32.6%)
VOTE SHARE	57.7%
CHANGE	+27.5%
2ND PLACE	Lab

http://johnny4falkirk.scot

JOHN MCNALLY WAS born in Denny in 1951 as one of seven children. Educated at St Patrick's Primary and then at St Modan's High School, he left school at the age of fifteen to become an apprentice hairdresser/barber. He has continued as the owner of a barbershop in Stirling Street since the early 1970s. He became a councillor for the Herbertshire ward of Falkirk Council in a by-election in August 2005, taking the seat from Labour with a 26% swing. He has represented the Denny & Banknock ward since 2007. He was SNP spokesperson on housing until October 2014, and is now leading for the SNP on community, leisure and tourism. He stood in Falkirk at the 2010 general election, winning 30% of the vote. He beat four other candidates to secure the Falkirk nomination, including Tasmina Ahmed-Sheikh (elected in Ochil & South Perthshire). He lives in Stirling with his wife Sandra, a health visitor, and they have two adult children. ■

Johnny Mercer

CONSERVATIVE MP FOR PLYMOUTH MOOR VIEW

FORMER MP	Alison Seabeck, Liberal Democrat, defeated
MAJORITY	1,026 (2.4%)
VOTE SHARE	37.6%
CHANGE	+4.3%
2ND PLACE	Lab

http://johnnyforplymouth.com   @johnnymercer81

POLITICAL NEWCOMER JOHNNY Mercer was born in Kent into a family with a strong military tradition: he had three brothers in the Royal Navy. He left Eastbourne College School in 2000 and went briefly into work, first as an intern with Eurolife Assurance in the City of London. He then departed from the family path and joined the army, rather than the navy, graduating from Sandhurst in 2002. He was with Plymouth Citadel-based 29 Commando, serving three tours in Afghanistan, and was also stationed in Belize, Brunei, Canada and Germany, leaving in 2013 as a captain. He met his wife Felicity at school and they have two young girls. They live in the Tamar Valley. ∎

Huw Merriman

CONSERVATIVE MP FOR BEXHILL & BATTLE

FORMER MP	Greg Barker, Conservative, stood down
MAJORITY	20,075 (36.4%)
VOTE SHARE	54.8%
CHANGE	+3.2%
2ND PLACE	UKIP

www.huwmerriman.org.uk

HUW MERRIMAN WAS born in 1973 and brought up in Buckingham, the son of a teacher mother and a local council worker father. Failing the entrance exam for the local grammar school, he attended Buckingham County Secondary Modern School. Ignoring advice not to continue his studies, he attended Aylesbury College of Further Education and won a place at Durham University to read Law. After graduating, he qualified as a barrister and worked in a criminal practice for a short time in London. Having decided that the Bar was not for him, he moved to an in-house legal position. He spent seventeen years working as a banking and finance lawyer. His last position was as managing director and lawyer at Lehman Brothers in administration, managing the team of lawyers tasked with unwinding the Lehman Brothers estate in Europe.

He moved to East Sussex in 2006 and was elected to Wealden District Council for Rotherfield. He stood for Parliament in the seat of North East Derbyshire at the 2010 general election. He became the chairman of Wealden Conservative Association. He owns a farm at Five Ashes, near Heathfield. He is married to Victoria and they have three daughters. ∎

Amanda Milling

CONSERVATIVE MP FOR CANNOCK CHASE

FORMER MP	Aiden Burley, Conservative, stood down
MAJORITY	4,923 (10.5%)
VOTE SHARE	44.2%
CHANGE	+4.1%
2ND PLACE	Lab

www.amandamilling.com @amandamilling

AMANDA MILLING WAS born in Burton-upon-Trent and brought up in Staffordshire. Her father worked for local manufacturing business Britool and she lives in the village of Brereton, Rugeley, in the constituency. After graduating from University College London in 1997 with a degree in Economics and Statistics, she forged a career in market research, specialising in qualitative research in financial services and the public sector, advising banks and building societies. Starting as a research executive with SW1 Research in May 1997, she joined Quaestor in August 1999. In January 2010 she joined Optimisa Research Limited and is currently a director and head of clients, operating out of their office in Leeds.

Active in the Conservative Party since her teenage years in London as a student, she has served as a councillor on Rossendale Borough Council in Lancashire since 2009 (retiring in 2015), representing the Helmshore ward, including as deputy group leader of the Conservatives since 2012. She has been deputy chair political of Rossendale Conservative Association and has also been a member of Bury North Conservative Association. Amanda Milling is married to Mischa, a child and adolescent consultant. Away from work and politics, she is a keen horse rider, competing in dressage events on horses bred on the family farm, and a long-distance runner. She is a governor of Helmshore Primary School. ∎

Carol Monaghan

SCOTTISH NATIONAL PARTY (SNP) MP FOR
GLASGOW NORTH WEST

FORMER MP	John Robertson, Labour, defeated
MAJORITY	10,364 (23.6%)
VOTE SHARE	54.5%
CHANGE	+39.3%
2ND PLACE	Lab

http://carolmonaghan.scot   @Carol4GlaNW

BORN AND BROUGHT up in Whiteinch
in north-west Glasgow, Carol Monaghan
graduated from Strathclyde University
with a BSc Hons in Laser Physics and
Optoelectronics in 1993. Having trained as
a teacher, gaining a PGCE in Physics and
Mathematics, she has worked in a number of Glasgow schools, including fourteen
years at Hyndland Secondary as head of
physics and head of science. She has also
spent two years as a Glasgow University
lecturer training future teachers. An SQA
consultant, she has been involved in developing physics qualifications at a national
level. She is the mother of three school-
age children. ▪

Dr Paul Monaghan

SCOTTISH NATIONAL PARTY (SNP) MP FOR CAITHNESS,
SUTHERLAND & EASTER ROSS

FORMER MP	John Thurso, Liberal Democrat, stood down
MAJORITY	3,844 (11.2%)
VOTE SHARE	46.3%
CHANGE	+27.1%
2ND PLACE	Lib Dem

http://paulmonaghan.scot   @_PaulMonaghan

BORN IN MONTROSE in 1965 before moving to Inverness when he was two, Dr Paul Monaghan has lived in Contin for the past thirty years. Educated at Inverness Royal Academy and at the University of Stirling, gaining a first-class honours degree in Psychology and a PhD in Social Policy, he has had a variety of jobs. He was a director of Catalyst (Highlands) Ltd between 1995 and 1997 and then Highlander Web Magazine Ltd from 1997 until 2008. Since 1997 he has been the director of Highland Homeless Trust. He is also a director of Inverness MS Therapy Centre (since 2010); a founder and director of Food for Families, based in Invergordon; a founder of North Highland College Foundation, based in Thurso; and a member of the SSE Fairburn Windfarm Community Fund. He is a graduate member of the British Psychological Society and a Fellow of the Institute of Leadership and Management.

He joined the SNP in 1994 and stood unsuccessfully in the Highlands Council elections in 2012. He founded the Yes Highland campaign during the Scottish referendum campaign. He lives in Ross-shire with his wife Stephanie and their daughter. ▪

Wendy Morton

CONSERVATIVE MP FOR ALDRIDGE-BROWNHILLS

FORMER MP	Sir Richard Shepherd, Conservative, stood down
MAJORITY	11,723 (29.7%)
VOTE SHARE	52.0%
CHANGE	-7.3%
2ND PLACE	Lab

http://wendymorton.co.uk   @morton_wendy

WENDY MORTON WAS born in 1967 and grew up in the Yorkshire Dales, where her father was a farmer. She attended the Wensleydale School, later gaining an MBA with the Open University. Her first job was as an executive officer in HM Diplomatic Service in London, where she became fluent in German and was posted to Bonn. She also represented the FCO on the Export Licence Committee, which reviewed applications for the export of British works of art. Leaving for the private sector, she worked in sales and marketing for an Italian company before setting up an electronics and manufacturing business, DM Electronics, in 1992 with her husband, a chief petty officer, who had just left the

Royal Navy. She was also an area manager selling optical products for Centrosytle Ltd between 2003 and 2010.

She served as a Richmond Yorkshire district councillor between 2001 and 2006. She stood in the seat of Newcastle upon Tyne Central in 2005 and in Tynemouth in 2010, returning to the family business after the election. She was appointed a vice-chairman of the Conservative Party in 2013, with responsibility for social action, and is closely involved with the Conservative's Project Umubano in Rwanda. ▪

Professor Roger Mullin

SCOTTISH NATIONAL PARTY (SNP) MP FOR
KIRKCALDY & COWDENBEATH

FORMER MP	Gordon Brown, Labour, stood down
MAJORITY	9,974 (18.9%)
VOTE SHARE	52.2%
CHANGE	+37.9%
2ND PLACE	Lab

http://rogermullin.co.uk   @RogMull

WHEN ROGER MULLIN gained an HNC in electrical and electronic engineering from Kilmarnock College in 1969, a career as an academic must have appeared very unlikely; that he would in the future be the MP of former Labour stronghold Kirkcaldy & Cowdenbeath perhaps more so. Returning to education in 1973, studying for an MA in Sociology at the University of Edinburgh, led to him working part time at the university as a sociology and social statistics tutor. He subsequently worked at Stevenson College in Edinburgh, Glenrothes and West Lothian colleges. He was a part-time social sciences tutor for the Open University for twenty-two years. In 1985 he established Inter-ed, a social research company, and he was a director of Momentous Change Ltd, focused around the referendum. Since 2010 he has been an honorary politics professor at Stirling University, where he teaches. He is a former trustee of the Adam Smith Foundation and also freelances as an education consultant.

He has contested four previous general elections and a by-election (Paisley North in 1990). He was also the SNP candidate in Ayr at the Scottish Parliament election in 1999. He is a former vice-convenor of the SNP. He is married to Barbara and the couple have three daughters. ■

Gavin Newlands

SCOTTISH NATIONAL PARTY (SNP) MP FOR PAISLEY & RENFREWSHIRE NORTH

FORMER MP	Jim Sheridan, Labour, defeated
MAJORITY	9,076 (18.0%)
VOTE SHARE	50.7%
CHANGE	+31.7%
2ND PLACE	Lab

https://gavinnewlandssnp.wordpress.com   @GavNewlandsSNP

BORN IN PAISLEY in 1980, Gavin Newlands has lived in Renfrew since he was four years old. He attended Trinity High School, Renfrew, and, while attending James Watt College (now part of West College Scotland), he was offered the chance of promotion in his part-time job in a Glasgow Airport restaurant, which meant leaving further education behind. He has been a business manager for the restaurant chain for seventeen years.

He first joined the youth wing of the SNP in 1992 and became a Renfrew community councillor in 2011 and an associate member of Maryhill Community Council for eighteen months. He stood unsuccessfully for election to Renfrewshire Council in 2012 in Paisley South. He played for Paisley rugby club for seventeen years. He is married to Lynn, whom he met at Glasgow Airport, and they have two young daughters. ▪

John Nicolson

SCOTTISH NATIONAL PARTY (SNP) MP FOR
DUNBARTONSHIRE EAST

FORMER MP	Jo Swinson, Liberal Democrat, defeated
MAJORITY	2,167 (3.9%)
VOTE SHARE	40.3%
CHANGE	+29.7%
2ND PLACE	Lib Dem

@MrJohnNicolson

BORN IN GLASGOW, John Nicolson is a television presenter and journalist. He studied English Literature and Politics at the University of Glasgow, graduating in 1984. He won a Kennedy Scholarship and Harkness Fellowship to Harvard University (John F. Kennedy School of Government). While in the US, he won the World Universities Debating Championship at Princeton, New Jersey. He was recruited by US Democrat Senator Daniel Moynihan of New York as a speech-writer on Capitol Hill. Returning to Glasgow, he joined BBC Scotland to present the BBC's youth affairs programme *Open to Question*. He has since reported for and presented programmes including *Newsnight, Panorama, Watchdog, Public Eye* and News 24. He was the main presenter of *BBC Breakfast* for a number of years. Although having joined the SNP at the age of sixteen, he has not been politically active previously, in large part due to his career. He lives in Bearsden, East Dunbartonshire. ▪

Brendan O'Hara

SCOTTISH NATIONAL PARTY (SNP) MP FOR
ARGYLL & BUTE

FORMER MP	Alan Reid, Liberal Democrat, defeated
MAJORITY	8,473 (16.3%)
VOTE SHARE	44.3%
CHANGE	+25.3%
2ND PLACE	Lib Dem

@BrendanOHaraSNP

BORN IN 1963, Brendan O'Hara is originally from Glasgow but has lived in the constituency since 2004. Educated at St Andrew's Secondary School in Carntyne, he then attended Strathclyde University, where he graduated in 1991 with a degree in Economic History and Modern History. Having worked for Glasgow District Council for several years, he moved into television and is an award-winning TV producer, having worked for STV, Sky Sports and the BBC. A director of Oh! Television Limited since 2009, his work has included the BAFTA-nominated *Football Years* and *Road to Referendum* (both for STV) and *Comedy Connections* for BBC One. He has made documentaries on *I, Claudius* and *Prime Suspect*.

He has been an SNP member for thirty-three years and stood for Springburn at the 1987 general election and for Glasgow Central in 1992. His brother is Diarmid O'Hara, producer, journalist and former editor of *Newsnight Scotland*, and he is the great-great-grandson of one of the founders of Celtic Football Club. He lives in Helensburgh with his wife and two teenage daughters. ▪

Melanie Onn

LABOUR MP FOR GREAT GRIMSBY

FORMER MP	Austin Mitchell, Labour, stood down
MAJORITY	4,540 (13.5%)
VOTE SHARE	39.8%
CHANGE	+7.1%
2ND PLACE	Con

www.melanieonn.co.uk   @OnnMel

MELANIE ONN WAS born in Grimsby to a family with a history in the fishing and docking industry. Her uncle still works on the docks. She attended the local Healing Comprehensive and Franklin Sixth Form college. She studied Politics, Philosophy and International Studies at Middlesex University. She helped as a constituency caseworker for Austin Mitchell, the former MP, and, moving to London in 2001, worked at Labour Party HQ. She left after ten years as head of the party's Compliance Unit. At the age of twenty-two she stood for election to be a GMB shop steward and was branch secretary. From the Labour Party, she joined Unison as regional organiser for Yorkshire & Humberside in 2010.

She stood as a Labour Party regional list candidate in the 2009 European elections. She is a governor at a junior school. She is married to a soldier. ∎

Kate Osamor

LABOUR MP FOR EDMONTON

FORMER MP	Andy Love, Labour, stood down
MAJORITY	15,419 (37.3%)
VOTE SHARE	61.4%
CHANGE	+7.8%
2ND PLACE	Con

http://kateosamor.co.uk   @KateOsamor

OFUNNE KATE OSAMOR was born in Nigeria in 1968 and arrived in the UK as a child. Her mother was an active left-wing activist in the 1980s who played a key role in establishing Labour's Black Sections. Having attended the University of East London, she worked in the NHS from 2002 until 2013, as a GP surgery practice manager in Hammersmith and as an executive assistant in a surgery in Camden.

She was elected to Labour's national executive committee in September 2014 and is a well-known party and trade union activist. She is a trustee of a women's charity based in Edmonton Green, the All Women's Welfare Association. She has lived in north London her whole life, spending the past fifteen years in Tottenham. ▪

Kirsten Oswald

SCOTTISH NATIONAL PARTY (SNP) MP FOR
RENFREWSHIRE EAST

FORMER MP	Jim Murphy, Labour, defeated
MAJORITY	3,718 (6.6%)
VOTE SHARE	40.6%
CHANGE	+31.7%
2ND PLACE	Lab

http://kirsten4eastren.org   @kirstenoswald

BORN IN DUNDEE, Kirsten Oswald grew up in Carnoustie, attending Carlogie Primary and Carnoustie High School. She has a degree and a Master's in History from the University of Glasgow. She worked in human resources for Motherwell College between 1998 and 2002 and has been head of human resources at South Lanarkshire College since 2002.

She joined the SNP in June 2014 and is a member of the Eastwood branch. She was an active Yes campaigner during the referendum and sits on the committee of the local East Renfrewshire Women for Independence Group. She is a community councillor and a parent governor. She lives in Clarkston with her husband and their two sons. ∎

Steven Paterson

SCOTTISH NATIONAL PARTY (SNP) MP FOR STIRLING

FORMER MP	Anne McGuire, Labour, deselected
MAJORITY	10,480 (20.1%)
VOTE SHARE	45.6%
CHANGE	+28.3%
2ND PLACE	Lab

www.stevenforstirling.com   @Steven4Stirling

STEVEN PATERSON WAS born and raised in Stirling, growing up in Cambusbarron. He attended Stirling High School and Stirling University, graduating in History and Politics. He spent nine years working for the local tourist board and ran his own tourism business, Scottish Visits, supplying guidebooks and arranging tours and vacations for tourists from North America until 2007. Before his election he worked as a parliamentary researcher for Stirling MSP Bruce Crawford.

He has been a member of the SNP since 1996 and has represented the Stirling East ward on Stirling Council since 2007. He is deputy leader of the SNP group and the portfolio holder for Communities, Culture and Community Planning. ▪

Matthew Pennycook

LABOUR MP FOR GREENWICH & WOOLWICH

FORMER MP	Nick Raynsford, Labour, stood down
MAJORITY	11,946 (25.6%)
VOTE SHARE	52.2%
CHANGE	+3.0%
2ND PLACE	Con

www.matthewpennycook.com   @mtpennycook

BORN IN 1982, Matthew Pennycook has a background firmly rooted in the third sector. He grew up in south London in a single-parent family. He attended Beverley Boys' Secondary School comprehensive in New Malden before gaining a First in History and International Relations at the London School of Economics, winning the C. S. McTaggart prize for best overall degree performance in any subject. He went on to take an MPhil in International Relations from Balliol College, Oxford, with the help of a scholarship. While at university, he volunteered with the Child Poverty Action Group. He has since worked for the Fair Pay Network, between 2008 and 2009, and the Resolution Foundation.

He has also been head of office and senior researcher for Karen Buck, Labour MP for Westminster North.

He was elected as Greenwich West councillor in 2010 on the London Borough of Greenwich Council. He is a former governor at James Wolfe Primary School and is a trustee of the charity Greenwich Housing Rights and Greenwich Pensioners' Forum. He is a member of the Living Wage Foundation's advisory board and was an adviser on Ed Miliband's living wage campaign for the Labour leadership. He is Greenwich Organiser for Hope not Hate. He lives in west Greenwich and his partner Joanna is private secretary/head of office to Lord Justice Gross. ∎

Jess Phillips

LABOUR MP FOR BIRMINGHAM YARDLEY

FORMER MP	John Hemming, Liberal Democrat, defeated
MAJORITY	6,595 (16.0%)
VOTE SHARE	41.6%
CHANGE	+9.4%
2ND PLACE	Lib Dem

www.jessphillips.org   @jessphillips

JESS PHILLIPS WAS born and still lives in Birmingham. She studied Economic and Social History/Social Policy at the University of Leeds between 2000 and 2003. She was business development manager for Sandwell Women's Aid, offering support to victims of domestic violence, sexual violence, child sexual exploitation and human trafficking. Between 2008 and 2010 she was project and events manager for Health Links, an events company working within the health, social and environmental sectors. She studied for a post-graduate diploma in Public Sector Management at the Institute of Local Government at Birmingham University between 2011 and 2013. She has also worked for Jack Dromey MP.

She was elected as a Birmingham city councillor for the Longbridge ward in May 2011 and was selected to be the Victims' Champion for Birmingham in June that year. She has been a member of the West Midlands Police and Crime Panel. She lives with her husband Tom, an OTIS lift engineer, and their two young sons. ▪

Chris Philp

CONSERVATIVE MP FOR CROYDON SOUTH

FORMER MP	Sir Richard Ottaway, Conservative, stood down
MAJORITY	17,140 (29.7%)
VOTE SHARE	54.5%
CHANGE	+3.6%
2ND PLACE	Lab

http://chrisphilp.co.uk   @chrisphilp4mp

CHRIS PHILP WAS born in 1976 and brought up in West Wickham. His father was an archaeologist and his mother was a teacher. He went to St Olave's Grammar School in Orpington and then University College, Oxford, achieving a First in Physics. His Master's thesis was on theoretical quantum mechanics. Upon graduating, he worked for McKinsey & Co., before starting his first business in 2000, distribution company Blueheath, which he sold four years later for £80 million. In 2004 he co-founded a training and recruitment business, which he sold in 2006. His latest venture is Pluto Capital, a financial investor/asset manager for the construction sector in the UK and south-east Europe.

He was chairman of the Bow Group from 2004 until 2005. He was a London Borough of Camden councillor for the Gospel Oak ward from 2006 to 2010, and stood in Hampstead & Kilburn at the 2010 general election, losing by only forty-two votes. After his father contracted the MRSA superbug in hospital, he advised shadow Health Secretary Andrew Lansley on the bug in 2005. He has also set up a charity, Next Big Thing, which encourages inner-city youth to set up businesses. He is married to Lizzy and they have twins. ∎

Rebecca Pow

CONSERVATIVE MP FOR TAUNTON DEANE

FORMER MP	Jeremy Browne, Liberal Democrat, stood down
MAJORITY	15,491 (26.8%)
VOTE SHARE	48.1%
CHANGE	+5.9%
2ND PLACE	Lib Dem

www.rebeccapow.com (work)   www.rebeccapow.org.uk   @pow_rebecca

REBECCA POW WAS educated at Le Sainte Union Convent in Bath before studying Rural Environment Studies at Imperial College London. Graduating in 1982, she spent the next twenty years as a BBC and ITV reporter, specialising in the environment, farming and gardening. She was the first environment correspondent on television in Britain while working for HTV. She also produced and presented *Farming Today* on BBC Radio 4. This led to her working for the National Farmers Union. Ten years ago she set up her own public relations consultancy, Pow Productions. She continues to write for publications about country living and gardening.

She has been a school governor for ten years, a parish councillor and a trustee of the Somerset Wildlife Trust. She was selected at an open primary. She has lived in Taunton for twenty-seven years and her husband Charles Clark was born and raised in rural Somerset. They have three children. ∎

Victoria Prentis

CONSERVATIVE MP FOR BANBURY

FORMER MP	Sir Tony Baldry, Conservative, stood down
MAJORITY	18,395 (31.7%)
VOTE SHARE	53.0%
CHANGE	+0.2%
2ND PLACE	Lab

www.victoriaprentis.co.uk

BORN IN BANBURY in 1971, Victoria Prentis grew up in nearby Aynho on the family farm. Her father is Tim (now Lord) Boswell, who was MP for Daventry from 1987 to 2010. She attended Malvern Girls' College and Downing College, Cambridge, where she was chairman of the Cambridge University Conservative Association. She qualified as a barrister in 1995 and initially was self-employed in chambers, before spending the past seventeen years working as a government lawyer for various departments. She was asked to join the senior civil service in 2009, and headed the Justice and Security team at the Treasury Solicitor's Department until shortly before the election. Between 1999 and 2012 she was a director of St Matthew's Conference Centre Ltd in Westminster.

Since 2008 she has been chair of the Benefactor's Board of the Oxford Children's Hospital Trust and is a founding trustee of the Northamptonshire Parent Infant Project. She is a director of Transport Sense, an anti-HS2 campaign group. She is vice-chairman of the Carlton Political Committee. She married Sebastian, a fellow barrister and former abstract landscape painter, in 1996 and they have two daughters. ∎

Tom Pursglove

CONSERVATIVE MP FOR CORBY

FORMER MP	Andy Sawford, Labour, defeated
MAJORITY	2,412 (4.3%)
VOTE SHARE	42.8%
CHANGE	+0.6%
2ND PLACE	Lab

www.votepursglove.co.uk   @VotePursglove

AT TWENTY-SIX YEARS old, Tom Pursglove is one of the younger members of the 2015 intake of parliamentarians. He was educated at Sir Christopher Hatton School in Wellingborough and studied at Queen Mary University of London. He has since been a parliamentary assistant to Chris Heaton-Harris MP and assisted Peter Bone MP at a constituency level. He is the director of Together Against Wind, the national anti-wind farm campaign.

He was first elected to serve the Croyland ward on the Borough Council of Wellingborough in 2007 at the age of eighteen, possibly the youngest councillor in the country at that time. He has served as chairman of the Appointments Committee. He is a former deputy chairman political of the Wellingborough Conservative Association. ∎

Jeremy Quin

CONSERVATIVE MP FOR HORSHAM

FORMER MP	Francis Maude, Conservative, stood down
MAJORITY	24,658 (43.3%)
VOTE SHARE	57.3%
CHANGE	+4.6%
2ND PLACE	UKIP

http://jeremyquin.com

JEREMY QUIN WAS born in Aylesbury in 1968. His mother was a state primary school teacher and his father an agricultural merchant before becoming the third generation of his family to be ordained in the Church of England. Brought up in Buckinghamshire and Hertfordshire, Quin attended St Albans School. He read History at Oxford University between 1987 and 1990 and was president of the Oxford Union. He has worked for Deutsche Bank and its predecessors since 1990, climbing to managing director of Deutsche Bank UK. He was seconded to the Treasury as a senior corporate finance adviser between 2008 and 2009, at the height of the financial crisis.

He has been actively involved with the Swan Credit Union (a not-for-profit credit union) since 2010 and a board member since 2014. He is a governor of a school near Buckingham. A party member for thirty years, he has been chairman of the Buckingham constituency party and has recently been deputy chairman of the Oxfordshire and Buckinghamshire Area Conservatives. He stood for election in Meirionnydd Nant Conwy at the 1997 general election and was shortlisted for Salisbury in 2010 but did not stand in the election. He lives in Quainton, North Buckinghamshire, with his wife, Joanna, a corporate lawyer. ▪

Will Quince

CONSERVATIVE MP FOR COLCHESTER

FORMER MP	Sir Bob Russell, Liberal Democrat, defeated
MAJORITY	5,575 (11.5%)
VOTE SHARE	38.9%
CHANGE	+6.1%
2ND PLACE	Lib Dem

www.will4colchester.org.uk   @willquince

BORN IN 1982, Will Quince studied Law at the University of Wales, Aberystwyth, between 2001 and 2005. He began work not in the legal sector but in industry, as a market development executive for Concur Technologies and as a customer development manager for Britvic Soft Drinks. He then decided to return to law, joining Asher Prior Bates (APB) as a trainee solicitor and studying for a postgraduate diploma in Legal Practice in 2010 at the University of West of England in Bristol. Since 2013 he has been a solicitor with Thompson Smith and Puxon (TSP) in Colchester, dealing with corporate and commercial law and commercial and residential property matters.

He was elected as an East Hertfordshire district councillor in 2007 and served for two years. In 2011 he was elected as the councillor for Prettygate on Colchester Borough Council, rising to become leader of the Conservative group. He is a trustee of Grassroots, the Colchester and Tendring Community Trust, and a governor at Montgomery Junior School in Colchester. He lives in Colchester with his wife Elinor and their young daughter. ▪

Angela Rayner

LABOUR MP FOR ASHTON-UNDER-LYNE

FORMER MP	David Heyes, Labour, stood down
MAJORITY	10,756 (27.6%)
VOTE SHARE	49.8%
CHANGE	+1.4%
2ND PLACE	Con

www.angelarayner.com   @AngelaRayner

ANGELA RAYNER HAD a tough childhood growing up on an estate in Stockport and was largely raised by her grandmother. She left her school, Avondale High, aged sixteen and spent the next ten years working in social care, looking after elderly people in their homes. She was seconded from her job to the position of assistant branch secretary for Unison. She was later elected as a Unison North West lay official and has been a Unison official/local government officer with Stockport Council since 2000.

A member of the Labour Party since 2000, Angela was actively supported by Unison in her efforts to become an MP. She first stood in Manchester Withington, where she was beaten at the selection process by Jeff Smith. She volunteered as a campaign worker for John Kerry at the 2004 presidential campaign. A single mother at the age of seventeen, she is now married and has three boys. ▪

Christina Rees

LABOUR MP FOR NEATH

FORMER MP	Peter Hain, Labour, stood down
MAJORITY	9,548 (25.7%)
VOTE SHARE	43.8%
CHANGE	-2.4%
2ND PLACE	Plaid Cymru

www.christinarees.co.uk   @Rees4Neath

CHRISTINA REES WAS born in south Wales. She attended Cynffig Comprehensive School, represented Wales Schools at tennis, hockey and athletics, and was a member of the GB Youth Team sent to the Munich Olympic Games. After university, she took up squash and soon became Welsh No. 1, with over 100 caps. For several years she was an auditor for South Glamorgan County Council. Married to Ron Davies, the former Labour Secretary of State for Wales, she worked as his constituency secretary for twelve years. Returning to education in 1991, she studied Law at Ystrad Mynach College and took a degree from the University of Wales. She was called to the Bar in 1998 and worked as a barrister for just over a year before returning to squash in 2003, becoming a national coach for Wales and a professional at the Vale Hotel.

She stood in Arfon at the 2011 Welsh Assembly elections and was a candidate in the European elections in 2014. A former Mid-Glamorgan county councillor, she was elected to represent the Newcastle ward on Bridgend County Borough Council in 2012. She is a member of the Welsh executive committee of the Labour Party. In 2011 she was divorced from Ron Davies, with whom she has one daughter. ▪

Marie Rimmer CBE

LABOUR MP FOR ST HELENS SOUTH & WHISTON

FORMER MP	Shaun Woodward, Labour, stood down
MAJORITY	21,243 (43.9%)
VOTE SHARE	59.8%
CHANGE	+6.9%
2ND PLACE	Con

www.marierimmer.org.uk   @marieerimmer

MARIE RIMMER IS a local government veteran and, according to Labour Uncut, is the 'grande dame of Merseyside Labour politics'. Born in St Helens, she grew up in a working-class family in the Gerards Bridge area. Leaving school at the age of fifteen, she joined Pilkington Glass in their Statistics and Accounts department. She later moved to Procurement, where she became a buyer of engineering equipment for the glass production lines. After an employment break, she re-joined Pilkington's to become a health and safety adviser. While at the firm, she became a trade union member and shop steward. She remains a member of Unite.

She was first elected to St Helens Council in 1978 and only stood down in 2015, having served for thirty-seven years. She was the council leader for almost twenty years until she was ousted in 2013 following a leadership challenge. She is a trustee of St Helens Hope Centre, which manages the local food banks. On the day of the Scottish referendum in September 2014, she was arrested and charged with assault after travelling to Scotland to campaign for the No vote. She denies the allegation but will stand trial in Glasgow in August 2015. ∎

Gavin Robinson

DEMOCRATIC UNIONIST PARTY (DUP) MP FOR
BELFAST EAST

FORMER MP	Naomi Long, Alliance, defeated
MAJORITY	2,597 (6.5%)
VOTE SHARE	49.3%
CHANGE	+16.5%
2ND PLACE	Alliance

@GRobinsonDUP

GAVIN ROBINSON WAS the 57th elected Lord Mayor of Belfast between 2012 and 2013, at the tender age of twenty-seven. A lifelong East Belfast resident, he read Law at Queen's University and attained a Master's in Irish Politics, before training as a barrister. He is a former special adviser to First Minister Peter Robinson, who is not a relation.

He was co-opted onto Belfast City Council in 2010 to replace Sammy Wilson, representing the Pottinger area, and was then elected in May 2011. He is currently a member of the East Belfast District Policing and Community Safety Partnership subgroup, having previously represented the council on the board of the Ulster Orchestra and the World Police and Fire Games 2013. He was designated an Alderman in 2012. Raised a Presbyterian, he currently attends the Church of Ireland. He is married to Lindsay. ∎

Mary Robinson

CONSERVATIVE MP FOR CHEADLE

FORMER MP	Mark Hunter, Liberal Democrat, defeated
MAJORITY	6,453 (12.2%)
VOTE SHARE	43.1%
CHANGE	+2.3%
2ND PLACE	Lib Dem

www.mary-robinson.org.uk   @MaryRobinson01

BORN IN 1955, Mary Robinson studied for a Law degree while bringing up her four children. She set up a firm of accountants, Robinson Rose, with her husband, which in 2008 merged with another firm. She has since run Mary Felicity Design with one of her daughters.

She was elected to South Ribble Borough Council for the Horwick & Priory ward in 2007 and served until standing down in 2013, following her selection. She has also been a Penwortham town councillor. Within the party, she has served as chairman of the South Ribble Association. She was the local authority governor of a primary school. Her husband, Stephen, is a former fellow councillor on both South Ribble District Council and Penwortham Town Council. ∎

Rt Hon Joan Ryan

LABOUR MP FOR ENFIELD NORTH

FORMER MP	Nick de Bois, Conservative, defeated
MAJORITY	1,086 (2.4%)
VOTE SHARE	43.7%
CHANGE	+5.2%
2ND PLACE	Con

@joanryanEnfield

JOAN RYAN HAS returned as MP to the seat she held between 1997 and 2010. Born in 1955 in Warrington, she attended local schools in the Warrington area before studying at the City of Liverpool College of Higher Education, where she gained a BA in History and Sociology in 1979. In 1981, she gained an MSc in Sociology from the Polytechnic of the South Bank. She worked as a teacher of Sociology and European Politics in Hammersmith and as a freelance oral history interviewer for the Imperial War Museum for a period of three years in the mid-1980s.

Elected to Barnet Council for eight years, she was deputy leader of the council until she was elected to Parliament as the Member for Enfield North at the 1997 general election. She served as a PPS, as a whip for four years and as a junior Home Office minister responsible for nationality, citizenship and immigration from 2006 until the election the following year. Appointed as the PM's special representative to Cyprus in 2007 and made a Privy Counsellor, she was fired the following year when she called for a leadership election to replace Gordon Brown. Since her defeat, she has worked as the CEO of the Global Tamil Forum and as a consultant with Butler Kelly. She is married. ▪

Alex Salmond

SCOTTISH NATIONAL PARTY (SNP) MP FOR GORDON

FORMER MP	Sir Malcolm Bruce, Liberal Democrat, stood down
MAJORITY	8,687 (14.9%)
VOTE SHARE	47.7%
CHANGE	+25.5%
2ND PLACE	Lib Dem

@AlexSalmond

WHEN ALEX SALMOND announced his intention to resign as Scotland's First Minister and leader of the SNP the morning after the referendum, few anticipated that he would be returning to Westminster within a year, and that he would be the leading figure among fifty-six SNP MPs. Born in Linlithgow in 1954, he attended Linlithgow Academy and took an HNC in Business Studies at Edinburgh College of Commerce and an MA in Economics and Medieval History at St Andrews University. Before his political career, he worked as an economist in the Department of Agriculture and Fisheries for Scotland and with the Royal Bank of Scotland for seven years.

He has been either a member of the House of Commons or the Scottish Parliament, and sometimes both simultaneously, since 1987. He represented Banff & Buchan in Westminster between 1987 and 2010. In Holyrood he represented Banff & Buchan between 1999 and 2001, Gordon between 2007 and 2011 and Aberdeenshire East since 2011. He was leader (national convenor) of the SNP from 1990 until 2000 and from 2004 until 2014, serving as the first Nationalist First Minister from 2007 until his resignation in 2014. He is married to Moira, a former civil servant, whom he met at the Scottish Office in the 1970s. ∎

Antoinette Sandbach

CONSERVATIVE MP FOR EDDISBURY

FORMER MP	Stephen O'Brien, Conservative, stood down
MAJORITY	12,974 (27.4%)
VOTE SHARE	51.0%
CHANGE	-0.6%
2ND PLACE	Lab

www.antoinettesandbach.org.uk   @ASandbachMP

ANTOINETTE MACKESON-SANDBACH WAS born in 1969. Her family has farmed in the Elwy Valley for six generations. She taught English in Indonesia before studing Law at the University of Nottingham. She gained a scholarship to Lincoln's Inn and was called to the Bar. She practised as a barrister at 9 Bedford Row Chambers, specialising in criminal law, between 1996 and 2006, and was an elected member of the Bar Council for two terms. She was a part-time senior researcher to David Jones MP, former Secretary of State for Wales, until 2010. The following year, she was elected to the Welsh Assembly for the north Wales region. She has been shadow Minister for the Environment and Energy since 2014,

having previously held the shadow Minister for Rural Affairs post. Since 2005 she has run two small businesses. She promised to stand down from the Welsh Assembly if elected to Westminster.

She has also been a councillor on Ynys Môn/Isle of Anglesey County Council. She stood unsuccessfully for Delyn at the 2010 general election. She is a governor of Packwood Haugh School and a former patron of the Chrysalis charity. She recently married and has a young daughter. ▪

Liz Saville-Roberts

PLAID CYMRU MP FOR DWYFOR MEIRIONNYDD

FORMER MP	Elfyn Llwyd, Plaid Cymru, stood down
MAJORITY	5,261 (18.2%)
VOTE SHARE	40.9%
CHANGE	-3.5%
2ND PLACE	Con

www.facebook.com/LizSavilleRoberts   @Miliast

BORN IN 1964, Liz Saville-Roberts grew up in London but is recognised as a leading pioneer in the development of the Welsh language in further education colleges. She moved to Wales from Eltham, London, upon going to Aberystwyth to study Celtic languages. She attended a Welsh language course at Nant Gwrtheyrn, or 'The Nant', in 1983. She spent time as a journalist for the *Caernarfon & Denbigh Herald* and also worked as a lecturer, project manager and director with further education colleges in north-west Wales. Since 2008 she has been a director of Cwmni Cynnal, where she works alongside her husband; the charity was first established in 1996 by local authorities to provide educational support services. She is the director of the Sgiliaith Centre, which promotes the Welsh language and offers support on bilingualism to schools and colleges throughout Wales.

She has been a councillor on Gwynedd Council since 2004 and portfolio leader for Education since 2008. She stood unsuccessfully for election to the National Assembly for Wales in 2011. She is married to Dewi, and they have twin daughters. ∎

Paul Scully

CONSERVATIVE MP FOR SUTTON & CHEAM

FORMER MP	Paul Burstow, Liberal Democrat, defeated
MAJORITY	3,921 (7.9%)
VOTE SHARE	41.5%
CHANGE	-0.8%
2ND PLACE	Lib Dem

www.scully.org.uk   @scullyp

PAUL SCULLY ATTENDED Bedford School before going to the University of Reading in 1986 to study Chemistry and Food Science. He worked in the financial services, property and telecoms sectors for twenty-five years. Since 2011 he has been a partner in the Nudge Factory, a public affairs consultancy, leading on government relations. He also worked in Westminster from 2005 until 2012 in the offices of three MPs, Andrew Pelling, Shailesh Vara and Alok Sharma.

A former member of Sutton Council, he was the leader of the opposition between 2006 and 2010. He is a governor at Sutton College of Learning for Adults (SCOLA), Stanley Park High School and the Federation of Victor Seymour Infants' School and Children's Centre and Camden Junior School in Carshalton. ▪

Naz Shah

LABOUR MP FOR BRADFORD WEST

FORMER MP	George Galloway, Respect, defeated
MAJORITY	11,420 (28.3%)
VOTE SHARE	49.6%
CHANGE	+4.2%
2ND PLACE	Respect

@NazShahBfd

BORN IN BRADFORD West, Naz Shah had a turbulent upbringing. The family was abandoned by their father when she was six. Having been sent to live with her grandparents in Pakistan at the age of twelve to avoid her mother's violent partner, she was subjected to a forced and violent marriage at fifteen and was not allowed to return to school. In 1993 her mother, Zoora Shah, poisoned her abusive partner after years of domestic violence and was sentenced to twenty years in jail, serving fourteen. Shah campaigned in support of her mother and other abused women and won the Emma Humphreys Memorial Prize in 1999 for campaigning on women's rights. After several low-paid jobs, she worked for Bradford City Council and later became a carer for children with disabilities. She joined the NHS, rising to become a commissioning manager for NHS Bradford & Airedale between 2003 and 2010, when she was made redundant. Between 2010 and 2013 she set up and ran a children's indoor play centre, café and ladies gym. Since 2012 she has been the chair of mental health charity Sharing Voices Bradford.

Having only been selected in March 2015 after the original candidate stood down, she comfortably defeated George Galloway, the victor of the Bradford West by-election in 2012. ∎

Tasmina Ahmed-Sheikh OBE

SCOTTISH NATIONAL PARTY (SNP) MP FOR OCHIL
& SOUTH PERTHSHIRE

FORMER MP	Gordon Banks, Labour, defeated
MAJORITY	10,168 (17.6%)
VOTE SHARE	46.0%
CHANGE	+18.4%
2ND PLACE	Lab

@TasminaSheikh

TASMINA AHMED-SHEIKH WAS born in Chelsea in 1970, and raised in Edinburgh. Her mother is half-Welsh, half-Czech, and her father was born in India and became a Conservative councillor. She studied Law at Strathclyde University and a Master's at Edinburgh University, qualifying in 1997. She joined Glasgow law firm Hamilton Burns in 2005, specialising in commercial conveyancing and private client work, and was made a partner in 2006. She founded the Scottish Asian Women's Association in 2012. Prior to her legal career, she was an actress and star of many Asian television series, produced by her husband, Zulfikar, and his firm Elysée Productions.

An active member of the Conservative Party at sixteen as chair of Edinburgh Central Young Conservatives, she supported Labour in the 1990s for two years, before re-joining the Conservatives and standing in the 1999 Scottish Parliament elections in Govan, finishing third behind Nicola Sturgeon. In 2000 she joined the SNP and has been the party's national women's and equalities officer since 2012. She joined the advisory board of Yes Scotland in 2012, is an elected member of the SNP's national executive committee and stood for the SNP in the 2014 European elections. She is a practising Muslim and has four children. ∎

Tommy Sheppard

SCOTTISH NATIONAL PARTY (SNP) MP FOR
EDINBURGH EAST

FORMER MP	Sheila Gilmore, Labour, defeated
MAJORITY	9,106 (19.3%)
VOTE SHARE	49.2%
CHANGE	+28.8%
2ND PLACE	Lab

http://tommysheppard.com   @TommySheppard

TOMMY SHEPPARD WAS born in 1959 in Coleraine, on the north coast of Northern Ireland. He went to the local grammar school and then Aberdeen University, initially to study Medicine. He graduated in 1982 with a degree in Sociology and Politics. He was elected vice-president of the NUS and moved to London. He stayed for eleven years working in PR. He was elected as a Labour Hackney borough councillor in 1986 and re-elected in 1990, becoming deputy leader. In 1992 he stood for Bury St Edmunds as a Labour candidate. Returning to Scotland in 1993, he joined a district council as a senior official. He was appointed assistant general secretary of the Labour Party under John Smith in 1994,

but was sacked by Tony Blair in 1996. He left the Labour Party in 2003.

Starting The Stand Comedy Club as a hobby in 1995, he turned it into a business in 1998. He also set up Salt 'n' Sauce Promotions Ltd and the Scottish Comedy Agency. He is a board member of the Edinburgh Festival Fringe. Sitting on the National Council of the Scottish Independence Convention during the referendum, he only joined the SNP in 2014. He lives in Edinburgh with partner Kate and daughter. ∎

Paula Sherriff

LABOUR MP FOR DEWSBURY

FORMER MP	Simon Reevell, Conservative, defeated
MAJORITY	1,451 (2.7%)
VOTE SHARE	41.8%
CHANGE	+9.6%
2ND PLACE	Con

www.paulasherriff.org.uk @paulasherriff

PAULA SHERRIFF WAS born in Glasgow and moved to Yorkshire as a teenager. After leaving school aged eighteen, she worked for ten years in Victim Support with the police. She joined the NHS, working first for Wakefield Primary Care Trust and then, when dermatology services were outsourced in 2013, transferring to Virgin Care. She was a workplace shop steward for over six years.

She was elected as a councillor on Wakefield Council for Pontefract North in 2012 and is chair of Pontefract Business Forum. She is also a governor of New College in Pontefract. She was chosen from an all-women shortlist. Her sister, Lee Sherriff, was the Labour candidate in Carlisle but lost out to the sitting Conservative MP, John Stevenson. ∎

Tulip Siddiq

LABOUR MP FOR HAMPSTEAD & KILBURN

FORMER MP	Glenda Jackson, Labour, stood down
MAJORITY	1,138 (2.1%)
VOTE SHARE	44.4%
CHANGE	+11.6%
2ND PLACE	Con

www.tulipsiddiq.com @TulipSiddiq

TULIP SIDDIQ IS the niece of Bangladesh Prime Minister Sheikh Hasina and granddaughter of the country's founding father, Sheikh Mujibur Rahman. She was born in Mitcham, London, in 1982, but spent her childhood in six countries due to her mother's job as a journalist. She returned to London in 1998, studied English Literature at University College London and took a Master's degree from King's College London. Later, in 2011, she completed a second Master's in Politics, Policy and Government. She has worked for Amnesty International, the London Labour Party (as press officer), Philip Gould Associates, the Greater London Authority, the MPs Oona King,

Sadiq Khan and Harry Cohen, and, most recently, the Brunswick Group.

She worked on Ed Miliband's leadership campaign and has been a policy adviser to Tessa Jowell. She was a councillor for Regent's Park on Camden Council and cabinet member for Culture and Communities. She has served as national BAME officer for Young Labour and women's officer for London Young Labour. She is an executive board member of Unite the Union and a school governor, and has been a governor on the Camden and Islington NHS Foundation Trust. She is married to Chris St John Percy, a strategy consultant and former civil servant. ▪

Ruth Smeeth

LABOUR MP FOR STOKE ON TRENT NORTH

FORMER MP	Joan Walley, Labour, stood down
MAJORITY	4,836 (12.5%)
VOTE SHARE	39.9%
CHANGE	-4.4%
2ND PLACE	Con

www.ruthsmeeth.org.uk   @RuthSmeeth

BORN IN 1980 in Edinburgh, Ruth Smeeth was brought up in Bristol and educated at Downend Comprehensive and the University of Birmingham, where she studied Politics and International Relations. She worked as a Unite trade union policy and research officer and spent a secondment with think tank the New Health Network. She was director of public affairs and campaigns for the pro-Israel lobby group Britain Israel Communications and Research Centre (BICOM). She then worked in the private sector as public affairs manager for Nestlé and for international catering company Sodexo. Most recently, she was director of HOPE not hate, the leading anti-fascism and anti-racist campaign. She joined the Labour Party at age sixteen and stood as the Labour candidate in Burton at the 2010 general election. She is married to Michael, who currently works for GEC Distributed Power. ▪

Cat Smith

LABOUR MP FOR LANCASTER & FLEETWOOD

FORMER MP	Eric Ollerenshaw, Conservative, defeated
MAJORITY	1,265 (3.0%)
VOTE SHARE	42.3%
CHANGE	+7.0%
2ND PLACE	Con

www.catsmith.co.uk   @CateySmith

CATHERINE 'CAT' SMITH was born in Barrow-in-Furness, and was educated locally at Parkview School and Barrow Sixth Form College, before moving to Lancaster to study Gender and Sociology at the university. After graduating in 2006 she spent a year in an elected sabbatical post as women's officer for the students' union. She has combined working for not-for-profit organisations with working part time in Parliament for a number of MPs and peers. She was the office and communications manager for the Christian Socialist Movement for two years, and since 2011 was parliamentary officer for the British Association of Social Workers. She has worked in the past for Bob Marshall-Andrews MP and Katy Clark MP, and in recent years has been a part-time parliamentary assistant to Jeremy Corbyn MP and Baroness Wilkins.

She stood as the Labour candidate in Wyre & Preston at the 2010 general election. A member of GMB and Unite, she is political officer of her Unite union branch and a workplace representative. She is a former vice-chair and women's officer of London Young Labour and has been national chair of Next Generation Labour since 2011. She is a monthly columnist for the *Tribune* newspaper and sits on the editorial board of *Chartist* magazine. ∎

Jeff Smith

LABOUR MP FOR MANCHESTER WITHINGTON

FORMER MP	John Leech, Liberal Democrat, defeated
MAJORITY	14,873 (29.9%)
VOTE SHARE	53.7%
CHANGE	+13.3%
2ND PLACE	Lib Dem

www.jeffsmith.org.uk   @JeffSmithetc

JEFF SMITH WAS born in Withington Hospital and has lived in his constituency all his life. His mother and father, a secretary and a joiner respectively, met as young Labour activists. He has a degree from the University of Manchester and was the first member of his family to go to university. He worked as a self-employed event manager and DJ, running everything from large concerts and festivals to sporting events until he entered local government.

He was elected in 1997 to the Old Moat ward on Manchester City Council, serving as executive member for Children's Services and, more recently, in the Finance and Human Resources role. He is a governor of two schools in Withington and serves on the board of Southway Housing Trust and Manchester Central Convention Centre. He is a member of USDAW, the Co-operative Party, Unite, Socialist Education Association, Friends of the Earth, and Withington Civic Society. ∎

Royston Smith

CONSERVATIVE MP FOR SOUTHAMPTON ITCHEN

FORMER MP	John Denham, Labour, stood down
MAJORITY	2,316 (5.2%)
VOTE SHARE	41.7%
CHANGE	+5.4%
2ND PLACE	Lab

www.roystonsmith.co.uk   @Royston_Smith

AFTER LEAVING HIS secondary school in Southampton, Royston Smith joined the Royal Air Force as an engineer in 1980 and served ten years, working with the Nimrod maritime reconnaissance fleet. In 1990 he joined British Airways and worked at London Heathrow for the next sixteen years. He is a director of 3SFire Ltd, a fire management consultancy, and has worked as a public relations consultant since 2006.

He was first elected to Southampton City Council in 2000 as the councillor for the Harefield ward. He served as cabinet member for Economic Development between 2007 and 2010 and then became leader of the council until 2012. He is the chairman of Hampshire Fire and Rescue Authority, is a trustee of the Blue Lamp Trust and sits on the board of Southampton Solent University as an Independent governor. He fought the Southampton Itchen seat at the 2010 general election, losing by just 192 votes. He was awarded the George Medal for bravery in 2012 for helping to tackle a gunman aboard the Royal Navy submarine HMS *Astute* during a civic visit. A lieutenant commander was killed in the incident. ▪

Karin Smyth

LABOUR MP FOR BRISTOL SOUTH

FORMER MP	Dawn Primarolo, Labour, stood down
MAJORITY	7,128 (14.0%)
VOTE SHARE	38.4%
CHANGE	-0.1%
2ND PLACE	Con

http://karinsmyth.com   @karinsmyth

KARIN SMITH WAS born in London to Irish parents who came to Britain seeking work in the 1950s. She attended a local grammar school and sixth form college, before studying Politics at the University of East Anglia between 1984 and 1988. She took an MBA at the University of Bath between 1994 and 1995. She was a political assistant to Valerie Davey MP between 1997 and 2001. She has worked in the NHS for a number of years, most recently as the manager of the South Bristol GP Consortium clinical commissioning group since 2010. She was non-executive director of Bristol North PCT from 2002 until 2006.

She joined the Labour Party in 1985. She is a member of Unison, a school governor and a former trustee of the Bristol Deaf Centre. She was selected by her local party from an all-women shortlist. She is married to Rob and is the mother of three young boys. ▪

Amanda Solloway

CONSERVATIVE MP FOR DERBY NORTH

FORMER MP	Chris Williamson, Labour, defeated
MAJORITY	41 (0.1%)
VOTE SHARE	36.7%
CHANGE	+5.0%
2ND PLACE	Lab

www.amandasolloway.co.uk   www.amandasolloway.org.uk   @Amanda4DerbyN

BORN IN 1961, Amanda Solloway attended Bromcote Hills Grammar before entering into employment. She spent eleven years in retail, working for Baird Clothing, rising to head of training and development, and then was director of the National Skills Academy for Retail until 2011. She has since worked as a management consultant, specialising in behavioural development and presentation skills. She is a fully qualified coach and a Fellow of the Chartered Institute of Personnel and Development. She is the co-author of *Emotional Intelligence*. She has been a director of the AIM Awards since March 2011.

She is regional chair and national deputy chair-elect for the Conservative Women's Organisation and is a parish councillor and a school governor. She is active in the Girl Guide movement, a board member for the Open College Network and a founder member and director of Million Trees Derbyshire. She is married with two children. ■

Sir Keir Starmer KCB QC

LABOUR MP FOR HOLBORN & ST PANCRAS

FORMER MP	Frank Dobson, Labour, stood down
MAJORITY	17,048 (31.0%)
VOTE SHARE	52.9%
CHANGE	+6.8%
2ND PLACE	Con

www.keirstarmer.com   @Keir_Starmer

SIR KEIR STARMER was Director of Public Prosecutions (DPP) and the head of the Crown Prosecution Service (CPS) from 2008 to 2013. Born in 1962, he was named after former Labour Party leader and socialist Keir Hardie. He was educated at Reigate Grammar School and studied Law (LLB) at the University of Leeds in 1985 and a Bachelor of Civil Law degree at St Edmund Hall, Oxford, the following year. He was called to the Bar as a barrister in 1987, became a QC in 2002, and co-founded Doughty Street Chambers. He previously prosecuted numerous cases for the CPS during his career, specialising as a defence lawyer with expertise in human rights law, and has worked on cases around the world. Since leaving the CPS he has returned to his chambers and joined Mishcon de Reya as a part-time consultant. He is the author and editor of several books about criminal law and human rights. He married Victoria, a solicitor, in 2007 and has a son and daughter. He comfortably won the seat of Holborn & St Pancras at the election, pushing Natalie Bennett, the leader of the Green Party, into a distant third behind the Conservatives, with only 13% of the vote. ∎

Chris Stephens

SCOTTISH NATIONAL PARTY (SNP) MP FOR
GLASGOW SOUTH WEST

FORMER MP	Ian Davidson, Labour, defeated
MAJORITY	9,950 (24.3%)
VOTE SHARE	57.2%
CHANGE	+40.8%
2ND PLACE	Lab

http://chrisstephenssnp.blogspot.co.uk   @CStephenssnp

THE SON OF a Glasgow shipyard welder, Chris Stephens was born in the city in 1973. A former mortgage loan processor for Genpact Mortgage Services, he most recently worked for Glasgow City Council and is a senior Unison negotiator.

He joined the SNP in 1989 at the age of sixteen. He is currently the secretary of the SNP Trade Union Group, a member of the party's national executive committee, and the convenor of the SNP's Glasgow Pollok Constituency Association. He previously contested the Westminster seat of Glasgow South West at the 2010 general election and stood in the Glasgow Pollok constituency at the 2007 and 2011 Scottish Parliament elections, coming a very close second to Labour. He was sixth on the SNP regional list at the European elections in 2014. ▪

Jo Stevens

LABOUR MP FOR CARDIFF CENTRAL

FORMER MP	Jenny Willott, Liberal Democrat, defeated
MAJORITY	4,981 (12.9%)
VOTE SHARE	40.0%
CHANGE	+11.2%
2ND PLACE	Lib Dem

www.jostevens.co.uk   @JoStevensLabour

JO (JOANNA) STEVENS has been a trade union solicitor all her working life. She was educated at Elfed High School in Flintshire before studying Law at the University of Manchester between 1985 and 1988. She qualified in 1989 from Manchester Polytechnic and joined Thompsons Solicitors the same year. She has worked with the firm for the past twenty-five years and was most recently people and organisation director.

She has been a member of the Labour Party since the mid-1980s. She is a member of GMB, Unison, the Fabian and Haldane Societies and the Co-operative Party. She has lived in Cardiff for twenty-five years and is the mother of two boys. ▪

Wes Streeting

LABOUR MP FOR ILFORD NORTH

FORMER MP	Lee Scott, Conservative, defeated
MAJORITY	589 (1.2%)
VOTE SHARE	43.9%
CHANGE	+9.6%
2ND PLACE	Con

www.wesstreeting.org   @wesstreeting

WESLEY 'WES' STREETING was born in 1983 in Tower Hamlets. He attended Westminster City School in Victoria and read History at Selwyn College, Cambridge, serving as president of the Cambridge University students' union. He was a beneficiary of support of the Sutton Trust. A vice-president of the NUS for two years, he was then elected as NUS president in 2008 and 2009. He worked for PwC as a public sector consultant until 2010. He spent a year working for the Labour organisation Progress, and was chief executive of the Helena Kennedy Foundation, an education charity. He was head of education at Stonewall between 2012 and 2013.

A Labour member since the age of fifteen, he was elected in a 2010 by-election to Redbridge London Borough Council for the ward of Chadwell. He was forced to give up his PwC job on his election, as PwC acted as the council's auditors. Only fifteen months later, he was elected as deputy leader of the Labour group and has served as shadow cabinet member for Resources. He worked for four months on Oona King's unsuccessful bid to win the Labour Party's nomination to be their candidate in the 2012 London mayoral election. ▪

Rishi Sunak

CONSERVATIVE MP FOR RICHMOND YORKSHIRE

FORMER MP	William Hague, Conservative, stood down
MAJORITY	19,550 (36.2%)
VOTE SHARE	51.4%
CHANGE	-11.4%
2ND PLACE	UKIP

www.rishisunak.com

RISHI SUNAK WAS born in 1980 and brought up in Hampshire. His father is an NHS family GP and his mother runs her own chemist's. He attended Winchester College, where he was head boy, and went to Lincoln College, Oxford, gaining a First in PPE. He joined Goldman Sachs in 2001 as an analyst, and had progressed to become executive director (merchant banking) by the time he left in 2004 to study for an MBE at Stanford University. In 2006 he became a partner with investment charity The Children's Investment Fund Management (TCI). In 2009 he co-founded a new £1 billion global family investment business, Catamaran Ventures.

At the age of nineteen he volunteered for work experience at Conservative Central Office. He set up and ran Policy Exchange's BME Research Unit and is governor of the East London Science School, a free school based in Tower Hamlets. He met his wife, Akshata, in California, where they lived for a number of years. They have two young daughters. His wife is the daughter of Infosys founder N. R. Narayana Murthy and Sudha Murthy, an Indian social worker and author, and has an estimated net worth of around $320 million (1.41% stake in Infosys). ∎

Alison Thewliss

SCOTTISH NATIONAL PARTY (SNP) MP FOR
GLASGOW CENTRAL

FORMER MP	Anas Sarwar, Labour, defeated
MAJORITY	7,662 (19.5%)
VOTE SHARE	52.5%
CHANGE	+35.0%
2ND PLACE	Lab

@alisonthewliss

BORN IN SEPTEMBER 1982, Alison
Thewliss joined the Scottish National
Party while still at school. She is a part-
time parliamentary assistant to Bill Kidd
MSP. She has been a Glasgow city councillor for the Calton ward since 2007 and
is a member of the executive committee.
A member of the Scottish Campaign for
Nuclear Disarmament (CND), she was
appointed to Nuclear Free Local Authorities (NFLA) Scotland in 2014. She has also
served on Glasgow Greenspace Partnership since 2012. She is a former director
of Glasgow Clyde Regeneration. She has
a young baby. ▪

Derek Thomas

CONSERVATIVE MP FOR ST IVES

FORMER MP	Andrew George, Liberal Democrat, defeated
MAJORITY	2,469 (5.1%)
VOTE SHARE	38.3%
CHANGE	-0.7%
2ND PLACE	Lib Dem

http://derekthomas.org @DT4Stives @DerekThomas2015

DEREK THOMAS WAS born to missionary parents in 1972. He grew up in Cornwall, attending Camborne Comprehensive. He left education to complete a traditional Cornish stonemason apprenticeship. In a career move, he re-trained and joined the voluntary sector, working as a development manager for Mustard Seed, a charitable trust. In 1997 he set up and continues to run SurviveAlive, a Christian outdoor adventure project for vulnerable young people. He continues to run a small local construction business.

He fought the St Ives seat at the 2010 general election and is chairman of the Cornwall Conservative Area Management Executive. He has been a Penwith district councillor, serving on the Audit Committee and as member champion for children and young people. He is a parish councillor and a school governor. He is a member of West Cornwall Healthwatch, a campaigning group defending healthcare provision. He lives in St Buryan and is married to Tasmin, and they have two young sons. ▪

Nick Thomas-Symonds

LABOUR MP FOR TORFAEN

FORMER MP	Paul Murphy, Labour, stood down
MAJORITY	8,169 (21.5%)
VOTE SHARE	44.6%
CHANGE	-0.1%
2ND PLACE	Con

http://nickthomassymonds.com @NThomasSymonds

BORN IN 1980, Nick Thomas-Symonds is from Blaenavon and attended St Alban's RC Comprehensive School in Pontypool. He read PPE on a scholarship at St Edmund Hall, Oxford, graduating in 2001. He became a college tutor in Politics at his old college at the age of twenty-one, specialising in British politics, and remains a lecturer, having won several academic awards. He has also lectured at Harris Manchester College. He took a law conversion course at the University of Glamorgan and a Bar Vocational Course at Cardiff University, called to the Bar in 2004. Since then, he worked as a barrister at Civitas Law in Cardiff Bay, specialising in chancery and commercial law.

A Labour Party activist for twenty years, he was secretary of Torfaen Constituency Labour Party. He is also a governor at his old school, St Alban's. He is the author of several books, including biographies of Aneurin Bevan and Clement Attlee. He lives in Abersychan in north Torfaen with his wife Rebecca and two daughters. ∎

Owen Thompson

SCOTTISH NATIONAL PARTY (SNP) MP FOR MIDLOTHIAN

FORMER MP	David Hamilton, Labour, stood down
MAJORITY	9,859 (20.4%)
VOTE SHARE	50.6%
CHANGE	+30.0%
2ND PLACE	Lab

www.owenthompson.scot @Owen_Thompson

BORN IN 1978, Owen Thompson was raised in Loanhead after moving there at the age of seven when his father became minister at Loanhead Parish Church. He attended Paradykes Primary School, Beeslack High School in Penicuik and studied Accounting and Finance at Napier University. After working in the financial services industry until 2007, he worked as an assistant to Rob Gibson MSP in the Scottish Parliament and then Clare Adamson MSP until 2011.

A member of the SNP since 1996, he was elected to Midlothian Council, representing Loanhead, in a 2005 by-election, one of the youngest councillors in Scotland. Re-elected in 2007 and 2012, he became leader of Midlothian Council in 2013 and cabinet member for Finance and Integrated Service Support. He has been the SNP's local government convenor since 2011, supporting councillors and councils across Scotland, and is secretary of the SNP CoSLA Health & Well-being Executive Group. He is director and vice-chair, since 2006, of the Loanhead Community Learning Centre and a board member of Rosewell Development Trust. He is married and is a brown-belt kick-boxer and a Tough Mudder competitor. ▪

Michelle Thomson

SCOTTISH NATIONAL PARTY (SNP) MP FOR
EDINBURGH WEST

FORMER MP	Mike Crockart, Liberal Democrat, defeated
MAJORITY	3,210 (5.9%)
VOTE SHARE	39.0%
CHANGE	+25.8%
2ND PLACE	Lib Dem

@MichelleThomson

MICHELLE THOMSON WAS born in 1965 and grew up in Bearsden, outside Glasgow. She studied at the Royal Scottish Academy of Music and Drama, graduating in 1985. She worked as a professional musician, playing the piano, for several years, before re-training in IT, taking a Master's at Abertay University. In 1990 she started working for Standard Life in Edinburgh as an IT project manager. She worked in further various roles in financial services, including with the Royal Bank of Scotland, until setting up Your Property Shop Ltd in 2009, providing buy-to-let properties for investors. She has also been a director of Edinburgh Global Property Investments Ltd and Michelle R. Thomson Consulting Ltd.

A member of the SNP since 1981, she was not politically active until the referendum. In 2012 she founded and became managing director of Business for Scotland, campaigning for support for independence among the SME business community. She is the mother of two children. ∎

Maggie Throup

CONSERVATIVE MP FOR EREWASH

FORMER MP	Jessica Lee, Conservative, stood down
MAJORITY	3,584 (7.4%)
VOTE SHARE	42.7%
CHANGE	+3.2%
2ND PLACE	Lab

www.maggiethroup.com   @mthroup

BORN IN SHIPLEY, West Yorkshire, in 1957, Maggie Throup won a scholarship to Bradford Girls' Grammar School. She has a degree in Biology from the University of Manchester, has professional qualifications in Biomedical Sciences and holds a diploma in Marketing. After graduating, she began her career in 1978 as a medical laboratory scientist for Calderdale Health Authority, and then moved into medical diagnostics, sales and marketing for Nycomed (UK). Since 1996 she has run her own successful marketing consultancy, Maggie Throup Marketing. She has also been company secretary of Graphic Valuers Ltd.

She contested the seat of Colne Valley in 2005 and stood for Solihull at the 2010 general election, losing by just 175 votes to the former Liberal Democrat MP Lorely Burt. She has had voluntary non-executive roles with Solihull-based charities, including Changes UK, a residential care community interest company for people with mental difficulties. She is divorced and has lived in Solihull since 1987. ▪

Kelly Tolhurst

CONSERVATIVE MP FOR ROCHESTER & STROOD

FORMER MP	Mark Reckless, UK Independence Party (UKIP), defeated
MAJORITY	7,133 (13.6%)
VOTE SHARE	44.1%
CHANGE	-5.1%
2ND PLACE	UKIP

@KellyTolhurst

BORN IN AUGUST 1978, Kelly Tolhurst has lived and worked in the area all her life. She grew up around her father's local boat-building business and attended Chapter High School (now Strood Academy). She was the technical sales director of Skipper Marine Coatings UK, a company that provides marine services (yacht paints) in Rochester, from 2002. She was also an independent marine surveyor and consultant.

She has been a councillor for Rochester West on Medway Council since 2011 and is the portfolio holder for Educational Improvement. She sits on Chatham Charities Trustees, Chatham Maritime Charitable Trust Ltd, Kent and Essex Inshore Fisheries and Conservation Authority, and Lower Medway Internal Drainage Board, and is a trustee/director of action for Borstal Community Project. She stood against Mark Reckless in the November 2014 by-election caused by his defection to UKIP from the Conservatives. ■

Michael Tomlinson

CONSERVATIVE MP FOR DORSET MID & POOLE NORTH

FORMER MP	Annette Brooke, Liberal Democrat, stood down
MAJORITY	10,530 (22.6%)
VOTE SHARE	50.8%
CHANGE	+6.3%
2ND PLACE	Lib Dem

www.michaeltomlinson.org.uk   @Michael4MDNP

MICHAEL TOMLINSON ATTENDED Hereford Cathedral School and King's College London, graduating in 2000. He was called to the Bar in 2002, having won a major scholarship at the Middle Temple. He practises as a barrister on the Western Circuit as part of the 3PB Chamber, undertaking a broad range of civil work including personal injury, property, public law and regulatory. He was appointed to the Attorney General's Regional Panel between 2007 and 2012 and worked for various government departments. He is a member of the Personal Injury Bar Association and the Property Bar Association.

He has lived in Mid Dorset since moving to the area ten years ago and was formerly deputy chairman political for the local association. He was then the constituency's campaign manager in 2010, helping to cut the majority to just 269. He became chairman of the association shortly after and was recently elected as the chairman for the Dorset area. He has been part of the Conservative Party's Project Umubano, visiting Rwanda in 2009 and in 2011, advising the judiciary in Sierra Leone.

He is married to Frances and they have three children. He and his wife have helped to run a Christian youth camp for the past seventeen years. ▪

Craig Tracey

CONSERVATIVE MP FOR WARWICKSHIRE NORTH

FORMER MP	Dan Byles, Conservative, stood down
MAJORITY	2,973 (6.3%)
VOTE SHARE	42.3%
CHANGE	+2.1%
2ND PLACE	Lab

www.craigtracey.co.uk   @craig4nwarks

BORN IN THE north-east in 1974 to a family with a mining background near Durham, Craig Tracey moved to North Warwickshire in 1997. He was educated at Framwellgate Moor Comprehensive. He has worked primarily in the insurance sector and is senior partner of Dunelm Insurance Brokers, a general insurance brokerage he set up in 1996. He also runs a small public affairs consultancy, Politically Correct, in Staffordshire with his wife Karen.

He has been a board member of Southern Staffordshire Employment and Skills Board since 2014 and is founder trustee of the Lichfield Garrick Theatre. He was the chairman of the North Warwickshire Conservative Association until the selection process for the seat. He has been the West Midlands co-ordinator for Conservative Way Forward and Conservative Voice and the treasurer of Tamworth Conservative Association. He lives in Shuttington in the constituency. He succeeded in fighting off the challenge from former Solicitor General and MP for the constituency Mike O'Brien, in what was Labour's no. 1 target seat. ∎

Anne-Marie Trevelyan

CONSERVATIVE MP FOR BERWICK UPON TWEED

FORMER MP	Sir Alan Beith, Liberal Democrat, stood down
MAJORITY	4,914 (12.2%)
VOTE SHARE	41.1%
CHANGE	+4.4%
2ND PLACE	Lib Dem

www.supportannemarie.com @annietrev

BORN IN 1969, Anne-Marie Trevelyan attended St Paul's Girls' School and studied Mathematics at Oxford Brookes University. She has been a chartered accountant and since 2011 has run her own renewable energy business, Netherwitton Heating Company Ltd, with her husband John.

A member of the Conservative Party for the past ten years, she is a regional co-ordinator for the Conservative Policy Forum. She previously contested Berwick upon Tweed at the 2010 general election. She is a trustee of the Belsay Trust, an elected governor of Northumbria Healthcare Trust and a governor of Berwick Academy. She is a former director of Alnwick Community Development Trust Ltd. She is chairman of iNorthumberland Advisory Group, campaigning with Northumberland County Council for improved superfast broadband for the county. ▪

Thomas Tugendhat MBE

CONSERVATIVE MP FOR TONBRIDGE & MALLING

FORMER MP	Sir John Stanley, Conservative, stood down
MAJORITY	23,734 (44.2%)
VOTE SHARE	59.4%
CHANGE	+1.5%
2ND PLACE	UKIP

www.tomtugendhat.org.uk   @lashkartom (old)   @TomTugendhat (new)

THOMAS TUGENDHAT GREW up in London and near Ashford. He is one of four sons of Sir Michael Tugendhat, a High Court judge, and is a nephew of Lord Tugendhat. He studied Theology at Bristol University and then took a Master's degree in Islamics at Cambridge University, including learning Arabic in Yemen. He first went to Beirut as a journalist before establishing one of Lebanon's first public relations companies. On returning to the UK, he was a management consultant and a Bloomberg energy analyst in the City. As a member of the Territorial Army since 2003, he was mobilised to serve on operations in Iraq and Afghanistan with the Royal Marines and was the military assistant to the Chief of the Defence Staff. He also worked for the Foreign Office and helped set up the National Security Council of Afghanistan and the government in Helmand Province. He served with Labour's Barnsley MP Dan Jarvis in Helmand and the two remain good friends. He returned to civilian life in 2013 and is a director of security and risk management firm Lashkar & Co. He remains a lieutenant colonel in the Territorial Army. He was selected in an open primary contest. He is married to Anissia and they have a young baby. ∎

Anna Turley

LABOUR MP FOR REDCAR

FORMER MP	Ian Swales, Liberal Democrat, stood down
MAJORITY	10,388 (25.4%)
VOTE SHARE	43.9%
CHANGE	+11.1%
2ND PLACE	Lib Dem

http://redcarlabourparty.org.uk   @annaturley

ANNA TURLEY IS a former special adviser to David Blunkett in the Department for Work and Pensions, where she focused on child poverty and equality, and to Hilary Armstrong at the Cabinet Office, with responsibility for social exclusion, transformational government and better regulation. She had a brief stint at the agency Ledbury Group before joining the New Local Government Network as its deputy director. Before her election, she was a senior research fellow for the think tank IPPR North. She is the editor of the blog Progressive Localism and co-ordinator of the Co-operative Councils Network, which supports councils in developing co-operative approaches to local public services. She had the backing of the Co-op Party and Community Union in her selection. She was selected from an all-women shortlist. ∎

David Warburton

CONSERVATIVE MP FOR SOMERTON & FROME

FORMER MP	David Heath, Liberal Democrat, stood down
MAJORITY	20,268 (33.6%)
VOTE SHARE	53.0%
CHANGE	+8.5%
2ND PLACE	Lib Dem

http://davidwarburton.org   @DJWarburton

DAVID WARBURTON IS an accomplished classical musician turned entrepreneur and now a politician. Born in 1965 in Burnham, Lincolnshire, he was educated at state grammar school Reading School and Waingels College, a comprehensive. He studied classical music composition and piano at the Royal College of Music for his degree and Master's degree, followed by doctorate studies under Sir Harrison Birtwistle at King's College London. He taught at the Royal College of Music Junior Department while his music was performed at the highest levels. After teaching music for five years at an inner London school, he founded the technology company The Music Solution Ltd in

1999. This became Pitch Entertainment Group by 2005, with operations across the world. In 2006 he moved to Somerset and sold Pitch. He was an independent Forex trader for several years, set up two building property restoration companies in 2009 and, in 2012, co-founded the online business MyHigh.St. He is also a partner in Oflang Partners.

He joined the Capital Executive Committee of the Shakespeare Globe Trust in 2007 and founded the charitable project The Pulse. He was a deputy chairman of Wells Conservative Party. He lives in Mendip with his wife Harriet and their two young children. ∎

Matt Warman

CONSERVATIVE MP FOR BOSTON & SKEGNESS

FORMER MP	Mark Simmonds, Conservative, stood down
MAJORITY	4,336 (10.0%)
VOTE SHARE	43.8%
CHANGE	-5.7%
2ND PLACE	UKIP

www.mattwarman.net   @mattwarman

MATT WARMAN ATTENDED Salcombe Preparatory School and Haberdashers' Aske's Boys' School before graduating from Durham University in 2004 with a degree in English Literature. Soon after, he joined the Telegraph Media Group as a writer and has remained there until his election. He was made consumer technology editor of the *Daily Telegraph* in 2008 and technology editor/head of technology in 2013.

The chairman of a Conservative association in Hertfordshire, he is a first-time candidate. His Labour-supporting father was a candidate in the 1960s and 1970s. He won in an open primary following four rounds of voting, with eighty-one people casting their votes. He is married to Rachel, who is from the area, and her family still live and work in Boston. ∎

Catherine West

LABOUR MP FOR HORNSEY & WOOD GREEN

FORMER MP	Lynne Featherstone, Liberal Democrat, defeated
MAJORITY	11,058 (19.1%)
VOTE SHARE	50.9%
CHANGE	+16.9%
2ND PLACE	Lib Dem

www.catherinewest.org.uk   @CatherineWest1

CATHERINE WEST WAS born in Australia to Italian ancestors, one of whom established the famous Italia Conti Academy of Theatre Arts. She also holds a degree in Social Science and Languages and a Master's degree in Chinese Studies from the School of Oriental and African Studies. She speaks five languages and taught as an English as a second language teacher, including a year in Nanjing, China. Coming to the UK in 1998, she worked in welfare and housing using her local language skills.

Elected as an Islington councillor, representing the Tollington ward, in 2002, she became leader of the Labour group in 2004 and leader of Islington Council in 2010. She led the Islington Fairness Commission and was elected chair of the London Councils' Transport and Environment Committee in 2010. She stepped down from the council at the May 2014 elections to focus on her Westminster election campaign. Since leaving the council she has worked with Tottenham's Labour MP, David Lammy. She lives in Archway in London and is the mother of two children. Her husband works at the London School of Hygiene and Tropical Medicine, researching malaria in sub-Saharan Africa. ■

Helen Whately

CONSERVATIVE MP FOR FAVERSHAM & MID KENT

FORMER MP	Sir Hugh Robertson, Conservative, stood down
MAJORITY	16,652 (36.4%)
VOTE SHARE	54.4%
CHANGE	-1.8%
2ND PLACE	UKIP

www.helenwhately.co.uk   @Helen_Whately

HELEN WHATELY (NÉE Lightwood) was born in 1976 and grew up near Crawley. Her father is a surgeon and her mother is a doctor. After Westminster School, she spent a year teaching English in a village school in Nepal and working with street children in Kathmandu. She studied PPE at Oxford University, graduating in 1998. She worked for PricewaterhouseCoopers as a consultant until 2001. She joined AOL Europe in 2003. During 2006 and 2007 she was an adviser to the shadow Secretary of State for Culture, Media and Sport on media policy, and a member of the Quality of Life Policy Group. She joined McKinsey & Co. as a management consultant in the health sector and was with the firm from 2007 onwards.

She stood in Kingston & Surbiton at the 2010 general election against the Liberal Democrat Ed Davey. This time round, she was a multiple finalist, in Wealden, North East Hampshire, South Cambridgeshire, Bury St Edmunds and Banbury, before being selected in Faversham & Mid Kent. She has been married to Marcus since 2005, whom she met at university. The couple have three children, a boy and two girls, and her husband runs the energy business Estover. ▪

Dr Philippa Whitford

SCOTTISH NATIONAL PARTY (SNP) MP FOR
AYRSHIRE CENTRAL

FORMER MP	Brian Donohoe, Labour, defeated
MAJORITY	13,589 (26.8%)
VOTE SHARE	53.2%
CHANGE	+34.1%
2ND PLACE	Lab

http://whitford.scot   @Philippa_SNP

BORN IN BELFAST, Dr Philippa Whitford arrived in Scotland at the age of ten. She studied Medicine at Glasgow University and went back to Belfast for a year to start her surgical training in 1983. Having completed her surgical training around the west of Scotland, she worked as a consultant breast surgeon at Crosshouse Hospital, Kilmarnock, for over eighteen years. She has worked in the NHS for over thirty years in total. In 1991 and 1992 she was a medical volunteer in a UN hospital in Gaza and then spent a short time in southern Lebanon doing project planning for the charity Medical Aid for Palestinians. She returned to work for the NHS in Aberdeen in 1994.

One of the new breed of SNP politicians forged from the referendum campaign, she rose to prominence with a controversial campaign warning that the Scottish NHS faced privatisation unless the country became independent. She was a leading figure of Women for Independence. She lives in Troon with her partner, Dr Hans Pieper, a local GP. ∎

Craig Williams

CONSERVATIVE MP FOR CARDIFF NORTH

FORMER MP	Jonathan Evans, Conservative, stood down
MAJORITY	2,137 (4.2%)
VOTE SHARE	42.4%
CHANGE	+4.9%
2ND PLACE	Lab

www.craig-williams.org.uk   @Craig_Williams

BORN IN 1985, Craig Williams has worked as a researcher to the former leader of the Welsh Conservatives Professor Nicholas Bourne. Prior to his election, he worked as a policy adviser to Byron Davies, the shadow Minister for Transport, Regeneration and European Affairs.

He serves the Pentrych electoral ward, having been elected in 2008 to Cardiff City Council and re-elected in 2012. He has been chairman of the council's Economy and Culture Scrutiny Committee since 2012. He is a non-executive director of Cardiff Bus and former director of Cardiff Community Health Council. He serves as a governor for local primary and secondary schools. He is chairman of South Wales Central Conservatives and stood for election in Cardiff West in 2007 and in the 2011 Welsh Assembly elections. He also stood in the Cardiff South & Penarth by-election in 2012, following Alun Michael's resignation to stand as Police and Crime Commissioner. He lives in Cardiff with his wife, Clare, and young son. ▪

Corri Wilson

SCOTTISH NATIONAL PARTY (SNP) MP FOR AYR,
CARRICK & CUMNOCK

FORMER MP	Sandra Osborne, Labour
MAJORITY	11,265 (21.6%)
VOTE SHARE	48.8%
CHANGE	+30.8%
2ND PLACE	Lab

http://corriwilson.scott   @CllrWilson

CORRI (CORRAINE) WILSON was born in 1965. Her family moved to Ayr in the 1970s and she was educated at Ayr Academy and the West of Scotland University. She spent the first ten years of her working life as a youth worker for South Ayrshire Council and then the next twenty years as a New Deal adviser for the Department for Work and Pensions and its predecessor. Between 2005 and 2009 she was a project worker for Barnardo's, supporting families in danger of becoming homeless. She is a director of her own Caledonii Resources, a business support and event management company.

She has been a councillor for Ayr East on South Ayrshire Council since 2012 and is a director of Septembayr (the Ayrshire Festival), Ayr Renaissance and Ayrshire Housing. She spent ten months in 2007–08 as a custody visiting officer for Strathclyde Joint Police Board, visiting prisoners in their cells. She has two grown-up children. ▪

Mike Wood

CONSERVATIVE MP FOR DUDLEY SOUTH

FORMER MP	Chris Kelly, Conservative, stood down
MAJORITY	4,270 (11.2%)
VOTE SHARE	43.8%
CHANGE	+0.7%
2ND PLACE	Lab

www.mike4dudleysouth.com   @mikejwood

MIKE WOOD MOVED to Dudley with his family when he was a toddler, the son of a retired policeman. He went to school locally at Old Swinford Hospital School and studied Economics and Law at the University of Wales, Aberystwyth, graduating in 1997. He worked for several years in the European Parliament, first as an assistant to the Earl of Stockton MEP and then as a policy adviser to the Parliament on internal market legislation and environmental legislation. He joined consultancy JDS Associates as a senior researcher in 2006, before becoming a constituency organiser for Stourbridge and Halesowen & Rowley Regis in 2009. He was then a caseworker for Andrew Griffiths MP and worked as a parliamentary assistant to James Morris MP from 2011.

Having previously stood unsuccessfully in six local elections in Halesowen and Dudley, he was finally elected as a Dudley councillor in 2014 for Pedmore & Stourbridge East and was the shadow cabinet member for Finance. He has said that he would probably retain his council seat until 2016 if elected. He has been a member of the West Midlands Ambulance Service NHS Trust and served as a governor at a special needs school. He lives in Stourbridge with his wife, Laura, and their two young children. ∎

William Wragg

FORMER MP	Sir Andrew Stunell, Liberal Democrat, stood down
MAJORITY	6,552 (15.2%)
VOTE SHARE	41.4%
CHANGE	+7.8%
2ND PLACE	Lib Dem

www.williamwragg.org.uk   @William_Wragg

IN HIS EARLY twenties, William Wragg became one of the youngest MPs in the House of Commons. He grew up in Hazel Grove and was educated at the local Poynton High School and Manchester University. He was a personal tutor for a couple of years and then a primary school teacher in Rochdale until August 2014. He was employed part time as a parliamentary assistant to David Nuttall MP until the election.

He is a school governor at his former school, Hazel Grove Primary School. He was elected to Stockport Metropolitan Borough Council in 2001, representing the Hazel Grove ward, and is a member of the Children and Young People's Scrutiny Committee. He was a local authority-appointed member of Hazel Grove Community Association and the Transport for Greater Manchester Committee. He is a former chairman of the Hazel Grove Conservative Association and a member of the Conservative Councillors Association and the Association of Teachers and Lecturers. ∎

Daniel Zeichner

LABOUR MP FOR CAMBRIDGE

FORMER MP	Julian Huppert, Liberal Democrat, defeated
MAJORITY	599 (1.2%)
VOTE SHARE	36.0%
CHANGE	+11.7%
2ND PLACE	Lib Dem

http://danielzeichner.co.uk   @DanielZeichner

DANIEL ZEICHNER WAS born in 1956 and educated at the independent Trinity School of John Whitgift in Croydon. He first came to Cambridge to read History at King's College, where he met his long-term partner, Barbara. Before politics, he had a career in IT with Shire Hall, Philips and Perkins Engines, before moving to Norfolk with Norwich Union. He was an MP's researcher between 1992 and 1997 and a researcher for Clive Needle, MEP for Norfolk, from 1994 to 1999. Since 2002 he has worked as national political officer for Unison, including as a Labour-link officer. He is a director of a small company, Pettitts Ltd.

He served as a South Norfolk councillor between 1995 and 2003 and represents the region on Labour's National Policy Forum. This is his fifth consecutive election as a candidate. He stood for Mid Norfolk in 1997, 2001 and 2005 and for Cambridge in 2010. Prior to the selection process, he was chair of Cambridge CLP. He has run an anti-apartheid group, chaired a school governing body for seven years and is a national executive member of SERA. He was a trustee of Cambridge Crossroads for Carers for four years. As organiser for Labour's campaign for a democratic Upper House, he worked closely with Robin Cook on Lords reform. ∎

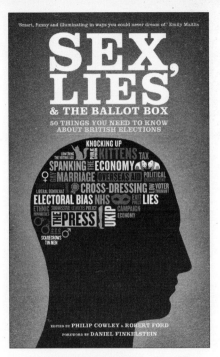

336PP PAPERBACK, £14.99

Shortlisted for the Practical Politics Book of the Year at the Paddy Power Political Book Awards 2015

In the aftermath of the most hotly contested and unpredictable election in a generation, this exhilarating read sheds light on the hidden world of British electoral politics. *Sex, Lies & the Ballot Box* delves into some of our more unusual voting trends, ranging from why people lie about voting to how being attractive can get you elected.

Each of the fifty accessible and concise chapters, written by leading political experts, seeks to examine the broader issues surrounding voting and elections in Britain. It is not just about sexual secrets and skewed surveys: it illustrates the importance of women and ethnic minorities; explains why parties knock on your door (and why they don't); and shows how partisanship colours your views of everything, even pets.

This fascinating volume covers everything you need to know (and the things you never thought you needed to know) about the bedroom habits, unconscious untruths and voting nuances behind our political choices.

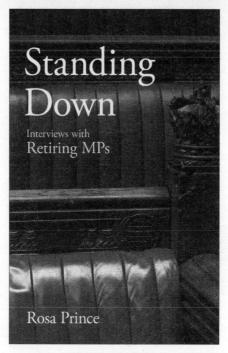

Standing
Down

Interviews with
Retiring MPs

Rosa Prince

EBOOK, £9.99

With big names such as Dame Tessa Jowell, Jack Straw and David
Blunkett all exiting the parliamentary stage in May, there is no
better opportunity to look back on the fascinating careers of some
of the most formative figures in UK politics in recent decades.

Speaking candidly about their highs and lows, their contributions and regrets, their
backgrounds and future plans, these twenty-six retiring MPs, interviewed by political
journalist Rosa Prince, provide frank and exclusive insights into their time in Parliament,
the seminal events they witnessed and their reasons for leaving.

With pearls of wisdom from Sir Menzies Campbell – 'MPs always know when it's time
to stand down, but they don't always admit it to themselves' – and David Blunkett –
'Knowing when to go is as important as knowing when to step up' – this timely farewell
to a generation of political heavyweights is a must-read for all.